SYRIA ————

D1504814

Hot Spots in Global Politics

Christoph Bluth, *Korea*
Alan Dowty, *Israel/Palestine 3rd edition*
Kidane Mengisteab, *The Horn of Africa*
Amalendu Misra, *Afghanistan*
Gareth Stansfield, *Iraq*
Jonathan Tonge, *Northern Ireland*
Thomas Turner, *Congo*

SYRIA

Samer N. Abboud

polity

Copyright © Samer N. Abboud, 2016

The right of Samer N. Abboud to be identified as Author of this Work has been asserted in accordance with the UK Copyright, Designs and Patents Act 1988.

First published in 2016 by Polity Press
Reprinted 2015, 2016

Polity Press
65 Bridge Street
Cambridge CB2 1UR, UK

Polity Press
350 Main Street
Malden, MA 02148, USA

All rights reserved. Except for the quotation of short passages for the purpose of criticism and review, no part of this publication may be reproduced, stored in a retrieval system, or transmitted, in any form or by any means, electronic, mechanical, photocopying, recording or otherwise, without the prior permission of the publisher.

ISBN-13: 978-0-7456-9797-0
ISBN-13: 978-0-7456-9798-7(pb)

A catalogue record for this book is available from the British Library.

Library of Congress Cataloging-in-Publication Data

Abboud, Samer Nassif.
  Syria / Samer N. Abboud.
    pages cm
  ISBN 978-0-7456-9797-0 (hardback) – ISBN 978-0-7456-9798-7
(paperback) 1. Syria–History–Civil War, 2011- 2. Syria–History–Civil War, 2011—Refugees. 3. Syria–Politics and government–2000- I. Title.
  DS98.6.A233 2015
  956.9104′2–dc23
                                                              2015018380

Typeset in 10.5 on 12 pt Sabon
by Toppan Best-set Premedia Limited
Printed and bound in the United States by RR Donnelley

The publisher has used its best endeavours to ensure that the URLs for external websites referred to in this book are correct and active
at the time of going to press. However, the publisher has no
responsibility for the websites and can make no guarantee that a site will remain live or that the content is or will remain appropriate.

Every effort has been made to trace all copyright holders, but if any have been inadvertently overlooked the publisher will be pleased to include any necessary credits in any subsequent reprint or edition.

For further information on Polity, visit our website:
politybooks.com

To the memory of Obaida al-Habbal, and all of Syria's martyrs

Contents

Acknowledgments viii
Maps xi
Abbreviations xiii

Introduction 1

1 The Rise and Fall of the Ba'ath Party 12

2 The Syrian Uprising 48

3 The Emergence of Armed Opposition 83

4 When the World Wades In 120

5 Fragmentation 162

6 The Humanitarian Crisis 188

Conclusion: Prospects for Resolution 215

References 229
Index 239

Acknowledgments

When I was twelve years old my parents took us on a family trip to Lebanon and Syria, my first time out of Canada. While only three days of that summer were spent in Damascus, they were among the most memorable days of my young life and stayed with me for the next few years. I was so captivated by the city—its sounds, smells, and aesthetics—that more than a decade later I would return, this time as a doctoral student conducting research into the rapid economic change occurring in the country after the assumption of power by Bashar al-Assad.

When I first arrived in Syria as a researcher I was greeted by someone at the Baramkeh car park in Damascus with the kindest words: "Welcome to Syria, this country is for everyone." For years, his welcome stuck with me and endeared me to the country and its people, if not the repressive regime that ruled over them. Over the last four years of the conflict I have spent many nights thinking about this man and the acquaintances, mothers, fathers, children, shopkeepers, taxi drivers, and servers I encountered over the years, and how the uprising has changed their lives. In some cases, I am fortunate to have my questions answered, but for the most part I am left only to speculate and fear the worst.

It is with a tremendous amount of sadness that I have written this book, which for me has been akin to recalling and retelling a tragic story that has played out for days, weeks, months, and years right before my eyes. As I, and so many others, have wandered helplessly trying to make sense of the Syrian tragedy, much of the world has watched with ambivalence befitting a weather report. I am certain that much of this stems from genuine confusion concerning the Syrian conflict and the ways in which it has been understood and analyzed in the West. Rather than delving into the complexities of the conflict, major media outlets, instant commentators, and the established pundits have preferred to frame the conflict in very convenient terms—regime versus rebels, good guys and bad guys, Alawi versus Sunni—then to offer sound analysis that contributes to understanding the main features, drivers, and dynamics of this extremely complex conflict.

In the pages that follow I attempt to provide a more complicated introduction to the Syrian crisis. This text does not present the conflict in rigid, dichotomous, and linear terms but aims to introduce you, the reader, to the different phases of the conflict and how it has evolved over the last four years. This book was written in relative solitude, but I am deeply indebted to a number of friends and colleagues who have provided me support over the years. First and foremost are Obaida al-Habbal, to whom this book is dedicated, and Zaher al-Saghir. Both Obaida and Zaher spent many hours with me in Damascus eating, laughing, walking, and talking about politics and history. Some of my fondest memories are of us on top of Mount Qasyun complaining about the inflated price of tea and coffee. I would also like to thank the many Syrians who took time to talk with me and introduce me to their beautiful country. There are far too many of them to name here.

Thanks are also in order for Pascal Porcheron and Louise Knight at Polity for their patience, kindness, and stewardship of the manuscript from beginning to end. Their encouragement throughout the process genuinely helped propel me in my moments of foundering. My research assistant, Josephine Lippincott, was not only an excellent and capable researcher who contributed immensely to this book but a wonderful motivator as well. My colleagues at Arcadia, Jennifer Riggan,

Warren Haffar, and Peter Siskind, have been excellent sounding boards for both ideas and complaints over the course of writing this book. Peter deserves special thanks for regularly reminding me that I was capable of synthesis. My deepest professional gratitude is extended to Miguel de Larrinaga, Can E. Mutlu, Marc Doucet, Mark B. Salter, and Benjamin J. Muller, whom I feel honored to call my friends and colleagues and who have provided me with many hours of laughter over the last few years. Our regular email exchanges about everything from the intelligent to the absurd sustain me in immeasurable ways. I would especially like to thank my trusted friend Benjamin for many things, including his professional mentorship, regular parenting advice, and for introducing me to Western boots.

I am deeply indebted to my parents, Rabab and Nassif, for not only raising me with unconditional love but for making sure that we never went a day in our house without talking about politics. Their care and selflessness have always made me feel safe in this world. My extended family in Syria and Lebanon have helped me in countless ways over the last decade while I traveled back and forth from the region and I am grateful for the loving relationships that I have with them despite the vast distance that separates us.

Finally, I would like to extend my deepest love and gratitude to my wife, Sonia, and our children Kalila and Nadim, who bring us so much happiness and joy. Kalila and Nadim spent many hours coloring, connecting dots, building structures, and drawing various animals while I worked my way through this book. Sonia's support has been invaluable and I have benefitted greatly from her insights and analytical sharpness that helped me craft many of the arguments in the book. Most of all, I appreciate her love and patience. I would not have been able to complete this book without either.

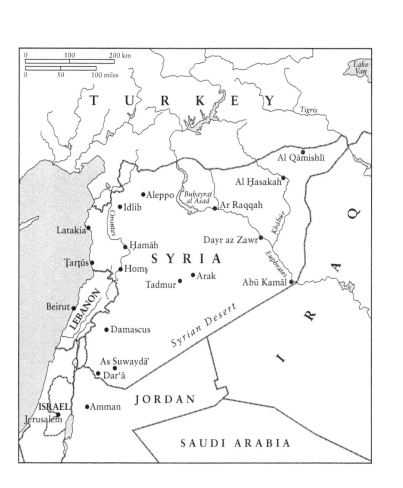

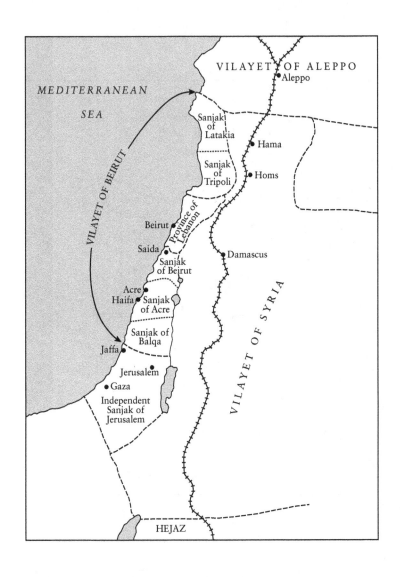

VILAYET OF ALEPPO

MEDITERRANEAN

SEA

Aleppo

Sanjak of Latakia

Hama

Sanjak of Tripoli

Homs

VILAYET OF BEIRUT

Province of Lebanon

Beirut

Saida

Damascus

Sanjak of Beirut

Acre
Haifa

Sanjak of Acre

VILAYET OF SYRIA

Sanjak of Balqa

Jaffa

Jerusalem

Gaza

Independent Sanjak of Jerusalem

HEJAZ

Abbreviations

AQI—al-Qaeda in Iraq
CBDAR—Canton Based Democratic Autonomy of Rojava
FSA—Free Syrian Army
GCC—Gulf Cooperation Council
IF—Islamic Front
ILF—Islamic Liberation Front
ISIS—Islamic State of Iraq and as-Sham
JAN—Jabhat an-Nusra
KDP—Kurdish Democratic Party
KNC—Kurdish National Council
KRG—Kurdish Regional Government
LAS—League of Arab States
LC—Local Councils
LCC—Local Coordination Committees
MB—Muslim Brotherhood
MSM—Majlis Shura al-Mujahideen
NATO—North Atlantic Treaty Organization
NCB—National Coordination Body for Democratic Change
NDF—National Defence Force
NRC—Norwegian Refugee Council
NSF—National Salvation Front
PKK—Kurdistan Workers Party
PPC—People's Protection Committees
PYD—Kurdish Democratic Union Party
SAA—Syrian Arab Army

SAMS—Syrian American Medical Society
SIG—Syrian Interim Government
SHRC—Syrian Human Rights Committee
SIF—Syrian Islamic Front
SILF—Syrian Islamic Liberation Front
SKC—Supreme Kurdish Council
SNC—Syrian National Council
UAR—United Arab Republic
UNHCR—United Nations High Commission on Refugees
UNSC—United Nations Security Council
UNSCR—United Nations Security Council Resolution
UOSSM—The Union of Syrian Medical Relief Organizations
UOSSM—Syrian Medical Relief Organizations
UOSSM—Union of Syrian Medical Relief Organizations
YPG—People's Defense Corps

Introduction

The daily lives of Syrians have changed dramatically since March 2011 when protests against the fifty-year rule of the Ba'ath Party began in the southern city of Dar'a. What began as a movement of sustained protest demanding regime change and political reforms has morphed into one of the most brutal and horrific conflicts in the post-World War II era. The conflict has become protracted, with the principal armed actors entrenched and a political and military stalemate consolidating. In the context of this stalemate, the humanitarian crisis wrought by the conflict is worsening: more than half of the total population killed, maimed, or displaced within only four years. The human tragedy of the Syrian conflict has no current end in sight. Sadly, and much to the detriment of Syrian society for generations to come, many local and regional actors seem content to fuel the horrors of the violence and do not invest in a meaningful process that could end the conflict. From the Syrian regime itself, which bears ultimate culpability and responsibility for the descent into maddening violence, to the various rebel groups, to Saudi Arabia, Qatar, Turkey, and Iran, there is seemingly no interest in ending the conflict.

Telling the story of the Syrian conflict is a complicated endeavor, especially in a context in which popular understandings of Syria reduce the conflict to simple binaries (Sunni/Shi'a or regime/rebel) that betray both the complexity of Syrian society and the conflict itself. In the pages that follow I attempt to confront these simplistic dichotomies and to introduce instead a broader picture of the Syrian conflict, one that moves back and forth between the meta-issues (such as regional rivalries, international involvement, and ideological and sectarian calculations) and the micro-issues (such as intrarebel cooperation and conflict, the humanitarian crisis, and the administrative fragmentation of the country) that are shaping and driving the military and political dynamics of the conflict and creating the current stalemate. In introducing the dynamics driving the conflict I also answer questions about who the main actors are, including the Islamic State of Iraq and as-Sham (ISIS), whose rapid and brutal rise in Syria and control of large swathes of Iraq and Syria have complicated the dynamics of the conflict as well as the possibilities of reaching a solution in the short term. One of my central goals is not only to trace the rise of groups like ISIS but to shed insight into the constantly shifting nature of alliances among rebel groups, the issues driving the political elements of the conflict, and the main actors (both local and international) who are playing key roles in the conflict. The goals for this book are to help the reader understand the broader dynamics driving the conflict, why it has persisted, who the main actors are, and why it has evolved in the way that it has.

In the popular understanding of the Syrian conflict it has morphed from a revolution into a civil war (see Hughes, 2014) but the conflict is not as linear as this suggests. There remains an active, robust, and committed movement of Syrians trying to rebuild their country, and to lead it free of the regime and the armed groups that now control it. At the same time, there is a slow fragmentation of the country and the retreat of armed groups into small areas under their territorial control, which has fueled civil violence that is worse in 2015 than it was in 2012. Thus the Syrian conflict is more than an uprising that morphed into a civil war; it is a conflict in which a revolutionary project to restructure society remains present.

The Syrian conflict is not one with a definitive beginning or a linear trajectory. What is at stake, analytically speaking, is the understanding of the parallel processes of revolution and civil war and their short- and long-term effects on Syrian state and society. This requires an attentiveness to the nuances and complexities of the Syrian conflict that most popular understandings lack (Rawan and Imran, 2013). From my perspective, such attentiveness requires an examination of the interplay of many factors: historical analysis, political economy, the role of international actors, the structure of networks of violence, and so on. With this in mind, the story I tell in the pages below begins in the Ottoman era with the formation of a landed elite that controlled the political and economic levers of society right through to the Mandate period. In the post-Mandate period of independence, mobilization of the socially disaffected classes overthrew the notable order. Out of the remnants emerged the Ba'ath Party, which has ruled Syria since 1963. The subsequent decades witnessed the consolidation of Baathist control of Syria and state institutions and the emergence of an authoritarian regime that ruled Syria through a combination of repression and clientelism. The lack of any sort of political freedoms, and the massive socioeconomic changes wrought in the 2000s by a shift away from socialist-era policies toward the market, fueled societal grievances that eventually propelled the protests that began in March 2011. The Syrian state and society have undergone three seismic shifts in the last century: the collapse of the Ottoman Empire, the Mandate period, and the era of Ba'athist authoritarianism.

Intersecting with this historical evolution are the social realities consequent on changes in the nature and structure of the Syrian state. The expansion of the state under the Mandate authorities fundamentally changed the relationship between state and citizen and brought the political authorities into the everyday lives of Syrians. Under the Ba'ath, the state was reoriented toward the dual goals of regime preservation and social mobilization through state institutions that would link different segments of Syrian society, especially those on the peripheries of Mandate politics, to the state and regime. The incorporation of new social actors transformed the material and political basis of Syria's social stratification and brought to political power a regime that was dominated by leaders from Syria's minority communities and rural areas. Ba'athist rule involved the distribution of social welfare in exchange for political quietism in Syria's incorporated social forces. By the 1990s this model had exhausted itself, and the regime slowly turned toward the market. By the time the uprising began in 2011, Syria had undergone a decade of dramatic economic transformation that had ruptured the economic links between state and society established from the 1960s to the 1990s.

Syria played a major regional role during this period as well, having fought two wars with Israel in 1967 and 1973 and then intervening in Lebanon's civil war later in the 1970s. The Syrian presence in Lebanon lasted until 2005, when a series of protests led to the withdrawal of the Syrian troops and security personnel who had exercised control over the Lebanese political system after the end of the country's civil war in 1991. The Middle East Peace Process in the early 1990s never realized a return of the occupied Golan Heights from Israel and a cold peace prevailed between the two countries up until today. Syria's regional alliances shifted considerably in the decades prior to the uprising, with the regime supporting various Palestinian factions against one another, Kurdish separatist groups in Turkey, and the Islamic Republic of Iran in its eight-year war with neighboring Iraq.

The legacies of Syria's historical evolution as a state, the transformation of its social stratification and political economy, and the changing geopolitical situation in the Middle East have all contributed to shaping the conflict today. The conflict itself has injected its own complexities into the Syrian arena with the arrival of armed groups such as ISIS and the emergence of Syrian Kurdish parties as major actors in the war. The role of regional actors in fomenting violence and supporting regime and rebel forces has internationalized the conflict in ways that decenter local actors from decision-making and power on the ground. Violence, fragmentation, and displacement are radically reshaping Syrian society.

Who are the Syrians?

Syria is an extremely heterogeneous society, with Sunnis, Alawi, Ismailis, Druze, Shi'a, Greek Orthodox, Maronite, and other Christian sects. Population breakdowns by religion are not entirely accurate, but close to 10 percent of the population was Christian and the remaining 90 percent Muslim, the majority of which are Sunni Muslims. In addition to religion or sect, class, ethnicity, and geography are also determinants of Syrian political and social identity. Syria is dominated by Arabs with a sizable Kurdish minority, which is no more than 8 percent of the total population. Prior to the uprising, Syria's population was around 22 million, with more than half of the population formerly concentrated in urban centers.

Syria shares borders with Iraq, Palestine/Israel, Lebanon, Jordan, and Turkey. The Golan Heights has been occupied by Israel since the 1967 war but is still home to many Syrian Druze who live under Israeli occupation. In the post-Mandate period, Syria's economy was dependent on agriculture and oil production. Agricultural production was central to the nation's social stratification in the Ba'ath period and oil revenues provided the regime with substantial rents to establish a strong central state and public sector. During the 1990s, there was a slow shift away from dependence on oil revenues and an attempt to diversify the economy. These reforms were accelerated in the 2000s when Syrian planners enacted policies to shift economic activity toward services. The shift in economic policy away from agriculture paralleled severe environmental degradation in the agricultural regions, including drought, which decreased agriculture's productivity and led to the transformation of the social basis around which agricultural activity occurred.

Unravelling the Conflict

The complexity and fluidity of the Syrian conflict does not lend itself to any quick-fix theoretical models. Larger questions about why it has evolved in this particular way and why a stalemate has taken root are not easily answered. Much of the academic literature on wars and conflicts focuses on variables and measurements that do not remotely fit the realities of Syria's conflict. More nuanced studies have drawn on different approaches to the study of the Syrian conflict (Hokayem, 2013; Lesch, 2013a,b; Sahner, 2014). The background of the protests and the early mobilization period encouraged many to draw on Social Movement Theory (SMT) (Durac, 2015) to help understand the organization and strategies of the early protest movement that morphed into the Local Coordination Committees (LCC). This research, which we will deal with substantially below, has been important in helping us understand the main players fueling the protests, what their socioeconomic backgrounds were, how they organized and mobilized protesters, and what their key roles were in the early stages of the uprising.

Other studies of the conflict attempted to explain the causes and background of the uprising by focusing on the long trajectory and exhaustion of Ba'athist politics in Syria (Wieland, 2012). Further research has been conducted into the causes of the uprising, with some arguing that environmental factors such as climate change and drought were major drivers of the protests (De Châtel, 2014). Others point to Syria's socioeconomic situation on the eve of the uprising, especially the effects of unemployment and declining standards of living, as causes of the protests (Dahi and Munif, 2011) while others argue that the contagion effect of initially successful Arab uprisings in such places as Tunisia and Egypt inspired Syrians to protest (Kahf, 2014; Lynch et al., 2013).

While the study of the causes of the uprising are important, the uprising cannot be reduced to one or two variables. Instead, it is the outcome of the interplay of all of these factors. Some research has focused on explaining the trajectory of the uprising through changes in the regime's behavior and its subsequent mutations during the conflict (Heydemann, 2013a,b; Seeberg, 2014).

The regional geopolitical situation can explain some dynamics of the Syrian conflict, and further studies have focused on the interplay between domestic and regional politics by privileging the penetrative role of regional actors in Syria (Salloukh, 2013; Hokayem, 2013). Finally, others, such as Khashanah (2014), have argued that the confluence of ideological and geopolitical interests of outside entities induced the Syrian crisis in an attempt to realign the country's foreign relations.

All of these explanations have been substantial and useful interventions into the study of the Syrian conflict and all serve to inform much of the analysis that follows below. The multilayered complexity of the conflict necessarily produces intellectual and analytical blind spots and an exhaustive study of this complexity would be impossible given the rapidly changing dynamics of the conflict. In order to address these larger questions about the Syrian crisis, I have drawn on but sought to look beyond some of the dominant approaches to the study of the conflict. Rather than focusing exclusively or predominantly on the transformations of the regime or on the international role in the conflict, I have drawn significantly on the idea of wartime political orders to explain the key patterns of the conflict, including cooperation and conflict between different actors, governance, politics, military activity, war economies (Staniland, 2012), and so on. In drawing on this notion of a wartime order, I am trying to explicate some of the more nuanced questions that help parse the conflict: Why do rebels sometimes cooperate and sometimes engage in conflict? What do the political and administrative structures of nonregime areas look like? Who is exercising violence and to what end?

The study of wartime political orders typically relies on analysis of two variables: territorial control and regime-rebel relations (Staniland, 2012). Most literature on wars tends to ignore how the diverse and contradictory interactions between regimes and rebels serve to construct political authority and control. Regime and rebel actors are not locked in a zero-sum game to control the monopoly of violence; rather, they engage in both cooperative and conflict relationships that shape

patterns of violence against civilians, governance, war economies, and, in important ways, postconflict politics. In this
study of the Syrian conflict I highlight the diversity of interactions between regime and rebel groups, and also between
rebel groups themselves. I look at how these groups control
territory, administer that territory, and exercise political
power and authority therein.

From the outset, then, it is important to clarify the meaning of "regime," "rebel," and "opposition," which are often
conflated. In the pages that follow, the homogeneity of these
categories will be broken down in favor of more pluralistic
and heterogenous explanations of what we call "the regime,"
"rebels," or "the opposition." In Syria today, there are multiple actors that constitute the parts of what we mean when
we refer to these categories. The analysis below highlights the
fragmentation of these categories and what that fragmentation means for the conflict.

The Syrian conflict is not simply about military wins and
losses or the contraction of regime territorial control. The
conflict has produced a political order structured by relations
among the different groups that produces patterns of violence
and governance that are contributing to the stalemate. The
relations produced by the conflict are themselves shaped by
a number of factors, including the role of outside actors,
sectarianism, territorial fragmentation, and the humanitarian
crisis. In the pages that follow the story of the Syrian conflict
is told through these lenses.

Structure of the Book: An Evolving Crisis

Chapter One begins with a historical overview of Syria's post-
Mandate state up until the period of the Baathist coup in
1963. The chapter looks at the rise and consolidation of
Baathist power from 1963 until the outbreak of the uprising
in March 2011. In this period, the social and material basis
of Ba'athist power shifted dramatically, especially in the
period of Bashar al-Assad's rule (from 2000 onwards), during
which the regime engaged in marketization that had acceler-

ated the Ba'athist shift away from its traditional social support base. The role of the regime's pillars of power—the Ba'ath Party, the security apparatus, and the state—are discussed throughout. Specific attention is placed on the wide range of social forces in Syria—the peasants, urban bourgeois, workers, and so on—and their differential positioning vis-a-vis the entrenched time Ba'athist regime. This will provide a substantive background from which to understand the context of the uprising and the social forces driving the movement to topple the regime.

Chapter Two covers the first months of the uprising until the period in which militarization began to take root and an armed opposition emerged. Here we examine the background of the protesters and of the uprising and answer questions about how the protesters organized and mobilized in the context of sustained regime repression. The central role of the Local Coordination Committees (LCCs) is highlighted, as is how the conflict gave rise to civil activity and organization more generally. The regime's response to the protests was to engage in a dual policy of repression and reform, the latter of which included substantial constitutional changes but had no immediate effect on the ground. This did not placate protesters. Continued repression forced the uprising to emerge as a nonhierarchical, decentralized movement loosely linking activists together throughout the country. In addition to the LCCs, a political opposition made mostly of Syrian exiles formed outside of the country and attempted to generate international support for the overthrow of the regime. As armed groups emerged inside the country within the first year, the movement against the regime suffered from "multiple leaderships" and the lack of a centralized structure that could serve as a serious and legitimate alternative to the regime. The failure of the protests of the first months of the uprising to initiate regime change would propel the conflict toward increasing militarization.

The main violent actors are introduced in Chapter Three. In Syria today, violence is highly fragmented and decentralized, and there are two different armed actors: fighting units and brigades. The former are usually small armed groups with limited mobility who usually operate in smaller areas of towns or cities, while brigades have hundreds of members and are active across Syrian governorates. These units and brigades are connected to larger networks of violence that are determined by an interplay of many factors: resource access, control of checkpoints and supply routes, ideology, and so on. These networks of violence are very fluid and there remains mistrust between many of the armed factions. Chapter Three explores the networked structure of violence and how this manifests within the Jabhat an-Nusra, ISIS, Kurdish, and regime networks.

The international dimensions of the conflict are taken up in Chapter Four, which discusses the main positions and approaches to the conflict of the major international players—the Arab countries, Russia, Iran, Turkey, Hizbollah and Western countries. Key issues that contributed to the internationalization of the conflict include debates over intervention and arming the rebel groups, the chemical weapons containment issue, and rival peace processes sponsored by the United Nations and Russia. These are highlighted. This chapter identifies, then, both how international actors are penetrating the Syrian arena and affecting the evolution of the conflict and how the conflict has been internationalized.

Chapters Five and Six ask how the conflict is redefining Syria. Chapter Five concerns the territorial fragmentation of the country into areas loosely controlled by rival armed groups, including the regime, Kurdish Democratic Party (PYD), Jabhat an-Nusra and other Salafist-jihadists, and ISIS; it looks also at the latter three groups' administrative apparatuses, and. the failure of the exiled political opposition's attempt at a transitional government. Finally, Chapter Five considers some of the impacts of fragmentation, including the rise of sectarianism and the regional impacts of fragmentation on neighboring states. Chapter Six is concerned with the humanitarian crisis, specifically the displacement of millions of Syrians and the effect this is having on the health care and education access of Syrians. This discussion opens issues and challenges associated with refugee protection in neighboring countries. Chapter Six concludes with a discussion of the failings of the international community to adequately address the Syrian humanitarian crisis.

1 The Rise and Fall of the Ba'ath Party

Syrian politics has been dominated by the Ba'ath Party since a bloodless coup brought military officers loyal to the party to power in 1963. The assumption of Ba'athist power in the 1960s initiated a period of relative political calm in Syria after decades of instability following independence from France in 1946. The social and economic transformations in Syria that made possible the rise of the Ba'ath Party are rooted in contradictions and consequences of the country's transitions from Ottoman governance to the French mandate and then through the independence period. These three political shifts have had profound impacts on the shaping of Syrian politics, society, economy, and the state. It is within the context of these major changes in political power and foreign suzerainty in Syria that the ideological and political conditions in which the Ba'ath Party came to power should be understood.

The shaping of contemporary Syria began in the later Ottoman period, when a series of reforms created and empowered a landlord-merchant class that formed the political elite of Syrian society at the turn of the century. The period of the French Mandate was one of relative continuity in the social composition of Syria's political elite, as the Mandate powers proved unwilling and unable to initiate major transformations in Syria's distribution of political power. It is not surprising, then, that after the collapse of the French Mandate, these same landlord-merchant classes continued to rule Syria and dominate political and parliamentary life. Rule by the nobility, however, was increasingly challenged by Syria's other major social forces. Such tensions between the ruling classes and those social forces that were on the peripheries of political life generated tremendous instability in the decades following independence. Indeed, the instability of the independence period that preceded the seizure of power by the Ba'ath was mostly the result of three parallel processes in Syria that would have profound effects on society: first, the rapid social transformations following integration in the global capitalist system; second, the expansion of state capacity and its penetration into society; and, finally, widespread social discontent and, eventually, mobilization, which would challenge and ultimately destroy the existing political structure. From the post-independence instability arose the Ba'ath Party. From 1963 until 1970 the party pursued a radical political agenda that reflected its leadership's commitment to comprehensive social transformation. In 1970, a "corrective revolution" led by Hafiz al-Assad would moderate some of the party's positions and initiate a process of consolidated state-building.

Ba'athist power in Syria arose in 1963 and was consolidated until the eve of the uprising in 2011. One of the key features of Syrian political life since the Ottoman times is the differential incorporation of Syria's social forces into political power and the often destabilizing and revolutionary implications of political peripheralization. The Ba'ath Party was largely successful in initiating major social transformation in Syria and uprooting the nobility-based order. This transformation was grounded in an attempt to overthrow the vestiges of nobility rule and to incorporate the disaffected classes—peasants, minorities, rural communities, and the petit bourgeoisie—into a new political order. The costs of such transformation, however, were high, and came at the expense of political democratization. During the period of Hafiz al-Assad's rule, a patrimonial state emerged whose stability rested on key pillars of authoritarian control, mainly the security apparatus, the army, the Ba'ath Party, corporatized actors, and the public sector. The pillars of authoritarian rule in Syria provided the institutions through which political mobilization of the disaffected classes and loyalty to the party could occur. By the 1980s, however, Ba'athist authoritarianism had shown signs of exhaustion, particularly after the financial crisis of 1986. Thereafter, gradual liberalization occurred and became a vehicle for the slow reintegration of commercial and bourgeois interests into the ruling coalition. By 2000, Hafiz al-Assad had died and bequeathed power to his son, Bashar al-Assad. Initially considered to be a reformer capable of steering Syria toward a more democratic system, Bashar al-Assad in the 2000s presided over further political contraction and crackdown, coterminous with economic liberalization. The decade preceding the uprising was one of intense and substantive economic change in Syria, in which the pressures of demographic growth, statist retreat, economic stagnation, and a shift toward marketization generated socioeconomic discontent with the regime that had no legitimate outlet. By the 2000s, the space for incorporation of social forces into the political system contracted and the social base that the regime had been based on from the 1970s had shrunk. Once again, in Syria, the peripheralization of social forces would have dramatic political consequences.

From Ottoman to Mandate Politics

The Ottoman Empire underwent substantial change in the 1800s. The period of reforms, known as the Tanzimat (1839–1876), attempted to wholly reorganize the state and the relationship between the Sultan and his subjects. A series of military defeats and nationalist movements that set European provinces on the path toward independence led to the territorial contraction of the Empire. In response, the state initiated the Tanzimat reforms to stave off internal collapse and to confront external pressures associated with European encroachment and the Empire's increasing integration into the global capitalist economy. These reforms were wide-ranging and had profound effects on social and political identities in the Empire. The attempt to eliminate distinctions between

Muslims and non-Muslims and to transform Ottoman subjects into citizens who would have a stake in the defense and
continuity of the Empire would radically alter relations
among political leaders and lay people. There would be,
however, two main outcomes of the reform that would shape
political life in Syria for years to come. The first was the
centralization of power in the expanding Ottoman state and
the stronger penetrative role for the state in the affairs of the
provinces. Such centralizing measures proved to be both a
threat and an opportunity to local provincial leaders who had
grown accustomed to relative autonomy and distance, both
politically and geographically, from the central Ottoman
state. The second was the introduction of private property
and landownership. The introduction of private landownership would ultimately form the economic basis of a new class
that would assume greater political power in the final decades
of the Empire and which had positioned itself for a role after
the Empire's collapse.

By the mid-1800s, the Syrian provinces of the Ottoman
Empire were being integrated into the global capitalist system.
Such integration meant increasing European penetration
of the provinces and economic pressure against traditional
industries. Such pressures stimulated the growth of agriculture, particularly for export to European markets. The importance of agriculture for the finances of the Empire was evident
in the passing of the Land Code of 1858, a policy meant to
encourage peasants to register state-owned land so that inter-
mediaries could not concentrate control over the productivity
of land (Khoury, 1983, p. 27). In fact, the opposite happened.
Peasants so feared the encroachment of the state that they
resorted to registering lands in the names of urban patrons
or rural notables, thus having precisely the opposite effect
of the Land Code's intentions. Even those peasants who
attempted to register their land found the costs prohibitive,
and their lands reverted to auction, where rural notables
could easily acquire them. Because the peasants were unable
to bear the costs associated with registration or agricultural
production, they quickly became sharecroppers and laborers
on land that they had only recently controlled. The effect of

the Land Code, then, was the gradual concentration of land in the ownership of urban families who had more secure property rights and who could more officially engage in commerce and trade.

As peasant proprietorship declined, land concentrations increased, and, after a series of political reforms, so did the political power of the landowning classes. In subsequent decades, class conflict became more apparent in the provinces, especially in agriculturally rich areas of Syria such as the Hawran, where conflict between peasants and landowners increased. In 1864, the Empire passed the Law of the Provinces, which established new administrative councils that would incorporate notables into the political system. P. S. Khoury (1983) held that the introduction of private property, the expanding Ottoman state, and new administrative councils provided the basis for the creation of a new kind of political leadership in Syria tethered to landownership. Political leadership in the latter half of the 1800s was almost entirely tethered to landownership. These leaders would be drawn from two sectors: first, the landowning scholars, religious families who controlled key religious posts in Syria; second, the landowning bureaucrats, who controlled the key political and administrative posts in the expanding Ottoman bureaucracy. The emergence of landowning classes would consolidate class structure in the Syrian provinces and more clearly demarcate divisions and conflict between landowners and peasants.

The Tanzimat reforms ultimately could not stave off Ottoman collapse, and by the end of World War I the victorious European powers were granted Mandates by the League of Nations to control former Ottoman lands and to midwife the new states into self-government. A unique form of suzerainty created by the League of Nations, the Mandates led to the creation of the modern states of Lebanon, Syria, Jordan, Iraq, and Palestine. Having assumed the Mandate for Syria and Lebanon (The British had a Mandate for the remaining countries), the French reinforced the landed elite rather than undermining them. In particular, the French authorities accelerated the private ownership of land through distributing formerly collectively held lands to the landed elite and tribal leaders in exchange for political subservience and commitment to the French project. In addition to increasing land holdings and wealth of the existing elite, they expanded the institutions of political representation to include a parliament, which, for the duration of the Mandate period, was dominated by landed interests. As the main site of political deliberation and decision-making, parliament became a site of inter-elite negotiation where landed interests were almost exclusively represented. Thus the landed elite's economic and political control was never seriously threatened during the Mandate period. It was not until the post-independence period that a political coalition would emerge that would challenge their authority.

French Rule and Independence

By the time the French had assumed the Mandate over post-Ottoman Syria in 1922–1923 after the deposition of the Syrian King Faisal in 1920, the country's social structure had begun to crystallize. The period preceding the deposition of King Faisal was one of mass politics and popular mobilization (Gelvin, 1999) in which new ideas about politics and nationhood permeated Syria's social and political landscape. During the immediate period of Ottoman collapse, popular committees emerged that reflected Syria's plural social mosaic and which began to articulate ideals of national community, a concept that was largely foreign until the late Ottoman period (Gelvin, 1999). As ideas of nationalism spread throughout (mainly urban) Syria, social stratification took shape around agricultural production and exchange, which dominated the country's economic activity. Owing to the active discouragement of industrialization by the French authorities, the class structure of Syrian society at the time revolved around land ownership and the marketing and exchange of agriculture (Hinnebusch, 1990). At the top were the large landowners, numbering around 3,000 notable families who represented less than one percent of the total population but owned more than half of all private land in the country (Hinnebusch, 1990, p. 39). The landed families also dominated all major political, professional, and bureaucratic positions. Immediately below the landowners were the merchants who controlled trade. Agricultural exchange provided the basis for the emergence of a new commercial class who facilitated Syria's entry into global capitalism. Merchants who were further removed from landowners and agricultural production and who were concentrated in and around urban areas made up the middle strata of society. These merchants held some land and positions within various professions and the bureaucracy, mirroring those of the landowners and commercial merchants. They did not develop social interests that could challenge the landed nobility-based order. The lower strata of urban Syrian society were made up of the petit bourgeoisie, artisans, and labourers who were at the extreme economic peripheries of the benefits of agricultural production. Finally, Syria's rural areas also were home to a very small group of notables who had either acquired some wealth from commercial activities or the *zu'ama* (political leaders). The overwhelming number of rural Syrians, however, were either share-croppers (around 30 percent of the total population) or landless peasants (around 60 percent) (Hinnebusch, 1990, p. 40) who earned wages cultivating land owned by the notables.

Syria's social stratification and the elite politics it underpinned would remain economically and politically dependent on agricultural production and elites' control of land. The relative continuity of the composition of the elite from the Ottoman through the Mandate period could not, however, remain stable amid more substantive political and economic changes introduced by the Mandate authorities. The growth of the state bureaucracy had created an entirely new class of middle-class professionals, mostly Western-educated and urban. The increasing penetration of the state into all facets of Syrian life and, more specifically, the increasing control of rural affairs by the urban political center, would further divide rural and urban Syria and breed hostility and resentment from rural communities against increasing state encroachment. Perhaps the most important change under the

French authorities was the introduction of formal institutions of political deliberation that would provide the framework for the exercise of a new kind of class cohesion among the landed notables. Unsurprisingly, the concentration of economic power in the landowning and commercial classes was mirrored in the new Syrian parliament. While political parties did emerge, they entirely reflected landed interests and did not seriously incorporate peasant or rural interests into the political system.

Beginning immediately after the Mandate authorities took power in the mid-1920s, there were signs of resistance to French rule from both the urban elite and the rural peasants. On the one hand, the elite found that French interests were increasingly inimical to their nationalism and that the French authorities had little interest in fulfilling the Mandate of midwifing Syrian self-government. Although the elite had benefitted tremendously from the French reluctance to upset the social structure and balance that had developed under the Ottomans, there was a contentious division between the French authorities and the elite that they ruled Syria through. Such tensions would ultimately culminate in the establishment of various institutions of political representation that offered the elite some degree of autonomy from their French overlords. On the other hand, peasants in the rural areas had become increasingly discontent with their socioeconomic plight as well as with French intervention into Syrian affairs. Such grievances were both complementary and contradictory, and did not provide the basis for cross-class mobilization against the French. Nor did they provide the basis for horizontal linkages among the lower classes and the development of a class consciousness that could mobilize peasants. Syria's many-layered identities—clan, sect, geography—prevented such a development among the lower classes. Clientelism and the dependence of many peasants on the landed elite for social and political gains further ensured that such mobilization could not occur and that peasants would remain subordinate to the elite-dominated system.

By 1925, a few years after the Mandate took effect, there was a Great Revolt that lasted until 1927. This cross-sectarian, cross-class revolt occurred throughout Syria and Lebanon and was largely uncoordinated and decentralized but had the common aim of overthrowing French rule. Peasants, tribespeople, rural notables, nationalists, and the elite had all developed grievances against the French after the deposition of King Faisal in 1920. By 1925, a call to arms by Syrian Druze leader Sultan al-Atrash led to battles against French forces. In the first weeks of the revolt the Syrian forces were successful and al-Atrash and the nationalists had formed an alliance that led to a National Provisional Government. However, reinforcements from France eventually pushed the Syrian forces into retreat and by 1927 the rebellion had been crushed and along with it the experiment in transitional government. The rebellion had changed French attitudes toward Syria and had encouraged authorities to reform the political system and begin responding to nationalist demands.

A series of policies followed that were meant to do precisely this, but they had not satisfied nationalist interests. In early 1936, National Bloc leaders had begun to publicly denounce the French authorities, which prompted the closing of the Bloc's offices and the arrest of two of its prominent leaders. The Bloc responded by calling for a national strike that began on 20 January and led to work stoppages and student protests in all major cities and towns. The strikes paralyzed the country. Initially, French authorities responded with violence against the protesters, which left many dead and forced the Bloc's leaders into exile. By March 1936, the French authorities began negotiations with the National Bloc that led to the signing of the Franco-Syrian Treaty of Independence.

Ideologically speaking, the Syrian elite had begun gravitating toward Arab nationalism. In the 1920s, in the aftermath of the collapse of the Ottoman Empire, the elite had not yet distinguished between Arab (transnational) and Syrian (territorial) nationalism or advocated for either, as their main political interests were in remaining as an intermediary between the French authorities and Syrian society (Mufti, 1996, p. 45). The Nationalist Bloc, a proto-party representing nationalist interests, had actively rejected Arab unionist plans, first by renouncing claims to Lebanon in 1936, and, second by rejecting unionist overtures from Hashemite Iraq and Transjordan (Mufti, 1996). The elite that controlled politics were thus navigating the space between French suzerainty and Syrian society that was increasingly being influenced by nationalism and the possibilities of mass politics.

By 1946 the French occupation of Syria had ended and the National Bloc elites had assumed control. The Bloc, however, immediately disintegrated into different factions— the National Party (Damascus-based), the Republican Party (Damascus-based), and the People's Party (Aleppo-based)— that represented the various interests of the elite. In addition to the remnants of the National Bloc existed the Communist Party, the Muslim Brotherhood, and the Youth Party, all of which had ideological backgrounds very different from Arab nationalism. Finally, the Syrian Socialist Nationalist Party (SSNP) and the Ba'ath Party represented transnational ideological interests, with the SSNP advocating for the integration of Syria into a greater Syrian political entity inclusive of Iraq, Lebanon, Palestine, and Jordan, and the Ba'ath Party advocating for Arab nationalism.

From Independence to the United Arab Republic

The post-independence period was one of tremendous political instability. Divisions among sectors of the political elite and agitation from the political parties opposed to elite rule made governance of the new state and the expansion of its political institutions difficult. The loss of Palestine in 1948 to Zionist forces had profound impacts on the radicalization of Syrian politics, especially for the nationalists. Meanwhile, the old elite had fragmented and was in political decline, while the new parties had begun to enjoy the support of large segments of the population. They could not, however, affect the distribution of power in society. They had not developed the distributive and patronage networks of the elite, which had allowed them to maintain support in both rural and urban areas. There was an emergent tension then between the elites governing the state and the political interests, demands, and ideological orientation of much of society. Such tensions led to different forms of political protest: street demonstrations, and, with remarkable frequency, coup attempts.

The 1950s was a period of intense political debate within Syria, mobilization of different societal interests, and the radicalization of Syrian politics. The elite political coalition that had sustained Syria from Ottoman times through the French Mandate had begun to collapse and be replaced with wider political coalitions that were inclusive of Syria's diverse political interests: rural peasants, the middle class, pan-Arab nationalists, and so on. The growth of state institutions created different centers of power beyond the elite-controlled institutions, and the army and bureaucracy emerged as two important sites of political control outside of elite capture. The army in particular, after a series of officer purges of Adib Shishakli (President of Syria between 1953–1954) loyalists, was dominated by Ba'athist officers.

Ba'athist influence was not confined to the army but had stretched to government, parliament, and among many individual Syrians, making the party a formidable force in Syria's emergent political landscape. The rise of Arab nationalism among Syrians had also benefitted the Ba'ath Party. The rise of mass politics and Arab nationalism in the 1950s was shaped by the advancement of economic interests outside of those of the traditional elite. Increasingly, the Ba'ath Party and others had adopted progressive social and economic policies that reflected the base of their support. This was especially the case in their advocacy of comprehensive agrarian reform and other policies that sought to break the economic stranglehold of the elites.

At the forefront of the rise of peasant politics in this period was Akram al-Hawrani, a Syrian from Hama who became engaged in politics in the 1930s. al-Hawrani came from Hama, an area in which feudal practices persisted and the landed elite remained strong. As al-Hawrani became a prominent figure in Syrian politics in the 1940s and then 1950s, he was a staunch advocate of agrarian reform aimed at breaking the strength of the landed elite. His calls for reform made him an extremely popular figure among Syria's peasantry. By 1950, al-Hawrani had established the Arab Socialist Party (ASP) and was credited with providing the space for the mobilization of Syria's peasantry against the old order (Batatu, 1999, p. 370). His influence on the Ba'ath Party was not only through his advocacy of peasant politics. In the aftermath of his exile in the early 1950s after the banning of the ASP, al-Hawrani agreed to merge the ASP with the Arab Ba'ath Party then led by party founders and ideologues Michel Aflaq and Salah al-Din al-Bitar (it was this unified party, renamed the Arab Ba'ath Socialist Party, that was disbanded by the United Arab Republic in 1958).

Despite the merging of the two parties, the plural landscape had led to the factionalization of politics and of state institutions. The army had begun to factionalize and disagreements between progressive and conservative politics led to state paralysis. It was in this context that many political leaders, including those of the Ba'ath Party, had begun to openly advocate for political union with Egypt as a means of stabilizing the country. Egyptian President Gamal Abdel-Nasser had reluctantly accepted the union but only under terms that would effectively circumscribe Syrian political mobilization and thwart radicalization. To this end, Nasser had imposed harsh political demands on Syria, including the dissolution of political parties and the concentration of all constitutional power in his presidency. Moreover, Egyptian officials had imposed on Syria a radical nationalization plan that made the state directly responsible for capital accumulation while restructuring private commercial and industrial sectors (Heydemann, 1999, p. 106). This followed a series of restrictions on Syria's business elite that were intended to disrupt the social and economic networks underpinning their power. Nasser's political and economic restructuring of Syria during this period would have profound impacts on the development of the Syrian state.

The new United Arab Republic (UAR) was declared in 1958 in an attempt to consolidate Syria's political institutions and end instability. Ba'athist leaders were actually given high positions in the new entity but many army officers had been transferred to Egypt and replaced with Egyptian personnel. Abdel-Nasser had viewed the Ba'ath with great suspicion and had actively tried to subordinate its leadership to his rule, despite the Ba'ath's insistence on shared governance of the Syrian region of the UAR. Pressures from Abdel-Nasser and from within Syria had slowly emasculated the Ba'ath Party and led to the migration of many supporters to other blocs.

Other parties had experienced similar fates as Abdel-Nasser had gutted the political system and put in place a Cairo-based bureaucracy. The UAR was never successful in incorporating the social backgrounds and basis of the major Syrian political parties into the new system. It thus lacked its own social basis from which to rule. Despite this, the UAR initiated radical reforms in Syria, especially land reform that gave land to peasants, a blow to the landed elite. A further legacy of the UAR was the authoritarian institutions and structures that were put in place and carried throughout in the post-1961 era (Heydemann, 1999). The state transformation that occurred during the UAR period was not reversed afterward but actually was reinforced and practiced right through to the Ba'ath Party coup in 1963.

1963 and the Rise of the Ba'ath Party

The failure of the UAR initiated a major transformation within the Ba'ath Party, including shifts in its ideological orientation and the social and sectarian composition of its supporters. When Nasser dissolved all political parties in 1958 as a prerequisite for the creation of the UAR, the provincial and national networks linking Ba'ath leaders and activists collapsed. After 1961, Ba'ath leaders were forced to reestablish the party's structures as well as to deal with the political and ideological fallout of the failed unification. Reestablishing the party's networks proved difficult in a climate in which Ba'ath supporters were split over the question of whether to seek re-union with Egypt or not. On the one hand, many Ba'athists, including co-founder Michel Aflaq, had supported re-union with Egypt in a federal model. The pro-unionists believed very strongly in Arab union and attributed the failure of the UAR to its undemocratic structure, and not to the ideals of pan-Arabism and unity. The unionists were largely drawn from the urban Sunni middle class, who had supported Ba'athism as the champions of Arab nationalism. They had ideological affinities with Nasserism and remained loyal to the Nasserist ideals of Arab unity and nationalism after the collapse of the UAR. They were joined by other segments of the middle and lower classes that had similarly supported Ba'athism for its pan-Arab ideals and leadership but had abandoned the party after its dissolution, or had questioned Ba'athist stewardship of Arab unity after the collapse of the UAR. The pro-unionists were more committed to the ideals of nationalism than to the party itself. On the other hand, the anti-unionists, while still committed to Arab nationalism, remained committed to the party and to reestablishing the pre-1958 Ba'ath networks. These activists were largely from rural areas, especially in Dar'a, Deyr az-Zor and Latakia, and were organized around the party's provincial branches. In addition, some Ba'athist military officers who were discharged after the formation of the UAR and who were overwhelmingly from Syria's minority Alawi, Druze, and Ismaili communities, similarly adopted opposition stances toward re-union. A "military committee" consisting of Mohammed Omran, Hafiz al-Assad, Abd al-Karim al-Jundi, and Salah Jedid was formed in order to transform the party and increase the political role of the military. Together with the rural activists, the military committee and other anti-unionist officers shared a rejection of the traditional Ba'ath Party model and the pre-UAR leadership, which they blamed for the dissolution of the party and the failure of union.

Two other major transformations occurred during this period that would have enormous consequences for the party and the future of Syria. First, the anti-unionists had drifted away ideologically from the traditional Ba'ath opposition to class struggle; they moved toward Marxism. Some Ba'ath leaders began to openly espouse socialism, which began a process of radicalizing the party and further distinguishing it from its pro-union elements. Moreover, the emergence of a new generation of Marxist-inspired activists led to the rejection of formal union as the vehicle of Arab unity; rather, mass political mobilization and social revolution were seen as the goal. For them, Arab nationalism was secondary and subordinate to the goals of socialism. Arab unity could only be achieved through mass socialist revolution, and not through the conservative, reformist approach adopted by Aflaq and the other pro-unionists within the party. Second, occurring parallel to the radicalization of the Ba'ath Party was the emergence of a minoritarian leadership. In the provinces and among the military officers, the new, younger generation of Ba'ath activists were overwhelmingly from Syria's many minority communities, especially the Alawi community. Moreover, the socioeconomic background of these activists was predominantly rural, thus making the reconstituted leadership of the Ba'ath Party rural and minoritarian.

On the eve of the 1963 coup there was no ideological coherency or consistency to the Ba'ath Party leadership. Rather, the party was splintering along social and ideological lines, with pro-unionists being largely drawn from the Sunni middle classes who had adopted more conservative, reformist positions, and the anti-unionists, who were increasingly radicalized and adopting socialism, drawn from the rural and minority segments of Syrian society. Under these circumstances of party fragmentation, Hinnebusch rightly states that "it is hard to imagine a more inauspicious juncture for a party to take power" (1990, p. 166). Nevertheless, fragmentation at the ideological and party level did not prevent military officers from organizing themselves to take power. Entirely divorced from the party's grass roots and lacking any sort of national character or mass social mobilization, military officers seized power in a bloodless coup on 8 March 1963. Circumstances prior to the coup had propelled an alliance of mistrust between party officials and Ba'athist military officers who were otherwise on opposite sides of the re-union question. The seizure of power by the Ba'ath in Iraq in February 1963 was a major catalyst, but a general climate of political stalemate and regime paralysis contributed as well. Almost immediately after the coup, internal fighting among members of the new Ba'athist regime occurred, and the new government was characterized more by factionalism than coherence. Factionalization and infighting contributed to a climate of political confusion and disarray. Eventually, however, after a few months, the Ba'ath regime was purged of most of its Nasserist elements and its leadership was drawn from a core of rural and minoritarian officers.

The rural-minoritarian character would fundamentally shape the structure and character of the Ba'ath regime for decades (Batatu, 1999). The party's revised form of pan-Arabism held that the road to unity could not be achieved through formal union but rather from mass political mobilization and social revolution that would bring about Arab unity. Together, rural activists and military officers had reconstituted the party, committed to radical socialism and to overcoming the political embarrassment of the dissolution of the UAR. What occurred during this period was a process Batatu (1999, p. 144) called the "ruralization" of the army, Ba'ath Party, and state bureaucracy.

The assumption of power by the Ba'ath Party in 1963 in a bloodless coup by its military committee on 8 March would eventually bring about a period of relative political stability in Syria. The turmoil and chaos of the immediate postcolonial period had given way to the Ba'athist model of authoritarianism-populism, which sought to "establish the authority of a strong state autonomous of dominant classes and external powers and to launch national economic development aimed at easing dependence and subordinating capitalist forces to populist goals" (Hinnebusch, 1990, p. 2). The Ba'athist regime had, in its early years, pursued a policy of radical social transformation that was to be brought about by the confrontation with, and suppression of, social forces underpinning the previous social order. The Ba'athists thus derived their legitimacy in part from their ability to organize and mobilize the peripheral classes, such as peasants, and to incorporate them into a political program aimed at destroying the vestiges of the previous political order and establishing a new, broad base of social support for a new political order (Batatu, 1999). For the Ba'ath regime, then, the origins of its social base and the social forces that were incorporated into Ba'athist politics are central to understanding the rise and consolidation of the regime and the strategies it employed to remain in power.

By the time that the Ba'ath Party had taken control of Syria in 1963 it was a radically different party than in the Mandate era. The UAR period had initiated ideological shifts in the party and had reorganized its social base. The party had emerged from UAR with varying ideological strands competing for control of the party. Eventually, the more radical strands won out and created a blueprint for Syrian society that was rooted in particular ideas about socialism—which was more important for the new leadership than pan-Arabism as a governing ideology.

The Ba'athist Coup

After coming to power, the radical Ba'ath officers had purged the army of Nasserist officers and had taken full control of the party. This was the beginning of a slow purge of party members who did not share their radical vision for the social transformation of society or who were loyal to other branches of the Ba'ath. In addition to internal conflict, the Ba'ath had to absorb dissent from within Syrian society, especially the remnants of the conservative parties that strongly opposed its radical socialist politics. The challenge for the Ba'athist leaders at the time was how to consolidate political power. As time would tell, however, there was an internal challenge that would also have to be resolved before power could be consolidated.

The initial years after the coup were thus a period of relative instability. The Ba'ath was able to survive in power because of the fragmentation of the opposition and the relative weakness of its conservative foes. The Ba'ath had to reinvigorate its relationship with its main social base in the rural areas to insulate itself from opposition and to enact its socialist revolution. By the mid-1960s, Ba'athist power had begun to consolidate as opponents were purged from key offices and the army and state apparatus were controlled by the party. Meanwhile, the government began a period of radical economic reforms through nationalizations of industry and finance and through continued land reforms that granted land rights to peasants and agricultural workers. Public planning would henceforth replace the market as the main distributive mechanism and the public sector became the main engine of economic development. Private enterprise was severely curtailed and economic relations with the West rolled back. Such policies provided the material basis of Ba'athist rule and allowed the party to consolidate a social basis of support outside of the urban areas, which had served as the traditional power centers from the Ottoman period.

The Ba'ath Party that came to power after 1963 had thus launched a revolution from above (Hinnebusch, 2001). Drawing on socialist ideals, they initiated a major social transformation of society, generated and mobilized popular support throughout different segments of society, and revamped institutions to ensure the stability of the regime. While the party had developed a cross-sectarian leadership and social alliances, sectarianism remained a factor in intra-regime politics. The regime was inclusive of Syria's historically excluded communities, especially the Alawi, but this was not enough to prevent sectarianism from playing an important role in the country. Alawi officers in the 1960s were keen to promote their co-religionists to positions of power and, along with many Druze in the party, had alienated Sunni leaders and taken clearly sectarian positions against them.

The Corrective Revolution and the Consolidated State

The consolidation of the post-UAR Syrian state was occurring amid battles internal to the Ba'ath Party. In 1970, Hafiz al-Assad led a "corrective revolution" that was motivated by the 1967 defeat in the Arab-Israeli war and the desire to end domestic conflict. Hafiz al-Assad led an ideological revision of the party while maintaining the cross-sectarian, civilian-military composition of the existing regime. This new "corrective movement" would maintain a commitment to socialism but would direct the state toward the liberation of the territories occupied in 1967. This entailed a reorientation of Syria's foreign relations and domestic policy to oppose antagonistic social forces. Rapprochement with the oil monarchies in the Arab Gulf would provide financial resources to al-Assad's efforts in exchange for Syria's ceasing to export socialist revolution to Arab countries, and economic policy would be slowly liberalized to provide some opportunities for the private sector.

According to Patrick Seale (1990, p. 172), Assad had two ideas about how to govern Syria after the corrective revolution: the first was that there was to be no challenge to his rule, that it would be absolute, and the second was that he would cultivate wide popular support for his policies. The corrective movement thus broadened the social basis of the new regime by placating and incorporating some elements of the traditionally hostile conservative social forces, especially the bourgeois. More important, however, was the institutional basis of the spread of these measures to expand Ba'ath Party reach and incorporate antagonistic social forces into the state. The first move was to create a parliament that successfully co-opted social forces beyond the regime's core rural constituency. The Ba'ath-dominated National Progressive Front (NPF, a coalition of parliamentary political parties) was created to incorporate socialist and communist parties, while Nasserists were also increasingly willing to cooperate with Ba'ath rule. Although Assad believed in his absolute power to rule Syria, he did so through the existing institutions of the state and party that were at his disposal.

Internal turmoil over the proclamation of a new constitution in 1973 that made the Ba'ath Party the leading party in society was eventually ignored after the beginning of the war with Israel. Although the army was unable to regain lost lands, they performed better than in 1967, and this won al-Assad a great deal of legitimacy in Syria. Equally important was the oil boom of the 1970s that followed the war. Petrodollars flowing into the Arab Gulf countries began to make their way into Syria in the form of grants to support the state in its war with Israel. Petrodollars allowed al-Assad to oversee the expansion of the state and the distribution of resources—jobs, services, and other economic opportunities—to fulfill the party's socialist goals.

The regime that al-Assad oversaw had four pillars of power (Hinnebusch, 2001, pp. 80–7). The first was the party itself (Seale, 1990, p. 174), which acted as an intermediary between the central state and the governorates and villages, ensuring the diffusion of state policy. The party emerged as the main agent of state policy. Moreover, the party was expanded to incorporate the regime's social base and to link party members to social institutions, such as unions. The second pillar was corporatism, a process by which different social forces are subordinated and incorporated into the regime. The regime had linked social forces by organizing hitherto demobilized groups, such as peasants and students, and incorporating them into state-controlled associations. The regime's control of these associations meant that they lacked any independence from the government; they were not autonomous. In exchange for financial support, these social forces were slowly incorporated into the state apparatus and thus created a large constituency committed to the survival of the state and regime.

The third pillar of al-Assad's rule was the state bureaucracy (Heydemann, 1999). The expansion of the state bureaucracy penetrated all facets of Syrian life, and the socialist policies in the 1970s and 1980s led to a bloating of the bureaucracy and public, which employed close to 25 percent of Syrians at one point in the 1980s. Finally, the fourth pillar of power in al-Assad's Syria was the army and security apparatus (Seale, 1990; Heydemann, 1999). The loyalty of the army and the security apparatus was ensured by placing regime loyalists, mostly Alawis, in positions of power. The army and security apparatus were effectively incorporated into the regime by the purging of non-Ba'athists and nonloyalists. In the late 1970s and 1980s the low-level civil war between the Muslim Brotherhood and the regime affirmed the loyalty of the army and the security apparatus, which, even throughout the current uprising, has remained loyal to the regime.

Fiscal Crisis and the "Liberalization" of Political and Economic Space

The consolidation of the Syrian state under Hafiz al-Assad's rule in the 1970s and 1980s withstood the turbulence of the period, which included regional wars (the 1973 Arab-Israeli war, and the Lebanese civil war that began in 1975) and civil violence. In the mid-1980s another source of turbulence occurred when the state suffered a fiscal crisis wrought by the rapidly declining price of oil. Syria's budget was heavily reliant on oil revenues derived from its own modest production and the recycling of petrodollars from Arab Gulf states. The need to generate revenues beyond oil led the regime toward a slow rapprochement with the private sector, one of its traditional antagonists.

With the exception of a few economic moguls connected to the regime, the 1970s and 1980s was a period of private sector stagnation. Most enterprises had to navigate a complicated and restrictive economic environment that was made even more difficult by the regime's open hostility toward bourgeois interests. By the late 1980s and early 1990s this had changed, as businesspeople started to develop stronger ties with the regime through patronage relations (Haddad, 2011). These emergent state-business relations grew in the 1990s and businesspeople were slowly incorporated into the web of political power, gaining seats in parliament and enjoying increasing access to the political elite.

The reintroduction of business interests into the political sphere was gradual as the regime elite continued to view the private sector with hostility. The main dilemma for the political elite was how to foster private-sector economic activity while suppressing their collective demands for access to political power and decision-making. The dilemma was clear: the political elite needed the private sector to stimulate the economy, to generate foreign exchange to compensate for lost oil revenues, and to create jobs to alleviate the employment bottlenecks in the public sector. In order to bring this about, the elite had to engage in compromises with the private sector. Thus the Ba'ath Party's historical antagonists were slowly incorporated into the regime.

In the early 1990s, the government had passed an investment law (No. 10) meant to liberalize investment restrictions. In 1992, the state budget included substantial restrictions on social welfare spending and tax incentives for private enterprises (Lawson, 1997). Such measures invited criticism from the General Federation of Workers Union, which accused the government of supporting private enterprises at the expense of the public sector. These reform policies, although gradual and piecemeal, reflected the slow strategic shift of the regime toward greater liberalization of private capital and a rollback of state spending to compensate for the loss of revenues.

Yet, despite these reforms, the private sector and the state remained antagonistic. The regime had never sanctioned associational activity, thus precluding the collective mobilization or articulation of interests by the private sector. Access to economic power was secured through access to the political elite and state bureaucrats who controlled the economic levers of the state. Patronage and economic networks were important to the cultivation of political networks and to the private sector's access to economic opportunities (Haddad, 2012; Haddad, 2004).

Like most other social forces in Syria, the private sector would not be autonomous from the regime. During the 1990s, the regime was successful in suppressing private-sector political demands and in incorporating the private sector into the ruling coalition. This inclusion was not total, however, as the majority of Syrian private-sector enterprises, often small, family-run, and with limited production, continued to operate outside of the networks of political power and within a web of complicated regulations, fear of asset seizure, and regime suppression. The benefits of the reforms then were only accrued by a select group of businesspeople who had direct access to the regime and were embedded in relationships with the political elite.

Consequently, the regime was only partially able to address the fiscal crisis of the 1980s. The liberalizations of the 1970s and 1980s had provided the space for private sector expansion but this had only benefitted an economic elite that was drawn from the urban Sunni bourgeoisie and, increasingly, from the sons and daughters of the political and security elite. The basis for the widespread distribution of wealth did not occur and the state's finances remained mired in stagnation. In the late 1990s, right before the death of Hafiz al-Assad, the state was facing potential economic crisis: a desperate need for widespread job creation, the alleviation of oil dependence, economic stagnation, and decreasing standards of living and increasing poverty (Perthes, 2001).

Bashar's Rise

By the time that Bashar al-Asad assumed power in Syria, the authoritarian populism that shaped the early years of Ba'athist rule in Syria had ceased to exist. Since independence, Syria had pursued forms of statist economic development whereby the state was positioned as the dominant economic actor. Under the rule of Hafez al-Asad, Ba'athist statism was underpinned by a model of social, economic, and political organization marshaled in support of state-building rather than economic development. The statist model placed the corporatist logic of inclusion, stability, and state dependence ahead of economic development. As Hinnebusch rightly argues, this model eventually exhausted itself because it fostered "consumption at the expense of accumulation" (Hinnebusch 2009, p. 17). The exhaustion of Ba'athist statism forced the regime to engage in a series of economic reforms in the late 1980s and throughout the 1990s, which were accelerated considerably after 2000 when Bashar al-Asad assumed power. Since 2000, economic reforms aimed at introducing market relations into the economy while gradually rolling back the policies, institutions, and distributional patterns of decades of central planning began. These reforms were motivated by neoliberal thinking about the economy and framed under the vague strategy of a "social market economy" that attempted to achieve social welfare through increasingly privatized and marketized mechanisms. As the period of marketization demonstrated, however, the reforms failed to address many of the social demands of Syrians. In attempting to do so, the marketization period severely disrupted the relationships between state and society that made material gains and social welfare possible.

The changes wrought in Syria during the 2000s led to the gradual deinstitutionalization of Ba'athism as a social, political, and economic model, and the decline of Ba'athism as a cultural and belief system designed to support its institutions (see Hsu 2007). The story of the social market economy in Syria, as elsewhere in the formerly centrally planned economies, is one of the gradual retreat of the state from its active and hegemonic role within society and the simultaneous dismantling of the institutions linking state and society, including the public sector, unions and syndicates, and the fiscal mechanisms supporting these links, such as the tax code or subsidy system. What was slowly occurring in Syria during the 2000s was a diffusion of economic authority from public to private sector through transfers of responsibility for social welfare from the state to the market. One of the consequences of the diffusion process is the undermining of traditional corporatist actors and the linkages they have developed with the regime and the state (Abboud, 2015). Economic policy then aimed at introducing the private sector as the main engine of economic growth and development. The state thus cedes authority to the private sector and rolls back many of its distributive policies that had linked other social actors, such as workers, to the state. Therefore, as a discourse and set of policy choices, the social market economy strategy was an attempt to alter the nature of the state's embeddedness in society relative to various social forces.

The government had failed to provide an explanation for what the social market economy actually was, beyond stating what goals they hoped to achieve through market reforms (Abboud, 2015). The basic structure of the policies was to rebalance public / private sector authority and to encourage private business interests to play a larger role in the economy. The state would adopt a more interventionist role to address market deficiencies while public-sector assets would be preserved in their current form. Private business interests would be addressed through the creation of new private-sector investment opportunities and not through the sale of public-sector assets. This method of dual-track liberalization was intended to create parallel and competing public and private sector actors in the economy, whether in finance, insurance, or service provision, such as schools and health care (Abboud, 2009), and to shift Syria's fiscal dependence away from oil revenues, which formed nearly half of all budgetary revenues in the 1990s.

Some of the key policies of the 2000s reflect the regime's strategy of dual-track liberalization and the shift toward a more marketized economy. Public-sector monopolies were slowly broken and new private-sector investments in banking, insurance, education, and other areas appeared. Meanwhile, the government's vast subsidy system was dismantled and price ceilings on everything from basic foods to housing prices were lifted. The economic volatility cause by the marketization of prices led to tremendous economic uncertainty among many households and businesses. The basic thrust of the reforms was to slowly remove obstacles to market activity and to subject prices to the market, all the while maintaining Syria's authoritarian political structures. The balance between the need for economic reform and regime stability was the main driver of the marketization period.

However, marketization did not broaden the basis of accumulation in Syria. Only very narrow private interests embedded in the regime's power circles benefitted from privatization. To be sure, many in the business community did reap peripheral benefits of marketization but the overwhelming majority (more than 96 percent) of Syrian business enterprises were small (less than ten employees) and were on the peripheries of the economic gains in the 2000s. Moreover, the marketization period initiated a series of economic shocks in Syria that would have profound impacts on the social and economic well-being of the majority of the population.

Most major socioeconomic indicators reflect a deteriorating of living standards during the 2000s and a reduction of the mechanisms of social mobility and social welfare. Unemployment rates continued to increase, wages were well below the increasing costs of living, and price volatility created economic uncertainty for millions of Syrians (Abboud, 2007). While the Ba'athist model of development contained structural flaws, the reforms in the 2000s did not necessarily address these. Instead, they have disrupted the institutions of social mobility, such as the public sector, and reconfigured Syria's social stratification that had taken root under Ba'athism. In the 1960s and 1970s, for example, redistributive policies had vastly improved the economic lives of peasants and the poor. Policies of nationalization and a robust distributive system that was focused on rural development and the privileging of agricultural production enhanced rural life. Meanwhile, public sector expansion created a massive social basis for the regime, middle-class jobs, and a strong state bureaucracy from which to govern the country (Haddad, 2012b). Public sector employees, urban workers, and rural peasants formed the social basis for the regime and the Ba'athist model of development was intended to shelter them from the market. In doing so, however, the regime adopted a purely distributive position in the economy and was not able, for political and social reasons, to extract wealth from these groups or make them a source of capital accumulation (Dahi and Munif, 2011).

By the 1980s, these mechanisms of rural support and public sector expansion were placed under pressure by the fiscal crisis and the state's distributive role was no longer fiscally sustainable. The regime was forced to begin to reorient the economy away from oil dependence and privileging the agricultural sector, and to move it toward the nonagricultural sectors of the economy (Hinnebusch, 2010). Eventually, a process of rural and agricultural neglect set in, a betrayal of the Ba'ath Party's primary social and economic basis of support. Three policies in particular would have substantial impacts on rural communities and their relationship to the regime: first, the rapid decline of agricultural subsidies;

second, new land laws that reoriented ownership and usage rights away from the cooperative models of the previous two decades; and, third, the government's incentives to produce a narrow few "strategic crops" which encouraged farmers to abandon diverse production of crops and instead concentrate on those that were heavily subsidized (Hinnebusch, 2010). Unsurprisingly, agricultural productivity declined as government attention turned toward the nonagricultural sectors of the economy. In the 1990s and into the 2000s there was a gradual movement of rural migrants into the urban peripheries. Most rural migrants had settled in slums around the major cities. This process was so pronounced that one Syrian economist suggested that around 20 percent of the total Syrian population lived in some sort of slum village by the late 2000s (Seifan, 2010).

In parallel to these policies were a set of neoliberal discursive shifts that redefined the relationship between state, society, and economy. The wholesale destruction of the institutions of the Syrian state or the privatization of public sector assets would have delegitimized decades of Ba'athist development. As a result, the new economic reforms had to be presented in a way that made them compatible with the Ba'athist policies of the 1970–2000 period, or, at the very least, did not discredit the decades of social policies that were the basis for Ba'athist rule. The social market economy emerged as a set of public narratives about the economy and allowed average Syrians to make sense of the turbulent economic transformations they were experiencing. These new narratives differed considerably from previous decades of Ba'athist rhetoric about the economy and reflected the government's strategic shift toward neoliberal policies by focusing on issues of personal responsibility, the central role of the private sector in economic development, decreasing dependence on the state for social welfare, and the greater integration of Syria into the regional and global economies through trade liberalization (Sottimano, 2008).

The policies pursued in the 2000s after Bashar Assad came to power were not simply representative of a new shift in economic thinking toward services or the urban economy at the expense of agricultural and the rural economy. The reforms introduced after 2000 blended neoliberal and authoritarian modes of governance, and in doing so had generated a new kind of politics that married the rhetoric of social welfare and protections with the benefits of liberalization and marketization. The regime had actively pursued economic transformation through a new coalition of the private-sector elites and a reinvigorated (but not autonomous) civil society. The new model of Ba'athist development would stress capital accumulation and not redistribution and would be diffused through these central social actors. The old model represented an alliance between the army, peasants, workers, the Ba'ath Party, and the public sector. However, this populist-authoritarian model had exhausted itself by the 2000s and gave way for a new model that instead reflected the economic interests of the urban classes, economic elites, and regime officials.

Bashar al-Assad had presided over not only a reorientation of the Ba'athist model of development but a reorientation of Syria's foreign relations as well. He had inherited from his father a collapsed peace process, hostile relations with Turkey and Iraq, and control over neighboring Lebanon. Syrian forces had been present in Lebanon since the civil war and the Syrian hegemonic role was consecrated in the Ta'if agreement that ended the Lebanese civil war in 1991. Syrian hegemony in Lebanon had bred resentment among many Lebanese while fostering a political elite that was dependent on Syria for political power (el-Husseini, 2012).

The events and aftermath of September 11, 2001, had radically changed the regional geopolitical situation. U.S.-led wars and occupations in Afghanistan and Iraq had disrupted an increasing rapprochement between Syria and Iraq, the latter having emerged as a major importer of Syrian goods and thus an important element of the government's trade liberalization strategies. The Syrian regime was active in fomenting the armed opposition to the occupation by supplying weapons and allowing the entry of fighters from its territory and had thus entered into indirect confrontation with the United States. Meanwhile, a similar rapproachment had occurred with Turkey. The threat of war in the late 1990s was replaced with "brotherly" relations between the two countries (Bank and Karadag, 2013) and the signing of a free trade agreement that was part of Syria's development strategy to achieve greater economic openness and foster market competition (Abboud, 2009). Syria's deepening ties with Iraq and Turkey contrasted the collapse of Pax Syriana after the assassination of former Lebanese Prime Minister on 14 February, 2005, which prompted a series of demonstrations in Lebanon that led to the withdrawal of Syrian forces from Lebanon. Finally, Syria had deepened its ties to Hizbollah in Lebanon. Hafiz al-Assad had been keen to keep Hizbollah's power in check by supporting another Shi'a based party called Amal. Bashar al-Assad, however, had actively deepened ties with Hizbollah and had drawn on their Secretary General's imagery to enhance his legitimacy inside the country.

By 2011, the Syrian state looked considerably different then it had merely a decade prior. There had been a radical reorganization of the country's foreign relations that had paralleled major transformation in the economy and the near abandonment of Baathist era socialist policies. The latter transformation had represented the growing convergence of regime-business interests and had further peripheralized those social forces that were central to the exercise of Baathist power and legitimacy from the 1960s, including the rural peasants and workers. Ba'athism had morphed considerably over the 2000s in ways that placed political and social pressures on the Syrian populace for which there was no political outlet to express discontent or mobilize.

Circumscribed Civil Society

Prior to the uprising, Syria did not have an autonomous civil society. There was very limited space for the expression of political dissent. From the 1960s onwards the only associations that were formed and licensed by the state were charitable organizations that were almost all religious. Political instability in the late 1970s and early 1980s altered the regime's tolerance of these associations, and, slowly, the licensing process was discontinued and charitable associations were sanctioned by the government. By the 1990s the government had renewed the licensing system and a number of legal, sanctioned associations began to operate alongside the remnants of the old associations that had remained in operation, albeit informally and without government permission.

Civil society organizations beyond charitable associations became a feature of Syrian political and social life during the marketization period in the 2000s. The opening up of political space for civil-society groups to form and operate was, however, severely restricted. The regime had fostered civil-society groups to bolster its reformist agenda but also as a means of alleviating some of the social hardships caused by marketization. Thus, many of the groups that emerged were focused on social service provision while very few advocacy or issue-based organizations were formed. While some rights groups were formed, these were limited and remained subject to regime repression. Those that were licensed and sanctioned by the government endured tremendous obstacles to legalization. Prior to receiving government approval, all thirteen intelligence agencies were required to approve the application, in addition to the Ministry of Social Affairs and Labour itself. Moreover, once approved, virtually all major projects needed approval from the Ministry. Such obstacles further restricted associational life.

Civil-society groups that were licensed were never entirely autonomous from the regime. In the early 2000s when the Declaration of One Thousand was signed and various political and cultural forums sprang up throughout the country, the regime was initially tolerant. Many of these forums actually planted the seeds for more organized forms of associational activity later in the decade, including human rights and charitable organizations. In the early parts of the decade, the most important was the Forum for National Dialogue that was started by Riad el-Seif, a parliamentarian. The success of the forum and the authorities' apparent sanctioning of its meetings led el-Seif to announce the establishment of a political party called the Movement for Social Peace. Riad el-Seif and his followers had overstepped the regime's limits with this declaration and el-Seif was stripped of his parliamentary immunity and convicted of bogus corruption charges. The attempt to create a new unsanctioned political party also led the regime to close all the remaining forums (except for one) in the country, effectively circumscribing the budding civil-society movement.

After this only few spaces existed for political and social discussion among Syrian elites. The Jamal Atassi Forum was never given a license to operate but remained active even though the remaining forums had been closed down by the regime. A second forum was the Syrian Economic Society (SEC), which held weekly meetings in Damascus where intellectuals, business leaders, and government officials came together to discuss the country's economic situation. The former forum was eventually closed down in 2005 while the SEC continued to offer lectures right up until the uprising.

In this period, Syria's civil society displayed two primary structural characteristics. The first is that it was mostly led by intellectuals and elites. This was especially true of the various forums. These civil-society organizations were predominantly elite gatherings and their political activity was confined to the exchange of ideas about reform and the future of the country. There were very few attempts at organization and mobilization of key segments of society around specific identities or issues. The second characteristic is that they were largely informal groupings with no established organizational structures, funding streams, or legal relationship to the state. The groupings were spontaneous to some degree and, aside from charitable organizations, had virtually no organizational precedent under the Ba'ath era.

By the mid-2000s these forums had made a return to the social and political arena and had begun to proliferate throughout the country. The growth of new, now formalized and licensed, civil-society organizations occurred within the context of the regime's shift to a social market economy of development (discussed earlier). This shift entailed a reorganization of the state's relationship to society. In particular, the social market economy model, in practice if not in theory, led to the gradual shifting of power from the state to social groups. For this reason, the regime had slowly begun to devolve power to groups that were hitherto excluded from the main centers of power, mainly, the business community (Abboud, 2012).

Thus, from the mid-2000s onwards, the regime had engaged in a process of authoritarian diffusion that shifted more power to social actors. The state would no longer be the central economic actor in society and would now rely on privatized actors (civil society, the business community) to provide social services, public goods, and economic growth.

Such a shift did not, however, entail a substantial loss of regime power. It instead forced the regime into codependent relations with social groups. For example, in the late 2000s, a major charitable organization called the Jama'at Zayd (Zayd Group), had become one of the largest and most organized charitable organizations in Damascus and operated a charitable network of more than thirty mosques (Pierret and Selvik, 2009).

For Pierret and Selvik, the growth of the Zayd Group represented a coalition of private-sector businesspeople working with local religious leaders to provide social and charitable works, or what has been referred to as the 'ulama-merchant nexus [Pierret & Selvik, 2009]. On the one hand, the regime had historically repressed such activities and thus had viewed the growth of these charitable organizations with extreme suspicion. On the other hand, the charities offered a social safety net to buffer against continued economic stagnation and the social effects of the shift toward a more privatized, marketized economy.

The need to pass social service responsibilities to private actors forced the regime to open up the space for civil-society groups. With the shift to a more marketized economy, civil-society organizations such as the Zayd Group proliferated. Some were, of course, less politically threatening to the regime than the larger Islamic networks. On the eve of the uprising there were hundreds of smaller charitable organizations that were registered with the Ministry of Social Affairs and Labour and which operated within a legal framework. Charitable organizations were by far the largest segment of civil society in the 2000s. The major sources of funding for these organizations were private donations from Syrians. There was virtually no Syrian government or foreign funding available to these organizations. The regime had also created a network of nongovernmental organizations that were controlled by the government and did not have any autonomy from the state. These Government Non-Governmental Organizations (GONGOs) were largely active in social issues, such as women's and children's rights, and in development issues. The GONGOs operated under the organizational umbrella of the Syrian Trust for Development and included different educational, social rights, and development organizations and were all organized under the patronage of First Lady Asma Assad, which gave the Trust relative protection from the authorities and a degree of social legitimacy to operate throughout Syria. The Syrian Trust was also the largest recipient of both government and foreign government funds, especially from the European Union. Perhaps not surprisingly, government efforts to engage civil society in the policy and development process were only inclusive of GONGOs.

In addition to the charitable organizations and the GONGOs, cultural and human rights organizations were established in the 2000s. While Syria has a long history of cultural forums dating back to the 1800s, many of these organizations disappeared after the Ba'ath Party took power in the 1960s. However, by the 2000s, they had begun to reappear but were mostly focused on music and art and had largely stayed away from engaging in political activity. Similarly, women's rights organizations were largely at arm's length from the government and were confined to focusing specifically on women's and children's issues. While some of the more prominent organizations, such as the Syrian Association for Women's Role in Development and the Syrian Women Observatory had engaged in activism around women's and children's issues, they were never treated as threatening by the regime because their activism was never directed at the structure of power.

These four types of civil-society organizations were largely tolerated by the regime (and in the case of the GONGOs, actively encouraged) in order to expand social service provision or to provide a small, circumscribed, and tolerated space for activism. In the 2000s, human rights organizations were also established that directly challenged the regime's repeated human rights abuses and engaged in activism for prisoners' rights and greater political freedoms for Syrians. A number of organizations existed in the 2000s, including the Syrian Observatory for Human Rights and the Syrian Human Rights Committee (SHRC), which had operated an extensive network of activists in the country up until the uprising. The human rights organizations, however, suffered from a number of problems that limited their political impact within Syria. First, many were underfunded and had failed to develop strong organizational capacities. Second, many had attempted, but failed, to pool resources and form larger associations to foster greater cooperation and activism. Unfortunately, personal rivalries among many of the activists led to splits between these organizations and a failure to coordinate activities. Most important, however, was the constant threat of repression, imprisonment, and closure from regime security forces, who viewed their work with hostility. Many of the key players in the human rights organizations in the 2000s spent time in prison, thus discouraging other activists and stunting the growth and efficacy of the organizations.

By 2011 the Syrian regime had undergone dramatic change in its social base and its economic orientation. Civil society organizations, especially GONGOs, were a small, but important element of this reorientation as they were incorporated into the state as social welfare providers and as alternatives to public sector provision of goods and services. The most important shift had occurred through the slow, gradual abandonment by the Ba'ath Party of its traditional rural constituency and the incorporation of the business community and the bourgeois into the new ruling bargain. While the business community did not represent civil society as such, the networks many of the urban business elite formed with the

Syrian *ulama* connected them deeply to associational life in pre-uprising Syria (Pierret, 2013).

Prelude to an Uprising?

Syria's post-Mandate history has been shaped profoundly by the Ba'ath Party. Having emerged out of a period of social discontent and popular mobilization, the Ba'ath Party had overseen the radical transformation of Syrian society and the dismantling of a political and economic system that favored landed notables. The seismic shifts in Syria's evolution from Ottoman province to French Mandate and through the independence period have at different times included and excluded various social forces whose antagonism with the state shaped politics. For much of the Ba'ath Party's control of power from the 1970s onwards, social discontent was dealt with through repression. The apparent stability of the Ba'ath period and the economic growth of the 1970s and into the 1980s was underpinned by a highly repressive and brutal security apparatus that ensured that political discontent would be suppressed. Such reliance on the security apparatus exposed the main structural flaw of Ba'athism that was masked by corporatism. The incorporation of social forces into the state did not occur organically or through popular acceptance and adherence to Ba'athist ideology, but rather through some combination of corporatism and repression.

While none of this historical discussion necessarily portends an uprising in Syria, it certainly suggests that the rapid social transformations and reorientation of the state's domestic and foreign policies had a profound impact on the Ba'ath Party's pillars of power and its ability to exercise control over society and suppress discontent. While there is no single, identifiable cause behind the decision of millions of Syrians to engage in protest and mobilization against the regime after March 2011, the changing nature of state-society relations, socioeconomic decline, and the suppression of political and associational life were all extremely important factors, alongside others such as climate change and the contagion effect of the Arab uprisings. While the Syrian uprising occurred within this larger context of the Arab uprisings, it has taken on a unique character and has evolved in radically different ways than in Tunisia, Egypt, Bahrain, and others.

Any inquiry into the nature, structure, and drivers of the Syrian uprising has to account for the uniqueness of the country and the specificity of its political, social, and economic landscape. The Syrian uprising was profoundly shaped by the historical suppression of party politics and the circumscription of opposition and associational activity. The absence of pre-existing institutions that could mobilize society gave the Syrian uprising the unique feature of being highly decentralized and uncoordinated. The absence of coordinating bodies gave rise to the need for greater organization among the protesters, which subsequently led to the creation of various groups both inside and outside of the country who attempted to organize and speak in the name of the uprising. Thus, from the very beginning of the uprising, the historical suppression of the political opposition would shape the limits and possibilities of the protesters and force them to create new structures from which to organize and mobilize against the regime.

2 | The Syrian Uprising   ——————

Political dissent had been effectively contained by the Syrian regime through a combination of repression and limited inclusion of social actors into the state. The corporatist relations that supported the Ba'athist model of development had begun to shift, however. In the absence of independent political parties or an autonomous civil society, there were no institutions for the expression and mobilization of political grievances. But socioeconomic decline, political inertia, and the continued state of emergency in Syria that had been in place since the 1960s all provided the basis for the articulation of political grievances and the mobilization of segments of the population within the broader context of the Arab uprisings. The mobilization of the 2011 period was markedly different than previous periods, during which political parties and patronage networks could cultivate and mobilize support around key issues and political demands. The suppression and incorporation of associational life precluded such mobilization in contemporary Syria. Nevertheless, in the absence of institutions, protests continued and social mobilization occurred in Syria.

This chapter focuses on the first months of the uprising, from March 2011 into the early period of 2012. We will examine the beginnings of the uprising and address how protests were able to sustain themselves in the absence of pre-existing institutions to mobilize the population. Here, the role of the Local Coordination Committees (LCCs) and other civil-society groups, in addition to social networks of protesters, was instrumental in giving the protests momentum and allowed them to continue in the face of sustained regime repression. We will also consider the role of the Syrian political opposition in exile and how the relations between opposition groups inside and outside of the country shaped the evolution of the conflict. The formation of the LCCs was vital to sustaining the protests as they took on multiple roles, first as organizers of the protests and as citizen journalists disseminating information about them, and, second in relief and governance roles when the regime's forces contracted throughout the country.

The regime's response throughout the first months of the process was to engage in sustained repression of the protesters while passing cosmetic political reforms. Both strategies failed to placate the protesters and a national movement quickly evolved. Yet despite the national character of the protests the movement was highly dispersed and decentralized, precluding effective coordination. Moreover, as the uprising continued the exiled opposition formed and attempted to exert its influence, to very little substantial effect, in large part because of its inability to suppress internal cleavages and to marshal material resources for the protesters. As the opposition became more militarized by the summer of 2011 and the exiled opposition fragmented into factions, the uprising had competing leaderships, all of which failed to coordinate and coalesce into a centralized command structure that could have placed military and political pressure on the regime. While these issues with the opposition help explain the regime's resiliency throughout this period, its ability to adapt to the changing circumstances of the protests, cultivate privatized violence, and consolidate its social base in 2011–2012 also helps explain why the regime did not succumb to the protests.

The Syrian Opposition

In the forty years of Ba'athist rule the domestic political opposition was severely suppressed. Political parties were essentially forbidden, except for those who accepted the leadership of the Ba'ath Party in the National Progressive Front, a coalition of parties represented in the ineffectual Syrian parliament. The emasculation of these parties and their subservience to the Ba'ath Party precluded the possibility of cultivating a base from which to mobilize against the regime. Political parties, such as the Muslim Brotherhood (MB), that did not acquiesce to this order were subject to repression. Simultaneously, the main associational institutions of society, such as unions and syndicates, were corporatized and brought under Ba'athist control, effectively circumscribing political autonomy and eliminating the possibility that they would function as vehicles for sociopolitical mobilization.

In this context, the only opposition to survive in any organizational form was the MB, but it did so outside of the country from the 1980s onwards. The Islamist opposition to Ba'athist rule was motivated by a number of factors, including opposition to Ba'athist secular policies, opposition to nationalization and modernization projects, and a rejection of state domination of the economy (Hinnebusch, 1990). The suppression of political activity and the deep cleavages between the regime and the Islamist opposition eventually led to violent confrontation, most dramatically in the attack by regime forces against Hama in 1982 that killed thousands of people. After 1982, the MB leadership was forced into exile and membership in the party remained punishable by death. The party would effectively cease to be a domestic opposition force as its leadership was effectively severed from supporters and constituents. With the elimination of the MB and the exile of its leadership the regime was successful in eliminating any popular threat to its hegemony.

With party life suppressed and the main opposition group in exile and its organizational capacity virtually eliminated, individuals emerged as the main oppositionists to the regime. The regime had effectively prevented the formation of an opposition and instead was left to deal with political opponents, who, as individuals, had no social base from which to mobilize. These individuals were typically academics or political writers. After 2000 and the assumption of power by Bashar al-Assad there was a general feeling among many within Syria that the new President was open to political dissent. Many of these figures thus began to more openly advocate for political reform. They ranged from academics to businesspeople to existing parliamentarians who may not have shared ideological affinities but were nevertheless committed to some form of political reform. Encouraged by what they believed to be a more open political climate after 2000, these "reformists" began organizing and in January 2001 produced the Statement of 1,000, a political document signed by 1,000 activists calling for reform. The increase of political dissent was to be short-lived, however. The Damascus Spring of 2001 was quickly suppressed by the regime, and many of the activists were imprisoned, threatened, or subject to physical violence by the *mukhabarat.*

The events of the Damascus Spring highlighted the structural weaknesses and realities of the political opposition. There were no parties to cultivate and mobilize a popular base of support. Politics and political dissent was left to individuals who were often risking their lives to make basic political demands. The heavy repression experienced by activists, many of whom were prominent figures in their respective professional fields, disincentivized any forms of activism by laypeople, let alone any attempts at organizing into political parties. The existing organizations consisted of small human rights groups and civil society forums, none with the capacity to challenge the regime. Human rights groups in particular suffered from a number of challenges that reduced their effectiveness, including the inability to recruit members and raise funds. Civil society forums were mostly meetings for people to come together and discuss social and political issues, leaving no room for collective organization and mobilization. The realities of regime repression and opposition weakness meant that the path to reform could not be taken through mass popular mobilization but only through incremental change and sustained demands against the regime regardless of the risks.

The plurality of the Syrian opposition is another factor that contributed to its overall weakness. Signatories of the Statement of 1,000 came from all corners of Syrian political life: Islamists, democracy activists, Kurdish figures, nationalists, leftists, social rights activists, and the business community. Although they agreed on the need for reform within Syria there was no institutional expression of their cooperation beyond their collective signatures. Many of the opposition figures remained wary of one another. Such mistrust precluded deeper forms of cooperation between opposition figures and rendered their attempt at making collective demands on the regime impotent and ineffectual.

This situation changed slightly in 2005 after the assassination of Rafik al-Hariri, Lebanon's Prime Minister, and the so-called Cedar Revolution in Lebanon that led to the withdrawal of Syrian armed forces from the country. From Syria's entry into the Lebanese civil war in the 1970s, and especially after the Ta'if Accord that ended Lebanon's civil war in 1990, the regime exercised hegemony over Lebanon. The collapse of Pax Syriana had seemingly weakened the regime and opened up another opportunity to opposition figures to make reform demands. In 2005 many of the opposition figures came together to form joint committees and initiatives that made space for cooperation (Landis and Pace, 2007: 54). The Muslim Brotherhood also played a prominent role in the attempts at unifying the Syrian opposition and many ideological adversaries from the secular or leftist political currents made very public overtures to the Brothers' leadership.

The move toward creating a broad opposition coalition culminated in the Damascus Declaration, a document envisioning democratic change in Syria. The Declaration expressed comitment to four guiding principles—nonviolence, democracy, oppositional unity, and democratic change—and was signed by five party coalitions, civil society groups, and a number of public figures. Eventually, many other groups and individuals from Syria's plural opposition landscape, including communists, nationalists, and Kurdish nationalists, pledged allegiance to the Declaration. For the first time in the modern history of Syria's opposition, secular and Islamist groups, Kurdish and Arab nationalists, and others from across the political spectrum had legitimized each other and committed to collective change in Syria.

Despite the importance of the coalition, the Declaration signatories were never able to translate their cooperation into sustained pressure against the regime or into an institutional arrangement that could take collective leadership of the opposition. Mistrust persisted among members, and accusations of cooperating with the regime undermined the legitimacy of others. Furthermore, fundamental disagreements over key national questions, particularly as they related to identity and citizenship issues, created schisms between some Arab and Kurdish figures. Perhaps most important, however, was the exile of the coalition. Many of the parties and figures who supported the Declaration lived outside of Syria and were disconnected from any wide support base. Those inside Syria were subject to heavy repression and increasingly found that exile was a safer and more politically strategic option from which to conduct their activities. It was thus in exile that Syria's opposition would crystallize in the 2000s. In late 2005, former Vice President Abdel Hallim Khaddam had defected to the opposition and formed an alliance with the MB. In 2006, Khaddam and the MB leadership created an opposition coalition called the National Salvation Front (NSF). However, the NSF was unsuccessful in generating public support from groups and figures inside Syria. The NSF was an entirely exile-led coalition that, while novel in bringing together Islamist and liberal currents into a political movement, lacked any wide social or popular base in Syria and was entirely ineffectual in advocating for reform and change within the country. For the most part, then, the regime was able to withstand opposition pressure for political reform. The impotence of the opposition and their lack of a popular base from which to mobilize Syrians made sure that the regime's repression of political activists and cosmetic political reforms would maintain Ba'athist hegemony.

Beginnings of the Uprising

There was no single cause of the Syrian uprising. The conflation of social, economic, and political factors alongside the breakdown of a culture of fear in the country (Kahf, 2014) all contributed to the protest movement. In the first few weeks, the protests were characterized by spontaneity and a lack of organization. Within months, the protests had spread throughout the country and it became meaningful to speak of a Syrian uprising that had national momentum, as protests were occurring throughout the entire country, from rural to urban areas. The lack of a unified or pre-existing Syrian opposition and the absence of a robust, autonomous civil society made organization and mobilization of protesters difficult.

Nevertheless, despite the absence of institutions that could mobilize Syrians, protests continued despite regime repression. This cycle—increasing protests inviting further regime repression—defined the first few months of the uprising prior to the militarization of the opposition later in 2011. The regime's response to the protests was twofold: on the one hand, regime forces engaged in brutal repression of protesters. On the other hand, the regime also rolled out a series of cosmetic political reforms. The rejection of these reforms by the protesters and the exiled political opposition fed into the regime's rhetoric that the protesters' only concern was destabilizing Syria and not political dialogue. In reality, the regime's overtures and reforms failed to placate the protesters because they were hollow: they never seriously threatened the regime's grip on power in the country or the impunity in which the security apparatus acted. In the remainder of this section, we explore the first months of the uprising and take a snapshot of key events that occurred in the first few months. The regime's dual response to the protests—reform and repression—simply accelerated the protests and set the stage for the deepening of the conflict.

The Arab uprisings were sparked by protests that began after the self-immolation of Tunisian street vendor Mohammed Bouazizi in December 2010 in the village of Sidi Bouzid. After suffering sustained harassment and humiliation at the hands of local police, Bouazizi ended his life in front of the local governor's office where he had gone to complain about his treatment, and where he had received no commitment from the governor or local government officials to end the harassment. His last words were, "How do you expect me to earn a living?" Within hours of his death protests began in Sidi Bouzid and then spread throughout the country. Though sparked by the suicide of Bouazizi, the protests were quickly framed around socioeconomic concerns and the endemic corruption and authoritarian rule of the incumbent regime led by President Zine el Abidine Ben Ali. After weeks of protests and the refusal of the Tunisian army to engage in violence against the protesters, Ben Ali fled the country on 14 January to Saudi Arabia, ceding to protester demands for his removal. The deposition of Ben Ali held promise that Tunisia could embark on a transition away from authoritarian rule and toward a more democratic political system. When similar protests spread throughout the Arab world, the hopes of the "Arab Spring" in Tunisia had been projected throughout the region.

Bouazizi's suicide "would change the course of Arab political history" (Sadiki, 2011) as protests gained momentum throughout the entire Arab world. There was not one Arab country that did not experience some form of protest, social mobilization, or political unrest that was motivated by the events in Tunisia. The entire Middle East state system and the geopolitical order that supported it seemed under attack. In January 2011 Hosni Mubarak, Egypt's long-serving president, stepped down after weeks-long protests throughout the country demanded his resignation, a dismantling of the regime, and a transition toward democratic politics. Although the removal of these "presidents for life" (Owen, 2012) was the first step in a long process toward dismantling the political and security apparatuses that constituted the regimes, the resignations nevertheless were seen as a transition away from authoritarianism. By February 2011, protests had spread to Libya. Although violence, especially state violence, was present throughout the countries experiencing protest, the Libyan case was the first one of the Arab uprisings that descended into what would be considered a civil war. Similarly, protests in Bahrain in the capital Manama led to the mobilization of the Peninsula Shield

Force, a Gulf Cooperation Council (GCC) military force, to quell the protests. In Libya, state violence against protesters brought the country to civil war and eventually international intervention by the North Atlantic Treaty Organization (NATO) that led to the removal of President Moammar al-Ghadafi. In Bahrain, the brutal, violent response would quell the protests but not without substantial social and political loss.

The militarization of the Arab uprisings in Libya and Bahrain would portend violence in Syria after protests began in February 2011. In January 2011, Bashar al-Assad gave an interview with the *Wall Street Journal* in which he dismissed the possibility of protests and large-scale violence reaching Syria, claiming, "We [Syria] have more difficult circumstances than most of the Arab countries [in reference to Western pressure and Syria's geopolitical alignments] but in spite of that Syria is stable" (*Wall Street Journal*, 2011). In the interview, he goes on to suggest that the conditions for an uprising in Syria do not exist because of the close ideological links between the government and the people.

Syria, however, was not immune from the contagion effect of the uprisings, as protests began in the southern city of Dar'a in February 2011. These protests came in response to the arrest and detention of fifteen middle-school-aged boys who had spray-painted the common Arab slogan of the protests "The people want the downfall of the regime" on their school wall. The detention of the young boys sparked immediate protest in Dar'a calling for their release. Eventually protests demanding their release along with that of other political prisoners morphed into anti-regime protests targeting emergency laws, poor socioeconomic conditions, corruption, police brutality, and arbitrary detention. On February 17, 2011, Dar'a experienced the first protests of the Syrian uprising, labelled the "Day of Anger." By March 15, 2011, a second protest had taken place. A third, after Friday prayers on March 18, gave the protesters increasing momentum in the city and put them in direct confrontation with the security forces who had begun to open fire and use live munitions on protesters. Meanwhile, around the same time in Damascus, hundreds protested and a female-led sit-in around the Ommayed Mosque in Central Damascus occurred, demanding the release of all political prisoners. By mid-March, protests were recorded throughout Syria in Damascus, Aleppo, al-Hassakeh, Dar'a, Deir ez-Zor, and Hama.

Within several weeks, the Syrian protests evolved into a movement that became more organized and which possessed a national momentum, but did not enjoy central coordination. Protests continued throughout the country and a shared language and set of demands emerged among the protesters. The principal demand was for regime change through the dismantling of the security apparatus, the resignation of President al-Assad, and the peripheralization of the political, security, and economic elite from the political sphere; a second demand called for the introduction of political reforms that would repeal emergency laws, lead to an independent judiciary and a new constitution, and create more representative political institutions and laws that were not subject to authoritarian control. Protests were quickly becoming more organized; local groups emerged to institutionalize the revolutionary energy and mobilize society against the regime. In the early stages of the uprising, these groups were mostly informal and used social, familial, and neighborhood ties. The first such evidence of institutionalized mobilization against the regime was the declaration of a group called The Youth of March 15 (in reference to the second major protest in Dar'a) who called for the dismantling of the regime, a series of political reforms, the release of political prisoners, and a range of socioeconomic measures to address poverty and inequality in the country. Other local groups reproduced such demands in the first months of the conflict and an uprising that was discursively and politically coalescing around demands for greater political rights was taking shape.

The inability of the regime's forces to quell the protests led to even more repression. The regime began to frame the protests as the work of foreign infiltrators and Islamist groups intent on destabilizing Syria (Ali, 2011). At this point, there was no evidence whatsoever that either the Syrian Muslim Brotherhood or any other Islamist movement was even remotely involved in the protests (Leenders, 2012; Leenders and Heydemann, 2012). Nevertheless, the regime maintained a policy of severe repression and the number of protester deaths increased through April into the summer months. In this period, the international community began to debate the Syrian conflict but the United Nations Security Council (UNSCR) failed to adopt a resolution condemning the regime's crackdown. The first signs of a Western–Russian/ Chinese split on the Syrian conflict had revealed themselves in the debates over the proposed resolution. Instead, Western states began imposing sanctions on regime officials in an attempt to place political pressure on regime elites to either defect or end the protests.

March and April 2011 were crucial months in the evolution of the uprising. While protesters were becoming more organized and LCCs were emerging to mobilize society, the Syrian regime engaged in a twofold response to the uprising. On the one hand, the regime enacted a series of cosmetic political reforms aimed at placating some of the protester's political demands. On the other hand, the security apparatus—the army, *mukhabarat* (intelligence services), police, and *shabiha* (thugs)—continued to engage in repression, including collective violence against protesters and against individuals participating in protest activity through arbitrary imprisonment, beatings, torture, kidnapping, and murder. The dual response of reform and repression suggests that the regime decision-makers were themselves divided over how to address the protests and that both security and political solutions to the crisis, no matter how cosmetic the political reforms actually were, had been contemplated by the regime leadership, both as a way to placate protesters and suggest to its supporters and the international community that the regime was capable of change.

Indeed, significant reforms were enacted on paper but these would have little consequence for the repression enacted by the security apparatus. On March 30, 2011, Bashar al-Assad addressed the Syrian parliament and categorized the protesters into those motivated and fuelled by foreign conspirators (a veiled reference to the Arab Gulf states, Israel, and the West) and satellite channels who were fomenting unrest in the country, and those who had serious political demands. Such a framing of the conflict by the regime would persist through the first years of the conflict. However, the failure of the regime's reforms to bring about an end to protests and violence would be taken as evidence by the regime and its supporters of the unwillingness of protesters to engage in dialogue and reform, and not as a failure of the regime itself. In that same speech, al-Assad dismissed the Cabinet and appointed a new Prime Minister. Later, 200 political prisoners from the notorious Saydnaya prison were released and granted clemency. On April 6, 2011, citizenship was extended to stateless Kurds and, later that month, the Emergency Law that had been in place since 1963 was repealed, satisfying a key demand of the protesters. The Higher State Security Court, the judicial body that tried cases in secrecy and was responsible for the detention and sentencing of security-related cases, was abolished, and a new law legalizing and regulating certain forms of protest was passed. In practice, however, the security apparatus continued to operate with impunity and these measures proved to have no effect on repression.

The regime's dual strategy of reform and repression would have no demonstrable effect on the momentum of the protests, which continued to increase during the first months of the uprising and which were spread throughout all major population centers of the country as well as throughout rural areas. Nevertheless, the regime continued to enact reforms meant to placate protesters. By the end of April, the weekly Friday protests that were occurring in unison throughout the country had resulted in increasing deaths at the hands of security forces. Meanwhile, activists and anti-regime supporters were arrested, imprisoned, beaten, and subject to other forms of repression. This did not, however, prevent the regime from establishing a committee in June to discuss the future of Syria—a move intended, yet again, to placate protesters and ostensibly provide a space for the expression of dissent. This occurred in the same week that internet service was effectively shut down in an attempt to prevent protesters from communicating with one another and the outside world. At no point in the course of these initial months had the security apparatus shown a commitment or adherence to the political track offered by the regime. Political reforms had no chance of being taken seriously while repression continued. The confrontation between the regime and activists was quickly spiraling out of control.

By June 2011, the violence in Syria was escalating. Protesters were regularly imprisoned and tortured and a campaign of repression was unleashed by the regime and its proxy security forces against anyone suspected of sympathy with the protesters. Thousands of Syrians were detained in this period and hundreds more killed. Regime violence became more brutal and involved much heavier weaponry, including an aerial campaign in June in the northwest of the country in Jisr al-Sughour after 120 regime soldiers were killed by armed rebels, which induced the largest wave of refugees into Turkey up until that point. Such large-scale violence would portend the coming months and years for Syrians. The brutality of the regime's response to the protests had pushed the uprising rather quickly toward militarization in a sort of self-fulfilling prophecy. The regime was unable to absorb the demands for political and economic rights and instead resorted to repression and demonization of protesters.

The regime's violent response to protests can also be understood within the context of intra-regime negotiations and debate about how to address the protests. Decision-making within regime circles is opaque and there is no way of knowing how larger strategic decisions are made, or whether there is coherency and agreement on the elite level about decisions. What is clear, however, is that there existed different options for regime decision-makers. The calculation that violence and repression was the best way out of the impasse was a clear victory for the more hardline decision-makers at the expense of those who may have been willing to offer some political concessions to stave off protests. From the early stages of the uprising, we saw a division between hardline and accommodationist positions (Valeriano and Marin, 2010) that continues today. While for the first years of the conflict the hardliners seem to have won, there are indications that the accommodationist position is perhaps not entirely dead. In particular, in late 2014 and early 2015, there have been a series of suspicious deaths and firings of key regime hardliners that indicates that the decision-making circles are in conflict with one another. In September 2014, for example, Hafez Makhlouf, the President's cousin and a hardliner who directed the powerful General Security Directorate in Damascus, was relieved of his duties and effectively exiled to Belarus. Rustom Ghazaleh, the head of Syria's political intelligence, was killed in 2015 when the bodyguards of Rafiq Shehadeh, head of military intelligence, physically beat him after a dispute between the two, reportedly over Iran's role in the conflict. These deaths and dismissals are but two in a series of recent reshuffles within the regime. At the moment, it is too early to tell what the long-term impacts of this reshuffling will mean but it does appear to reflect the growing strength of the accommodationists.

The trajectory of the Syrian uprising from this period onward would largely be determined by the transformations of the opposition groups and the adaptability of the regime to the uprising. In the remaining sections of this chapter, I consider both issues by examining the background of the growth of the opposition movement, the problems faced in the organization and mobilization of the protests, and how the regime responded to the new opposition movement. Unlike in previous periods of mass mobilization in Syria, the social and political background of the disaffected was not clearly defined. Syria's social stratification in the decades of Ba'athist rule and the shifts occurring during the 2000s discouraged and prevented the formation of cross-class, regional, or sectarian linkages between different social segments. Indeed, while many different social segments of Syrian society were disaffected and had grievances against the Ba'ath Party, these had never coalesced into a set of singular grievances or demands. As we will see below, the widespread disaffection with the Ba'ath Party may have fostered discontent and led to mobilization, but it was insufficient to generate coherency among the protesters.

Social and Political Backgrounds of the Protesters

The postcolonial Syrian political landscape was extremely plural, with many political parties and social networks vying for the allegiance of different segments of Syrian society. Syrian society on the eve of the uprising was no less segmented or fragmented than in those periods, with one key factor missing: by the 2000s, the Ba'ath Party had been successful in suppressing all forms of organized politics and had rendered all political parties inside of Syria and other associational groups, such as unions, impotent and unable to challenge the Ba'athist monopoly on political power and control of the state apparatus. The absence of formal political institutions in pre-uprising Syria should not be equated with the absence of political discontent. Rather, it points to the emasculation of political institutions and subsequent weak mobilization capacity of Syrian society. Political discontent was prevalent throughout Syria in the 2000s but, unlike in the postcolonial, pre-Ba'ath period, there were no parties or associations that could capture, represent, and mobilize this discontent.

As a result, the protests that began were completely decentered and leaderless, and were not organized by any national associations. They were more, however, than spontaneous demonstrations. From the early stages of the uprisings, demonstrations quickly spread throughout the country and adopted remarkably similar narratives despite the lack of central leadership. The expansion of the protests and the articulation of shared political grievances and aspirations gave the early protests the characteristics of coherent mobilization and not merely sporadic, spontaneous, and fragmented protests. Indeed, for the uprising to have occurred, to have assumed a national character, and to have spread throughout the country, mobilization first had to occur. The key question in the Syrian case is how mobilization occurred in the absence of institutionalized leadership. Or, in other words, how did the Syrian situation morph from a series of protests in Dar'a to more coherent mobilization and then an uprising with a national character when there were no political parties or associations to lead?

In the early stages of the uprising, Leenders and Heydemann (2012) have argued, the social networks of protesters and the "miscibility" of these networks, "or their ability to dissolve easily into one another because of their intense interconnectedness" (140), served as a substitute for formal institutions of mobilization and allowed the mobilization to spread and be sustained. Prior to this, there were significant barriers to collective action beyond the absence of political parties. In particular, widespread repression by the security apparatus had discouraged any form of nonviolent or violent collective action, with even political gatherings of nonviolent activists sometimes leading to long prison terms handed down by Syria's security courts.

There are at least five distinct social groupings (Abbas, 2011) that took part in the early protests and formed the dense social networks that sustained mobilization.

1. *Secular, educated, urban middle classes.* This group consisted of mostly young people who were professionals or were involved in cultural activities. They were mostly university educated and came from urban or semi-urban centers and had very few political linkages to the exiled opposition or domestic political activists (see below) who made up the pre-uprising opposition. In the early stages of the uprising, this group was heavily involved in media related activities as well as organizing protesters on the ground.

2. *Tribes (kinship based networks).* Al-Ayed (2015) has estimated that there are around 7.5 million Syrians (or 30 percent of the total population) of tribal background mostly concentrated in Deir ez-Zor, Raqqa, al-Hasakeh, and Dar'a but also located in the rural peripheries of Aleppo, Idlib, Hama, Homs, and Quneitra. Leenders and Heydemann (2012) have preferred to refer to these kinship networks as "clans" instead of tribes. These tribes were mostly concentrated in socioeconomically deprived areas and had borne the brunt of years of drought and

agricultural decline. Tribal leaders were instrumental in recruiting volunteers and protesters in the early stages of the uprising who could mobilize members based on existing socioeconomic grievances and historical exclusion from Ba'ath Party power. There has been no discernible political strategy from the tribes during the uprising, with some pledging allegiance to the opposition and others to the regime. The geographic concentration of the tribes has meant that they have been forced into conflict or partnerships with the main jihadist groups, Jabhat an-Nusra (JAN) and ISIS. In the case of an-Nusra, some tribes in the Deir Ez-zor area had been integrated into Nusra's command and military structure giving the organization a tribal character. In the case of ISIS, many tribes were initially targets of violence and repression and have, as of 2015, largely acquiesced to ISIS's rule in their areas, instead choosing to find accommodations with the organization.

3. *Political Islamists.* Members of this group are adherents of political Islam. Their affiliations and allegiances, however, are very diverse and not confined to the main Syrian Islamist Party, the Muslim Brotherhood. As membership in the Brotherhood was punishable by death, many of their activists inside Syria had been forced underground and were largely unable to recruit and organize supporters. Thus, many of the protesters in this group can be considered to support and adhere to some version of political Islam. They were typically supporters of particular religious sheiks who supported the uprising, or they were compelled to activism and protest by their religious beliefs. In the initial stages of the uprising and throughout its duration to the present, there has been no single Islamist party that dominated this group and offered a coherent vision and organizational structure. As Jabhat an-Nusra and ISIS entered the Syrian scene, many of the more militant activists from this grouping have migrated and joined them, while others who took up arms stayed in local, neighborhood groups affiliated with the Free Syrian Army or other brigades. Many other Islamist activ-

ists have also remained active in non-violent strategies and have participated in local councils and administrative structures.

4. *Political Activists.* The suppression of formal party politics by the Syrian regime led to the suffocation of political activity in the decades preceding the uprising. Nevertheless, there were many independent, non-affiliated political figures within Syria who had more or less made up the domestic opposition during Ba'ath Party rule. These activists were mostly intellectuals, professionals, or businesspeople. Their main institutional expression came in the early 2000s with the Damascus Declaration and the call for greater political freedoms within Syria, which only invited heavier repression by the regime and the imprisonment of many of their members. This grouping also consisted of social activists, such as human rights or prisoner rights activists, as well as political activists from leftist and Kurdish groups. Some activists from this group had been active in regime-sanctioned civil society organizations prior to the uprising.

5. *The Unemployed, Marginalized and Urban Subalterns* (Ismail, 2013). Unemployment and informality were key features of the Syrian economy before the uprising. The growing numbers of unemployed and underemployed Syrians grew considerably during the decade of marketization when public-sector opportunities effectively ceased, agricultural production (a main source of employment) plummeted, and the private sector was unable to provide jobs for the hundreds of thousands of Syrians entering the workforce each year. Informality and underemployment were not only urban phenomena but affected rural and semiurban areas as well, leading to a slow migration of many job seekers to the peripheries of Syria's main cities. Many of these migrants lived in informal housing, which have been estimated as high as 40 percent of total housing in the urban peripheries. Many of these people, who were on the outside of economic reforms and had very few job prospects, shared the socioeconomic and political grievances of other protesters and were natural participants in

the initial protest phases. Paradoxically, many Syrians in this grouping were also drawn into the *shabiha* and other paramilitary groups.

There was no common demographic (young/old), religious (Sunni/minority or secular/religious), social (urban/rural), or economic (upper/lower class) background to the protesters. The protesters shared common political and economic grievances against the regime even though they came from all geographic regions of Syria. While these protesters had perhaps dabbled in opposition politics they were largely not the veterans of Syria's pre-uprising political dissent (as described above) but, rather, newcomers to the political scene who were forced to forge ad hoc organizational structures under conditions of extreme repression and without the organizational, financial, or logistical capacity to do so. The difficulty of organization was compounded by the withdrawal of regime forces from certain areas of the country and the need to maintain and provide food and services to the local populations who had supported their political efforts. The withdrawal of regime security forces often paralleled the paralysis of state institutions in these areas that no longer functioned, further exacerbating the pressures placed on the protesters.

LCCs and the Problem of Mobilization

The establishment of the Local Coordination Committees (LCCs) in Syria came as a direct response to the need to organize protesters and to mobilize them against the regime. In the absence of pre-existing structures from which this could occur, the LCCs grew rather spontaneously in the various Syrian locales that were experiencing protest. They initially lacked any form of central organization and for many months remained decentralized and nonhierarchical. This afforded the LCCs some form of shelter from regime repression and gave them flexibility to adapt to the specific circumstances of their areas free from centralized control. Over time, the LCCs developed a much more networked structure that gave them the appearance of a national movement but, even today, much of the LCCs' work is focused on specific villages, towns, or city neighborhoods. In their brief history, the role of the LCCs has shifted and morphed considerably from being focused on activism (media outreach and protest organization) to providing relief to affected Syrians, and eventually into governance.

As protests raged throughout Syria in early 2011, there were no institutional apparatuses, such as political parties, unions, or professional syndicates, which were able to organize and mobilize protesters. The varying social and geographic backgrounds of the protesters made organization between their immediate networks difficult, if not impossible. For the most part, protests were occurring independently of each other and of any central coordinating body even as they were spreading throughout the country and increasing in their size and momentum. To begin to address the problems of organization and coordination, Tansiqiyyat, or the Local Coordination Committees (LCCs), were created in the first months of the uprising by activists who were seeking greater coordination of protest activity, to increase media visibility inside and outside of Syria of the uprising, and to enhance cooperation with other activists within Syria. In the initial weeks and months after the Dar'aa protests, the LCCs were focused on communication and logistical issues. The LCC activists took assumed responsibility for setting up sound systems, creating banners, fundraising, distributing information, and agreeing on common slogans for the protests.

The LCCs typically began as small gatherings of one or two dozen activists and them morphed in membership well into the hundreds, depending on the locale. They were entirely spontaneous in their formation and born out of the immediate needs of the moment. As they grew, solidarity between activists increased and the roles of the LCCs slowly began to expand. These early efforts created what Doreen Khoury (2012) has called "networks of solidarity" among LCC activists. Activists were similarly bound by their commitment to preserve and continue the uprising while creating a new national narrative that provided an alternative to the regime's own sectarian policy and their labeling of the protesters as sectarian agitators.

The role of the LCCs began to shift as regime power contracted throughout the country. The LCCs had morphed in some cases into Local Councils (LCs) which assumed responsibility for governing areas outside of regime control. The LCs had assumed responsibility for providing services, such as health care and education, maintaining the legal system, and attending to administrative issues. A shift was thus underway among the LCCs who were incorporating governance roles into their activities and had begun to morph into administrative actors. The vacuum created by the withdrawal of regime forces and the collapse of state institutions in certain parts of the country was initially filled by the LCs that had used the opportunity to begin to organize and govern society along revolutionary lines.

There are three central functions that the LCCs and LCs have played in the Syrian uprising. The first is that of activists, organizers, and citizen journalists. The initial protests would not have been sustained without the work of the LCCs and local activists. Citizen journalism was crucial to communicating information about the protests to other Syrians and to the outside world. While maintaining a focus on media efforts and protest organization, the LCCs began to work together to unify their political messages and slogans and to present a unified, cross-sectarian, and national voice with which to counter the regime's accusations that protesters were foreign infiltrators bent on disrupting Syria's stability. In articulating a new national story for Syria, the LCCs were putting forth an alternative vision for the country that could, in their hope at least, serve as the basis for a new political community free from Ba'athist hegemony (Ismail, 2013). Citizen journalism was essential to legitimizing the revolution for many Syrians as reliable, credible information was communicated from protests throughout the country. The activists had developed a sophisticated system of verification that allowed them to establish and maintain credibility among

Syrians and, less important, international media who were reporting on the conflict.

The second function that they provided was that of relief work. The LCs have consistently focused efforts on providing relief work to Syrians affected by the conflict through a series of civil-society organizations devoted to relief efforts. These organizations have been involved in providing medical services, schooling, and housing for displaced Syrians. Finally, the LCs have served a governance function in the nonregime areas. In the absence of functional state institutions, the LCs have served as de facto government in many areas. Unfortunately, the LCCs have not yet been sufficiently integrated into a centralized structure so much of this governance work is unstructured and unsustainable. In 2014, there were well over 400 LCCs in Syria operating throughout the country. In larger cities, there are often multiple committees who focus their work on specific neighborhoods or locales. While they often developed horizontal institutional linkages with other LCCs through the creation of different Majlis Thawar (Revolutionary Councils) that provided a space for LCC activists from different committees to meet and organize, these larger councils never materialized into bodies with national reach.

Notwithstanding the inability of the LCCs to evolve into a centralized structure, the activity of the Committees throughout Syria has been remarkable under the circumstances. Having evolved from a series of citizen journalists and protest organizers to taking on responsibilities for governance, the LCCs and their supporters were trying to organize a society in revolt in exceptionally violent circumstances. Making this task even more challenging was the absence of a pre-existing network of support or any history of collective activism. The spontaneity of the LCCs' rise and the limited horizontal integration between them has meant that there is no clear institutional structure that is replicated across governorates. There is no hierarchy as such beyond three offices that organize the three main functions of the LCCs: a relief office, media office, and an executive committee that deals with political and governance activities.

In addition to the LCCs, dozens of Syrian civil society organizations were established during the uprising. These organizations work in multiple fields, including media and relief, and have formed both inside and outside of the country. The uprising has given them the opportunity to grow autonomously, unlinked to the government. However, the new organizations were all born out of the conflict conditions and driven by the dire humanitarian situation. They operate in extremely difficult and dangerous environments and largely without sustainable financial and organizational resources. Nevertheless, the LCCs and civil society organizations have formed the backbone of the uprising from 2011 until now and have been caught between regime repression and rebel violence. For many, this has not prevented continued work toward realization of the uprising's goals.

A New Civil Society

Civil society in Syria prior to the uprising was severely circumscribed. The majority of organizations were devoted to charitable works. Those that organized issues of social and political rights were either extensions of the government (and thus not a serious threat to the regime's grip on political power) or were severely repressed and limited in the scope of their activities. Thus, when the uprising began in March 2011, there were no independent, autonomous civil society associations that could organize and mobilize protesters. Associational life in Ba'athist Syria had been severely repressed and the effects of the absence of robust associational life was evident in the early phase of the uprising.

The growth of Syrian civil society organizations since the uprising began has been necessitated by the demands of the uprising and the opportunities presented by the regime's contraction. Today, Syrian civil society organizations are active in all fields of social rights, relief and aid services, advocacy, governance, capacity-building, and economic reconstruction. They work very closely with the LCCs and the LCs in many areas. There are also dozens of organizations who operate in neighboring countries to provide relief work for Syrian refugees.

Some of the civil society organizations were started by existing activists who had experience. The majority of organizations, however, were started by activists who had no experience in civil society organizing whatsoever and who had been politically inactive in the years prior. In this way, the civil society groups shared a common trajectory with the LCCs, which were more or less spontaneous outgrowths of the uprising. Like the LCCs, many civil society groups started out very small and were loosely structured around familial and social networks. The LCCs focused on media, then relief and governance efforts; civil society groups focused on a range of other services and activities.

These groups were engaged in different forms of activism and work. They quickly became embedded in larger networks of activism, such as Najda Now (Assistance Now) or Mussalaha (Reconciliation), which focus, respectively, on bringing aid to Syria and bringing together community leaders to engage in reconciliatory dialogue. Other networks focus exclusively on aid provision, such as the Union of Syrian Medial Relief Organizations (UOSSM), which operates in the diaspora, or nonviolent civil disobedience, such as Ayyam al-Hourriya (Freedom Days). Given the dire situation, networked activism has become the most effective way for Syrian civil society to affect the humanitarian situation.

The growth of a Syrian civil society during the conflict is a testament to the resiliency of Syrian society in the face of ever-increasing violence and brutality and the persistence of Syrians in their pursuit of a better future. The civil society organizations that have been created since 2011 have faced a number of major challenges during the course of the conflict. The contraction of regime authority and the collapse of state institutions created a dire need for the administration of nonregime areas and for the provision of aid and services to the population. Civil society organizations have attempted to fulfill the dual role of administration and aid providers during the conflict. The major obstacle to this role is the deteriorated security situation in the country and the hostility with which most armed groups, from the regime to ISIS, view the civil society organizations. Most armed groups have actually refused to cooperate with many of the civil society groups and have instead established alternative institutions to exercise authority and provide aid. These groups are much better funded than the LCs and other civil society groups and are thus able to embed themselves in Syrian society more deeply. Today, civil society activists are engaged in a sort of perpetual revolution against the regime and against the armed groups that now dominate areas in which they operate.

In addition to the security situation, civil society groups face the challenge of providing aid and services in wartime. There is a severe shortage of basic necessities in Syria. The armed groups are able to procure goods through the war economy, while civil society groups are dependent on them for access to these goods. Such dependence severely compromises the groups' ability to provide relief services and to support Syrian communities. They are thus faced with a dire humanitarian situation which they have very few resources to remedy.

The difficulty of civil society's aid provision is also a function of their limited resources and their reliance on the Syrian National Council (SNC) and private Syrian donors for their financial resources. These have been largely insufficient to help support social service provision, especially in major areas such as water, electricity, and communications. The absence of financial and technical resources (such as phones and computers) has impeded the work of civil society organizations. Although financial resources are perhaps the most important challenge facing Syrian civil society, other factors have also made their work extremely difficult, including the challenges of mistrust and corruption, the lack of cooperation between groups, and political and ideological divisions that preclude collective action.

Perhaps the largest challenge facing Syrian civil society is in being taken seriously as a political actor in the uprising. The militarization of the uprising has deflected attention away from civil initiatives and the resiliency of nonviolence in Syria. The focus on militarization has thus ignored the profound impacts on Syrian society that have occurred in the development and networking of civil society initiatives. The absence of civil society groups from any negotiations, for example, suggests that they are irrelevant to the larger political answers that will decide the evolution of the Syrian crisis.

The Syrian National Council

The Syrian National Council (SNC) was the first coalition of the political opposition formed after the uprising. Aside from the LCCs, the SNC was composed entirely of parties and political currents outside of Syria and included the Muslim Brotherhood, the Damascus Declaration, the National Bloc, the Kurdish Bloc, the Assyrian Bloc, and independents. The SNC was officially created in October 2011 after a summer of deliberation between Syria's various exiled political factions came together to form an alternative to the regime. A charter was quickly passed that delineated power sharing among the parties and created various offices to liase with the protesters and the international community.

Despite the common goal of removing al-Assad from power, the SNC was fraught with internal divisions from the outset and was never able to develop into a serious and legitimate alternative to the regime. Council members had openly argued with one another and there were repeated threats (some acted upon) by members to resign over key questions of political strategy. In February 2012, for example, twenty SNC members resigned over the SNC's rejection of working with the armed opposition. Such internal division has continued to plague the SNC and the various exile political coalitions since the beginning of the uprising.

Multiple Leaderships

Although there is a long and rich history of political opposition in contemporary Syria, for all intents and purposes the opposition today is new. The three main networks that emerged in the months after the uprising—the Local Coordination Committees (LCC), Syrian National Coalition (SNC), and the Free Syrian Army (FSA, discussed in Chapter Three)— were nonexistent prior to the uprising and thus owe their creation to the political opportunity provided by the protests. In 2011 and 2012 especially, there were multiple attempts to unite the political opposition but these attempts largely failed to bring about coherency or affect political change, leading to a fragmented inside/outside opposition divided over issues of political legitimacy and questions of political strategy. On almost every key political strategy question facing the opposition in the first year of the uprising—whether to engage in dialogue with the regime, support violence or nonviolence, or call for military intervention—the opposition is divided along inside/outside lines (Sayigh, 2012). Activists within Syria (mostly represented by the LCC) were far removed from the politics of the exiled opposition that formed under the SNC.

The emergence of opposition groups inside and outside of the country had a significant effect on the ability of the opposition to affect the course of the uprising because it created multiple leaderships within the opposition. The absence of a pre-existing opposition that could organize and mobilize protesters forced oppositionists inside and outside the country to provide some organizational structure to their political demands. Mistrust and a lack of coordination between the different opposition groups created the conditions for fragmentation and the emergence of even more opposition groups as the uprising progressed. The multiple opposition groups were not only defined by their lack of horizontal coordination among groups but even a lack of vertical coordination *within* the movements themselves. Coordination between different LCCs or even within the SNC was not effective. The LCC and the FSA had highly decentralized structures, with each local committee or group operating independently. There is some coordination between different cells but not enough to speak of an organized, linear chain of command. In the case of the FSA, there was no military strategy adhered to by fighters and even less coordination over the distribution of material support. The opposition movement then was more a collection of nodes and networks of opposition than a coherent, coalesced movement with a clear hierarchical command.

The fragmented and networked structures of the opposition led Hassan Abbas (2011) to refer to this as the problem of a head without a body. The body of the uprising, represented by the demonstrators, has grown more apart from the head, represented by the different exiled opposition groups. The opposition in 2011 was thus structurally and politically weak. More important, however, was that the Syrian exile opposition suffered from an early legitimacy deficit that can be traced to two factors (Abboud, 2012). The first concerns the inability of the exiled opposition to formulate a discourse and narrative of a post-Ba'athist Syria that could resonate across Syria's wide social spectrum. Even in the early stages of the uprising, there were legitimate fears among many Syrians that the sectarianism dynamics of the uprising—a mostly Sunni-led protest movement against a predominantly minority regime—would lead to a bloody civil war and the sectarian fragmentation of the country. The fear of sectarianism very early on shaped how the protest movement was constituted (Ismail, 2011). Many Syrians did indeed despise the regime and perhaps wished for it to be overthrown, but their fear of sectarian violence and the division of the country along sectarian lines prevented many from openly supporting the political opposition. Groups such as the LCC engaged in what Ismail (2011) calls "political community making" in which they have publicly taken strong positions against sectarianism and for civil rights for all Syrians regardless of sect. This, however, has failed to resonate throughout Syria and the fears of sectarianism remained strong.

The second factor contributing to the legitimacy deficit was the inability of the exiled opposition to ensure the provision of material support to the demonstrators. For all intents and purposes, the SNC had no on-the-ground presence in Syria and were not able to provide resources to demonstrators. While the material relationship is important here, the more important factor is that the exiled opposition was made up of oppositionists who were largely unknown to the protesters. They were thus unwilling to politically support the SNC when there was no immediate social basis of support or material benefit to doing so.

All of the early opposition groups were united in their desire for a political transition in Syria. They were not united, however, around questions of political strategy and how to achieve that transition. There were two main questions concerning violence that divided the opposition in the first year of the uprising and which continued to plague the opposition in subsequent years. The first questions concerns whether to pursue violence or nonviolence as a political strategy. Virtually all the main opposition groups inside the country, including the LCC, rejected the role of the FSA in militarizing the conflict. The LCC and the National Coordination Body for Democratic Change (NCB) (a Syria-based opposition group) had advocated for nonviolent political strategies to confront the regime. Smaller opposition groups such as the al-Watan coalition and the Building the Syrian State Party had similarly criticized militarization. However, the SNC, which initially supported nonviolent strategies, began to shift and openly support arming the opposition and the militarization of the uprising. A second question concerned whether to advocate for military intervention. The case for military intervention was motivated by what oppositionists saw was a successful NATO-led campaign in Libya to oust al-Ghadafi's regime. The LCC, NCB, and other groups inside Syria were initially staunchly against Western intervention while the SNC leadership was increasingly supportive of intervention. Having limited access to the protesters, the SNC resorted to appealing to the international community as a means of affecting political transition. For the SNC, the only substantive strategy they could pursue was to have the western powers intervene into Syria and collapse the regime.

The multiple leadership problems of the Syrian opposition were compounded by a severe legitimacy deficit and disputes over political strategy. However, the most important factor explaining the opposition's inability to bring about political transition in the first year of the uprising is a combination of regime resiliency and insufficient resources to organize society and maintain security in nonregime areas. On the one hand, as I discuss below, the regime proved able to adapt to the changing situation on the ground and was successful in drawing on military and financial resources to stave off collapse. On the other hand, the regime's adaptability and resiliency was partially due to deficiencies in the opposition and the inability to provide a stable and sustainable alternative to the regime in the liberated areas.

Authoritarian Adaptibility

What explains the regime's resiliency during the course of the conflict? There are broadly two factors that can answer this question: the first external to the regime, that is, in the deficiencies and weaknesses of the opposition; and, second, in the ability of the regime to adapt to the changing circumstances wrought by the uprising. Indeed, even prior to 2011, the Syrian regime and other Arab authoritarian states had been undergoing transformative processes that were meant to consolidate authoritarian rule. In this period in Syria (as discussed in Chapter One), and throughout the Arab world, significant economic reforms had been undertaken that disrupted the material basis of postcolonial authoritarianism. These shifts had intended not to destabilize authoritarianism but rather to consolidate and strengthen it. These transformations gave rise to an area of inquiry concerned with authoritarian upgrading (Heydemann, 2007) and how shifting domestic and international political economies were changing patterns of authoritarian rule.

As the outbreak of the Arab uprisings suggests, the authoritarian upgrading project has largely failed, with many states in the region unable to stably balance neoliberal economic policies with authoritarian politics. The new modes of authoritarian governance ushered in during the 1990s and accelerated during the 2000s had the long-term effect of destabilizing the authoritarian states of the region. The Syrian regime's adaptability in the context of the uprising must be understood within the larger trajectory of authoritarian upgrading, with this stage defined by a more militarized, sectarian, and repressive core (Heydemann, 2013a,b: 63). For Hinnebusch (2012), authoritarian upgrading had significant costs that, as the uprising demonstrated, could not be contained in Syria. However, this upgrading was unbalanced and while it fostered grievances, it had not led to the withering or contraction of the regime's social base into a specific segment of society. Thus on the eve of the uprising the regime still had a strong social base of support that remained largely loyalist throughout the course of the conflict. The regime's survival is dependent on the support of these social groups, and the support has remained more or less intact throughout the conflict. These groups include the army and security apparatus, the crony capitalists (Hinnebusch, 2012), public sector employees (Haddad, 2012), religious minority groups, and the middle classes. These social groups have supported the regime because of a combination of sectarian/social, socio-economic, and security factors (Haddad, 2012). Perhaps the most important factor contributing to continued regime support has been how the regime has successfully fomented fear of the opposition and portraying them, particularly the militarized opposition, as foreign agents intent on destabilizing Syria. The regime's narratives about the protesters have also been overly sectarian and have played on minority fears of an Islamist takeover of the country. The fear of a Salafi-jihadist takeover of Syria has frightened both religious minorities and Syrian Sunnis who share fears about what Salafist rule would mean for them. Such fears have been profoundly strong among many Syrians, including those who have supported the uprising.

Yet, the regime's resilience cannot solely be explained by Syrian fears of a Salafist-jihadist takeover of the country. Stephen Heydemann has argued that the regime's resilience can be explained through authoritarian adaptation that has allowed the regime to adapt to the demands of the uprising while maintaining its own survival (2013a). For Heydemann, the regime's adaptation was multifaceted and included a series of institutional and policy transformations while simultaneously maintaining violence against protesters. On the international front, the regime was forced to maneuver around increasing international isolation and a restrictive sanctions regime by relying extensively on its main international supporters, Iran and Russia. Shifts in international alliances and a rapidly transforming geopolitical landscape have been central features of not only the Syrian regime's adaptability but that of other states as well (Aras and Falk, 2015). Domestically, the regime mobilized its social base by appealing to their fears of a broad Islamist takeover of the country. The regime responded to the contraction of the economy by rolling back market reforms and reasserting the state's role in the economy through the re-establishment of subsidies and other forms of economic welfare. This has not stemmed the tide of economic decay but has nevertheless been useful. Finally, the regime reorganized the security apparatus and military to better confront the tactics and strategies of the armed opposition (Heydemann, 2013a,b: 62).

The regime's adaptability has thus been structured by many domestic and international factors that have allowed its mutation and transformation in the face of rapid change on the ground. Its ability to navigate the conflict and to remain in control of large parts of the country suggest that regime elements, whether government or security officials or the business elite (Abboud, 2013), will be positioned to remain key players in the postwar reconstruction of the country. While some regime elements will undoubtedly survive into the post-conflict period, the regime's longevity or survival is uncertain and indeed even unlikely given the fragmentation of the country and the multiple military, economic, and political pressures on it. Nevertheless, the regime has remained resilient and adaptive as the conflict has grown and transformed.

The strength of the Assad regime's social base, the fear of sectarianism, the cohesion of the security apparatus, and the adaptability to the changes in the opposition movement have all contributed to the government's longevity during the conflict. A second factor—the weaknesses of the opposition—also helps explain the government's resilience throughout the conflict. Opposition weakness should be understood broadly here to refer to the inability of the opposition to bring about regime collapse but also to how the opposition has been unsuccessful in fracturing the regime's social support base or disincentivizing support for the regime. For many Syrians, support for Assad does not arise out of loyalty or commitment or even agreement with the regime's strategies during the war, but rather out of an objective fear of the opposition and a mistrust in the opposition's ability to provide a reasonable alternative. The weaknesses of the opposition and the horrors of violence in which all major armed groups are implicated have placed many Syrians in the unenviable position of having to choose between the lesser of two evils.

From Peaceful Protest to Violent Conflict?

The protests that began in Dar'a in March 2011 created and propelled a national movement of protests against the Syrian regime. The regime's response to the protests was to engage in sustained repression while passing cosmetic reforms, both of which failed to placate or stop the protests. Over the course of the Ba'ath Party's rule over Syria, they had been effective in suppressing all forms of associational activity. When the protests began, there were no institutions such as political parties that could organize and mobilize the protesters. This role was left to the newly created LCCs, a network of local activists who had come together to try and organize a society in revolt. However, the continued repression and the challenges of mobilizing under conflict conditions kept the LCCs fragmented and decentralized. The failure of the political opposition in exile to provide material or political support to the protesters on the ground contributed to the weakening of the LCCs and the inability of the opposition inside and outside of the country to coalesce and form a unified movement.

At the same time, the regime demonstrated its resiliency and adaptability during the conflict, which helps explain why the pressure of the protests did not lead to its immediate collapse. The fragmentation of the opposition and its multiple leaderships contributed to the regime's longevity, which can be explained as much by the weaknesses and shortcomings of the opposition as it can by Assad's military or political strength. The regime's resiliency then represents something of a paradox: on the one hand, it has lost control of large parts of Syria and no longer has the administrative capacity to govern in areas that it ostensibly controls. It has been under tremendous pressure from within its support base from segments of Syrian society that are increasingly fatigued by the war and are demanding its end (Dark, 2014).

On the other hand, the inability of the opposition to cohere and form a structured movement that has the political power and legitimacy to overthrow Assad and put forth a feasible transition plan has allowed the regime to maintain control over key areas of the country amid tremendous political and military pressure.

It has become common in most analyses of the Syrian conflict to draw a clear division between the period of popular, nonviolent mobilization and that of militarization. As I have maintained throughout the book, this is a false periodization of the conflict, as both nonviolent mobilization and armed insurrection or regime violence have been present since the outset. However, in the initial months after the uprising when the nonviolent mobilization had proved unable to overthrow the regime and the political pressures brought to bear by the external opposition proved futile, many in Syria chose the path of militarization as the option most likely to bring about the regime's overthrow. Thus, the seeds of militarization were planted in the initial stalemate that defined the conflict during 2011, a period in which the internal and external opposition was still in its infancy and had proved unable to bring about an end to the conflict.

In the next chapter, I explore the dynamics driving the militarization of the conflict. In doing so, I am trying to situate the rise of an armed opposition in parallel, rather than in opposition to, the nonviolent, popular mobilization that began in 2011. Syria's conflict has morphed considerably from 2011 and while militarization has contributed to territorial fragmentation and a humanitarian crisis (both discussed below) there has remained an active and robust nonviolent movement that is committed to the initial ideals of the Syrian revolution. Militarization has not meant the collapse of the early mobilizers discussed in this chapter, but has contributed to the expansion of the wider landscape of the Syrian opposition and the expansion of groups operating inside Syria. Whereas many in the nonviolent opposition had more or less consistent goals around regime change and political transitions, as we see below, armed actors inside Syria have wildly contradictory and conflicting goals. Such conflicts between groups have fueled further violence inside Syria and made the possibilities for immediate resolution even more remote.

| 3 | The Emergence of
Armed Opposition |
|---|---|

The militarization of the Syrian uprising began in June 2011 when army defectors formed brigades under the banner of the Free Syrian Army (FSA). Over the next few months, the main armed opposition in Syria grew under the FSA umbrella and quickly spread throughout the country with units and brigades emerging in major cities and in the rural peripheries. Much like the LCCs discussed in the previous chapter, this gave the FSA the appearance of having a vertical and horizontal command structure and, most importantly, a national character. With the creation of the FSA and the presence of an external and internal opposition the Syrian uprising expanded into political and military wings that had as their ostensible common goal the overthrow of the regime. However, such coherence between the political and military wings of the uprising was a mirage, and no substantive forms of cooperation that could affect political change ever emerged.

Since then, violence has proliferated throughout Syria. The conflict has become bloodier and more deadly, with thousands of Syrians murdered or displaced each month. In this chapter, we will explore the growth and use of violence in the Syrian conflict by both regime and nonregime forces. The militarization of the uprising—and the subsequent inability of the political and military opposition to overthrow the regime—led to the dramatic expansion of violence, the proliferation of different armed groups, and the territorial fragmentation of the country. The FSA's failure paved the way for the emergence of other armed groups, including but not limited to the Islamic Front, the Army of Islam, Jabhat an-Nusra, and the Islamic State of Iraq and as-Sham (ISIS), all of whom had conflicting agendas and strategies. Meanwhile, the Syrian Arab Army (SAA) has withered and the regime has been forced to rely on homegrown armed groups such as the National Defence Forces (NDF) and regional groups, such as Hizbollah and Iraqi and Iranian militiamen, to achieve its military objectives. In this chapter, we will explore the landscape of violence in Syria with specific reference to who the main actors are, why there is a lack of coordination between rebel forces, why regional states are supporting opposing sides, and how the diffused violence in Syria is not only precluding both military and political solutions to the conflict, but also contributing to continued stalemate and the slow fragmentation of the country into areas controlled by armed groups.

Understanding Violence in the Syrian Context

The nonviolent nature of the uprising gave rise to a number of studies drawing on Social Movement Theory (SMT) (Droz-Vincent, 2014; Leenders and Heydemann, 2012) to help explain the mobilization of large segments of Syrian society. Such approaches to mobilization and conflict do not sufficiently explain the militarization of the Syrian conflict or the nature of violence since 2011. Indeed, the proliferation of armed groups and the diffusion of violence throughout the country and beyond any central regime or rebel command structure is an important factor in explaining the continuity of the Syrian conflict, the profound violence being inflicted on civilians, and the current stalemate. How then can we understand the proliferation and nature of violence in Syria?

Mary Kaldor (1999; 2012) has proposed understanding contemporary civil violence through the perspective of "new wars" theory, an approach arguing that contemporary wars have four defining features: (1) they are fought by combinations of state and nonstate violent networks; (2) these networks are motivated by identity politics and not ideology; (3) networks attempt to achieve political, rather than physical, control of populations through fear; and (4) violence is financed through predatory measures that perpetuate violence. Kaldor's approach attempts to understand and theorize how we should understand contemporary warfare. Her approach is not without its critics, who argue that there is very little of anything "new" about the kinds of war and violence she explains (see Utas, 2012; Henderson and Singer, 2002). Moreover, the new wars approach has limited explanatory capacity in the Syrian context because of how its proponents downplay the role of geopolitics and ideological factors in perpetuating conflict, instead identifying globalization as the main structuring factor of new wars.

This is not the space to engage in the new wars debates (for a discussion of new wars and Syria see Malantowicz, 2013) but rather to weed out how these debates have provide analytical tools to help us explain the nature of violence in Syria. There are three main analytical tools in particular that can help us understand the proliferation and diffusion of violence, the structure and interrelations of armed groups, and stalemate and the continuity of conflict. The first concerns how war has become increasingly civilianized. The new wars debates have emphasized the civilianization of war, understood as the increasing involvement of civilians, rather than soldiers, in violence and war. This refers not only to civilians as armed actors, but as victims and supporters of violence (Steenkamp, 2014: 58). Civilians become instrumental to the proliferation of violence. The civilianization of violence is in part a response to the threats that emerge from outside communities. As we will see throughout this chapter, many of the rebel and regime armed groups formed initially to protect their locales. Today, many of the localized units in nonregime areas are made up of only a few dozen fighters at most and are concentrated in specific geographic spaces with virtually no mobility. The same is true of many proregime militias who are not directly connected to any central command. These units, whether in rebel or regime areas, are embedded and entrenched in their communities. In many contemporary wars, including Syria's, civilians, with little to no prior military training, have formed armed units and are connected to other armed groups in an intricate, networked structure that gives violence an organized character.

A second, related analytical tool concerns how the civilianization of war allows for the multiplicity of violence because it expands the social basis of violence (Steenkamp, 2014). Violence is no longer perpetuated by state actors, or even a small number of nonstate actors, but by a plethora of fighting units that all have different social backgrounds, strategies, goals, and capacities. New wars, then, are characterized by violence perpetuated by independent, autonomous groups, rather than state armies. These autonomous groups include militias, warlords, jihadists, armed insurgents, mercenaries, armed smugglers, and regular civilians. The members of these groups who exercise violence often lack military training. The nature of violence is often small-scale, including light weapons, and does not involve heavy artillery or air attacks and, as such, is not conducive to overrunning and defeating military forces. The objective for perpetrators of violence becomes to consolidate and control specific areas and to entrench themselves there.

A third final tool concerns the political economy of war. Maintaining violence and controlling territories requires material resources that are not readily available to many armed groups in the absence of state sponsorship or funding. Conflict provides economic opportunities to finance and profit from it. How armed groups finance their violence is central to understanding new wars and to the role of informality and criminality therein. Contemporary wars create the opportunities for networks to emerge that are engaged in both violence and economic profiteering, giving rise to organized structures of exchange, transportation, and consumption that are structured by war and violence. In wars such as Syria's, virtually all armed groups are dependent on war economies and the opportunities afforded by war. With this in mind, the remainder of the chapter identifies the main armed groups fighting in both the rebel and regime camps.

The Rise of the Free Syrian Army

The militarization of the Syrian uprising can be attributed to two main factors: first, the sustained and brutal violence inflicted on protesters by the regime and its armed proxies that encouraged Syrians to take up arms, and, second, the failure of the protests to initiate a political transition process, such as that which occurred in Tunisia and Egypt. Despite the regime's cosmetic political reforms in the months following the outbreak of the uprising, it was clear by the summer of 2011 that they were committed to a military solution to the uprising. As violence increased, protests expanded. And so went the vicious cycle. The initial protests were strongly committed to nonviolence as a political strategy, but in the months following the uprising this strategy was put under tremendous strain as some in the external opposition began advocating for international intervention and the creation of an armed wing. As these debates were ongoing within opposition circles, groups of army defectors began forming in their respective locales and began confronting regime forces with violence. Eventually, during the summer of 2011, these groups would form under the banner of the Free Syrian Army (FSA) and would form the core of the militarized opposition.

While some heralded the formation of the FSA as a necessary step toward bringing about political transition, in reality, the FSA was fraught with the same contradictions that characterized the political opposition. Even after five years of conflict, it is misleading to speak of the FSA as an army as such, with a horizontal command, a vertical communication structure, common command, shared resources, or even any real sense of esprit de corps among its members. The fragmentation of the FSA and the lack of coherency and centralization within its ranks suggests that the brigades form more of a network of violence than an army. An army has a central and hierarchical command, whereas a network of violence can be understood differently: as a decentralized form in which the various nodes of the network operate independently from one another but in relative cooperation. The lack of hierarchy or integration between the nodes makes their relationships precarious and contributes to the constant shifting of alliances.

The FSA was officially declared on 29 July 2011 when a group of defected officers led by Colonel Riad al-Assad declared the group's existence, pledging to support the uprising's goals of overthrowing the regime. The FSA consisted of only a few hundred, and perhaps thousands, of army defectors who were loosely organized in their respective geographic locales. Defectors from Homs, for example, were predominantly active in and around that city, and their operations were initially focused on protecting protesters and civilian areas from repeated regime attacks. The FSA's weapons were entirely drawn from stockpiles and caches they had confiscated from regime bases or taken with them when they defected. As such, they had very limited offensive capabilities to engage in sustained battles with regime forces in the major cities. In the late summer of 2011 the FSA had concentrated its activities on defensive activities to protect civilians, raids to capture weapons, and limited attacks on regime forces in areas of the country where they were deemed militarily vulnerable, such as in the urban and rural peripheries.

These military limitations paralleled the fragmented organizational structure of the armed opposition after the formation of the FSA. Broadly speaking, two types of armed groups emerged under the FSA umbrella. The first group consisted of highly localized and geographically concentrated armed groups made up largely of civilians and army defectors who were active in their towns, villages, and cities. These localized units are overwhelmingly underresourced. While they operate independently of central command they are nevertheless ostensibly loyal to the FSA as they receive some of their material resources through the FSA. At the very least, they pledge support and allegiance to the FSA in order to convey solidarity and cohesion among rebel ranks. The second group consisted of self-proclaimed brigades that were distinguishable from the localized units in many ways. They tended to be larger and contain many civilians as well as army defectors. Their material resources were drawn from international donors, and these brigades tended to be more ideologically and eventually religiously motivated, serving the interests and political strategies of their patrons, who mostly came from Gulf countries (Hassan, 2013). Perhaps most important is that these brigades were mobile and could conduct activities across much larger areas of the country, especially across provinces. This put many of the brigades in regular conflict with one another as they fought for control over key distribution routes, such as highways, checkpoints, and border crossings, and other strategic areas. Such infighting between brigades ostensibly loyal to the FSA exposed the weaknesses of the FSA structure in commanding and controling armed groups.

Infighting, resource and material deficiencies, and the geographical diffusion of the FSA units all precluded the unification of the fighters into a hierarchical command. There were major problems with the FSA's leadership from the beginning, with the founding officers, including the Commander Riad al-Assad, establishing themselves in Turkey and not in Syria. This made control over the local units and brigades as well as communication with field commanders much more difficult, if not impossible. The leadership's location in Turkey meant that they were heavily influenced and controlled by the Turkish government and its intelligence apparatus. This influence would be limited, however, as the exiled commanders exercised less and less control of the units and brigades that continued to sprout after July 2011. Over time (as we will see below) the FSA and the political opposition made multiple, failed attempts to unify the command structure of the rebel groups to provide coordinated military strategies and resources. The presence of such hierarchies should not be confused with their functionality, however. To date, the FSA hierarchy remains severely disconnected from events on the ground.

The FSA model, then, was never well suited to its goals of centralizing leadership and military strategy and serving as a political umbrella for the armed groups. In addition to disconnections between the FSA hierarchy and fighters on the ground, the commanders also enjoyed very little support and legitimacy among the fighters within Syria, in large part because of their inability to marshal resources to the front lines or provide sound military strategies. Attacks against regime forces were increasingly uncoordinated between the different FSA brigades and there was no coherent military strategy to speak of. What then occurred almost instantaneously after the creation of the FSA was the rapid spread of violence and the concentration of violence in specific locales.

Despite the FSA's structural weaknesses and military limitations, a year after its founding many of the FSA-affiliated brigades found themselves in control of large areas of northern Syria along the Turkish border where regime forces had retreated. This included a number of important border crossings, such as Bab al-Salameh. Control of the border crossings allowed the fighters access to more direct supply routes to bring in weapons and goods, which facilitated greater international involvement in the arming of rebels. By the summer of 2012, almost all of the rebel support from the international community was flowing from Turkey, where regional states such as Qatar and Saudi Arabia funneled resources and weapons to the rebels. The so-called liberated areas in the north quickly became an experiment in nonregime governance and control.

To this end, the rebel military commanders took advantage of having a direct link to the FSA leadership and secure supply routes to attempt to unify rebel ranks and coordinate command. Although the rebels had taken over large areas of northern Syria, they remained highly fragmented and infighting had threatened to erase any of their territorial gains and undermine the rebel claim to forming a legitimate alternative to the Assad regime. In September 2012 a Joint Command for the Revolution's Military Council was established in order to organize rebel groups inside the country and better link them to the external leadership. The Joint Command proposed an organizational structure to direct all rebel operations, beginning with a five-person General Command that was made up of five Brigadier Generals: Mithaq al-Bateesh, Abdel Majid Dabis, Zaki Lolu, Ziad Fahd, and Salim Idriss. Below the General Command were fourteen provincial Military Councils that would be responsible for activities in each province and would report back to the General Command.

Despite the new structure, the General Command was never really able to exert its full control over the rebel groups. Increasingly, rebel groups formed outside of the FSA structure or broke off from it when they were able to secure resources from international patrons or when alliances with other rebel groups broke down, such as over control of key highways, checkpoints, or border crossings. Infighting among the rebel groups paralleled a lack of communication between the Command's leadership and increasingly autonomous decision-making from the provincial councils. This contributed to further fragmentation of the rebel groups and more withdrawal from the General Command. More important, however, was the growth of rebel groups that did not adhere to the FSA's larger strategies, particularly around the inclusion of minorities and their alliances with the external opposition. The increase in violence after the summer of 2012 led to more and more sectarian groups motivated both by an increased religiosity permeating the rebel ranks and a desire to exact revenge for the regime's brutality. Thereafter, more Islamist-leaning commanders came to prominence in the rebel movement. The rise of sectarian and ideological commanders did not in and of itself immediately lead to the collapse of the Command structure, but disagreements over the administration of nonregime areas, particularly around issues of law and governance, as well as disagreements over military strategy, did so as well.

Toward the end of 2012 many of the brigades that were previously under the FSA umbrella began to break off and form independent brigades, further spreading and decentralizing violence and making attempts at consolidation difficult. The political and material relationships with the General Command were increasingly of limited benefit and international patrons were willing to provide resources to brigades outside of the FSA model. This was particularly the case after Saudi Arabia and Qatar were lukewarm about their support for the General Command, with each country accusing the other of exercising undue influence within the Command.

Both countries were thus reluctant to provide full political and military support to the Command and found identifying and resourcing particular brigades to be a more fruitful and advantageous strategy. Such a strategy would end up dividing the more powerful brigades and turning them against one another, fostering mistrust among the commanders and between them and the General Command. With Qatar and Saudi Arabia jockeying over control of the appointment of commanders and other leadership positions, fighters on the ground grew disillusioned with the FSA model and began holding alternative, parallel elections for military leadership roles. Many provinces very quickly had more than one military council leader. Rivalries ensued and infighting between rebel groups under the FSA umbrella increased. Splits among the brigades contributed to further defections from the FSA model, but, paradoxically, did not always lead to internal fighting, with some groups choosing to cooperate militarily in certain areas.

Networked Rebel Groups

With the defection of larger brigades from the Joint Command, alternative networks of violence began to emerge toward the end of 2012. The facade of rebel coherence and unification was put to rest at this time, with rebel groups sprouting throughout the country, particularly in the nonregime areas where territorial, political, and administrative control was contested by different and competing rebel groups. Interrebel relations were defined both by cooperation and conflict, depending on the particular situation. What was consistent, however, was that the relations between rebel groups were quickly unraveling and that they failed to cohere. As outlined above, the differences among the rebel groups involved questions of legitimacy and leadership, access to resources, and strategy. Increasingly, however, ideological differences emerged among the rebel groups and the cleavages between them became increasingly acute. While conflict and cooperation continued to define interrebel relations, conflict actually increased with the arrival of more rebel groups. As the rebel landscape widened, so did violence and the fragmentation of the country into smaller cantons controlled by different rebel groups.

In each governorate, the networks of violence looked and interacted differently. Some FSA brigades were stronger in the south and northwest, while the emergent Islamist groups were powerful in the north and east of the country. The slow spread and decentralization of violence made attempts to establish an FSA central command pointless. As time passed, the General Command became more insignificant on the ground and unable to exercise influence over local units and brigades. Relations among rebel groups would be determined by their specific interactions in different parts of the country.

It is virtually impossible to determine how many brigades and local units exist in Syria now. The Carter Center estimated in 2013 that there were at least 1,050 brigades and 3,250 battalions or companies (smaller localized units) operating in Syria (Carter Center, 2013, 24). The localized units often consist of a few dozen fighters with limited training and limited resources. The brigades have a few hundred fighters and have slightly more resources. Both the units and brigades are typically associated with larger structures that bring together a network of fighters (networked rebels) versus those outside of any broader structure (independent rebels). Particularly after the collapse of the General Command model, many of these groups are independent of any larger central command, with the more preferred association occurring through the creation of various Fronts that serve more as regional conglomerations of fighters then they do hierarchical commands. Loyalty to the Fronts is often weak, with different brigades pledging and withdrawing allegiance with alarming frequency. The example of Liwa al-Tawhid (Tawhid Brigade) is an excellent example of the fluidity of allegiance and coordination during the conflict. Tawhid was originally formed in and around Aleppo and was made up of thousands of fighters who had initial success on the battlefield. Their original affiliation was with the FSA but, owing to their increasingly Islamist leanings, they broke off from the FSA in 2012 and formed a coalition called the Syrian Islamic Liberation Front (SILF). Within a year, Tawhid, along with two of the other larger and more powerful brigades in the SILF (Jaish al-Islam and Suqoor al-Sham), were withdrawing from the SILF (which subsequently ended all joint operations and dissolved its command structure) to join the Islamic Liberation Front (ILF), a newly formed group of Islamist brigades. By August of 2014, the ILF, with Tawhid still a member, had joined the Majlis Qiyadat al-Thawra al-Surriya (Syrian Revolutionary Command Council), an alliance of more than seventy armed factions from across the geographic and ideological spectrum.

The basic function of the Fronts is to provide leaders a space for coordination and joint decision-making and resource sharing. The Fronts sit as the central node of networks of violence and include groups such as the Syrian Revolutionaries Front, the Syrian Islamic Front, Jabhat an-Nusra, and ISIS, all of which share remarkably similar characteristics in their networked structure. They are composed of smaller, less mobile fighting units who are active in geographically concentrated areas, and larger brigades of a few hundred members who are more mobile, more active, and have greater power on the battlefield.

The landscape of violence looks very different throughout Syria's governorates. Smaller, localized units are concentrated in specific areas of the governorates. The network of violence in Syria is thus extremely spread out and decentralized, and coordination across governorates, let alone on a national scale, is extremely difficult. In each governorate, then, there is a common structure to the armed groups. There are the larger brigades who are made up of smaller units. These brigades are often associated with a Front that gives the appearance of a national character when in reality the coalitions are amalgamations of entrenched brigades. The reason for this entrenchment is complicated but mainly due to resource and capacity issues. On the one hand, many brigades are strong enough to defend areas, hold territory, and establish some semblance of an administration there. On the other hand, they are not strong enough to make significant advances across territories because of the presence of other, hostile armed groups and the regime forces. However, because coordination is weak and mistrust among the groups remains very high, the coalitions do not exercise national power and have differentiated capacities across governorates. Thus different brigades exercise power in their specific locales—town, city, village, governorate—rather than on a national level. Such national limitations have largely driven coalition-making in the Syrian conflict. The inability to make larger military advances, coupled with the demands of administering and governing held territory, has fostered coalition building.

The fragmentation of the militarized opposition and its effects can best be seen in the city of Aleppo, where all of the major coalitions exist. Aleppo and its surrounding areas is perhaps the most strategic region of Syria because of the Turkish supply routes, which are essential to the survival of the armed groups. This is why many of them engage in conflict to control highways, routes, checkpoints, and border crossings. Such geographic control allows these groups to reap the benefits of the war economy and maintain their military entrenchment in Aleppo. The FSA's Command is strong in Aleppo but shares control of the nonregime areas with the SILF, the SRF, PYD, and Jabhat an-Nusra, all major coalitions with affiliated brigades scattered throughout the city and its countryside. Relations between these groups are rarely cooperative and they are mostly engaged in conflict with one another as they attempt to expand their geographic and military control. In addition to this, regime forces, including the SAA, NDF, and militia groups, are present in Aleppo.

While the case of Aleppo is perhaps unique, it is indicative of the larger fragmentation and division of the militarized opposition. The city and its countryside are home to thousands of fighters, all of whom have fluid affiliations with larger units and brigades. The many fighters divided into smaller groupings have never coalesced into a larger unit capable of coordinating and overtaking regime forces. Rather, the opposite has occurred. Most fighters turn against each other and allow the regime forces to remain entrenched in the parts of the city under their control. All of these coalitions alternate between conflict and cooperation but are ultimately vying for as much control of the city as possible.

But these coalitions are very rarely coherent in terms of their ideological leanings and often contain brigades that have different loyalties. An excellent example of this is the Jaish al-Mujahideen (Mujahideen Army) that was formed in early 2014 and is concentrated in the strategic corridor between Aleppo and the Turkish border. This coalition of Islamist-leaning brigades largely grew out of the FSA command structure but contains brigades that were created and operated outside of the General Command. The main reason for coming together was geography.

By March 2015 the FSA was a patchwork of armed brigades and local units that were scattered throughout the country but had begun to concentrate in the southern parts of Syria where they control large areas of Dar'a, Quneitra, and al-Sweyda. The FSA's retreat and entrenchment into the south reflects their weaknesses and repeated military setbacks throughout the rest of the country, especially in the north and northwestern parts of the country, where rival armed groups, especially ISIS and JAN, have inflicted major losses on FSA brigades. Despite the retreat and consolidation in the south, many of the same problems plaguing the FSA have remained. The lack of centralized leadership and sustainable resource flows make the FSA's control over southern territory tenuous.

The inability of the FSA to overthrow the regime and the losses of its affiliated brigades on the battlefield opened the space for the entry of larger, more powerful competing networks of violence to emerge. Had the FSA been successful in consolidating its control of nonregime areas the conditions that allowed for the entry of other groups would not have existed. Moreover, as the FSA brigades began to lose legitimacy among Syrians, who were increasingly weary of the FSA's own brutality and criminality, many groups were able to step in and fill a void. In addition, the arrival of newly formed armed groups who were often better equipped and more disciplined than the FSA led to the migration of fighters to these groups. While the FSA formed a distinct network of violence, the movement among different brigades and across networks would become a common feature of the composition of the armed groups.

Jabhat an-Nusra and Other Islamist Fighters

The landscape of Salafist-jihadist violence in Syria is large, with dozens of fighting units and brigades that adhere to Salafist-jihadist ideals. At the pinnacle of this large network of violence is the al-Qaeda-affiliated Jabhat al-Nusra, which is the largest and most organized Salafist-jihadist group in Syria. Although these groups share ideological affinities and cooperate with one another in military and administrative activities, they have not coalesced into a larger structure and still operate independently of one another. Many Salafist-jihadist groups are concentrated in the southern parts of the country as well as the northwest, but are active in and around Damascus and in the eastern areas where they have engaged in repeated battles with YPG and ISIS fighters. Thus, the Salafist-jihadist networks of violence are spread throughout the country but exercise a great deal of power in the northwest and southern parts of Syria.

Relations between the Salafist-jihadist groups vary depending on the geographic area. The lack of a centralized leadership and the failure of the groups to coalesce into a larger unit reflect the mistrust that continues to plague intrarebel relations. Cooperation and joint administration by the groups, on the other hand, demonstrate their pragmatism and a recognition that the diffusion of power in their geographic areas means that governance and administration must be cooperative and shared.

Although JAN is the largest and most powerful brigade and has engaged in many battles with ISIS, YPG, FSA, and regime forces, they have pursued largely cooperative relations with other brigades that share their ideological commitments and who are sympathetic to the basic tenets of al-Qaeda's ideology. These larger brigades, such as Ahrar al-Sham (who are part of the Islamic Front), enjoy friendly, strategic relations with JAN that have led to military and administrative cooperation. Infighting between these groups over territorial control has not occurred on a wide scale (see Chapter Five); violence between them has been rejected in favor of shared governance of areas under their control. Thus the larger brigades have not attempted to subordinate others but have instead worked together to achieve common goals.

There are other Islamist groups who may not share JAN's ideological affinities but who are nevertheless embedded in shared governance models and who engage in military battles together. These are Islamist groups that are largely part of the Islamic Front (IF) and the SIF before it, such as Suqour al-Sham. In Aleppo and Dar'a where Shari'a Committees have been established, JAN shares membership with multiple groups, including those Islamist brigades that do not necessarily adhere to Salafist-jihadist ideology but who are nevertheless sympathetic to JAN. There are smaller fighting units outside of the IF structure that JAN similarly coordinates with on the battlefield but these relations have not translated into their integration into JAN or IF, on the one hand, or the Shari'a Committees in Aleppo or Dar'a. Relations among these Islamist groups are confined to coordinating military activities. Many of the smaller Islamist fighting units are locally based and do not have the fighters or resources to expand beyond their specific locales. Cooperating with JAN and IF in local battles shores up their military strength.

Generally cooperative relations between the major Islamist brigades contrasts with the fluidity of relations with the FSA and other armed groups. The four major networks of violence—JAN, ISIS, FSA, and YPG—are in regular conflict with one another. However, the FSA has, depending on geographic area, entered into associations with both JAN and the YPG. This reflects the weaknesses of both networks but also the desire of groups such as JAN to incorporate opposition activities into their own. In many parts of the country, JAN operates side-by-side with FSA brigades such as the Hazm Movement and different brigades under the SRF umbrella (although relations between the SRF shift between conflict and cooperation quite regularly). The main difference between Islamist-FSA relations is that they are largely mutually beneficial and strategic and have not evolved into any administrative structures. Groups such as JAN and the IF may share resources, ensure the security of supplies, and exchange intelligence, but, beyond this, cooperation is nonexistent.

While the majority of Islamist groups beyond ISIS have proved remarkably flexible in entering into military cooperation with each other and with other armed groups, this has largely been a necessary by-product of their battlefield and administrative weaknesses. Intrarebel relations are extremely complicated and cooperation should not be confused with solidarity, cohesion, or centralization of command. The relations between JAN and other networks of violence are mutually beneficial and are prone to changes based on the evolution of the conflict. For example, JAN's largest and most powerful ally is Ahrar al-Sham. The ideological backgrounds of both groups have facilitated cooperation and thus both have interest in shared governance and the establishment of Shari'a courts. Militarily speaking, they support each others' activities and coordinate across multiple battlefronts. The majority of groups that JAN has good relations with are Salafist-jihadist groups, as shared ideology facilitates cooperation on military, social, and legal matters. Throughout Syria, there are many networks of Salafist-jihadist violence that coordinate closely with JAN, including Ansar al-Din, a coalition of smaller Salafist groups, and then smaller fighting units in different parts of the country.

However, ideological affinities and military coordination notwithstanding, these alliances are not concrete and therefore do not necessarily represent JAN's overall strength vis-à-vis other rebel groups. In March 2015, Ahrar al-Sham leaders began carving out boundaries of influence between them and JAN (al-Ali, 2015). Prior to this, Ahrar al-Sham had entered into an informal agreement to cooperate and coordinate with the YPG, who have been in regular battles with JAN. It appears, then, that JAN's closest military and ideological ally is slowly shifting away from its orbit of influence. A severing or reduction of relations between JAN and Ahrar al-Sham would have substantial consequences for JAN's military capacities and their administrative influence within nonregime areas. Currently, areas in the northwest and south in which JAN are active are considered to be very fluid and subject to multiple authorities' control, as evidenced by the cooperation around social service provision and courts. However, the severance of the relations that form the network of violence and authority could radically reshape nonregime areas and contribute to further fragmentation, as groups such as JAN and Ahrar al-Sham lay claim to specific territories and exclude other groups from their administrative structures. Further splits between JAN and other groups have been revealed on the battlefield, as battles between them and Hazm Movement and the SRF have dampened JAN's relations with other groups, exposing the fragility of their relations.

By 2015, JAN's influence and strength in Syria was based on its military capacities and its ability to provide social services. By entering into cooperative relations with other armed groups, JAN was able to extend its influence throughout the nonregime areas. However, the fragility of these relations has been exposed more recently and JAN's alliances are shifting quite rapidly. This pattern is highly consistent with rebel relations throughout the conflict, with certain brigades' strength rising and waning based on the power of their alliances. JAN is no different.

The PYD and the Kurdish Political Landscape

Syria's Kurdish population had long suffered the denial of basic rights in Syria, including the denial of citizenship and thus forced statelessness for hundreds of thousands of Kurds. The Kurdish population has historically been concentrated in the north and northeastern parts of the country but the major cities, including Damascus and Aleppo, have sizable Kurdish populations. Kurdish participation in opposition politics prior to the uprising was traditionally very limited, as many Kurdish oppositionists and political parties had closer ties to the regime and were also skeptical of opposition politics. The complicated relations between Kurds and their Arab compatriots continued in the first stages of the uprising.

Despite their collective frustrations with the regime, many Kurds and political parties attempted to steer a neutral path in the first stages of the Syrian conflict. Although many Kurds did participate in protests and were included in opposition structures, the political parties purposely steered clear of formally joining the opposition while simultaneously maintaining some political distance from the regime. The largest and most powerful Kurdish political party, the Democratic Union Party (PYD), is an offshoot of the Turkish-based Kurdistan Workers Party (PKK), and has been very reluctant to confront the regime throughout the conflict (International Crisis Group, 2013). There are other parties in the Syrian Kurdish areas that also exercise some influence among the population. Many of these parties operate under the larger umbrella of the Kurdish National Council (KNC). Although under the KNC umbrella, they are an ideologically diverse group with different social bases of support and different external patrons. The dominant parties within the KNC, the Kurdish Democratic Party of Syria (an offshoot of the Iraqi Party of the same name), and the Kurdish Democratic Progressive Party of Syria (an offshoot of the Iraqi Patriotic Union of Kurdistan), are heavily influenced by their Iraqi Kurdish patrons. The KNC and the PYD are the main political competitors within the Syrian Kurdish population and are outgrowths of the two competing versions of Kurdish nationalism espoused by their regional patrons in Turkey and Iraq.

Syrian Kurds have also supported different factions of the opposition during the conflict and have joined the ranks of FSA- and JAN-affiliated brigades, although, generally speaking, many of the armed and political opposition groups have not been inclusive of Kurdish political interests. Intra-Kurdish competition and coordination, then, has been an important determinant in Kurdish participation in the Syrian conflict. While the PYD is the stronger of the political parties and has taken the administrative and military leadership of the Kurdish regions, their strong ties to the PKK have made the Turkish authorities reluctant to accept their increasing autonomy within Syria. Conversely, the KNC, while not enjoying the same level of domestic support among Syria's Kurds, has stronger ties to both Turkey and the Iraqi Kurdish groups. Massoud Barzani, leader of the Kurdish Democratic Party (KDP) in Iraq, brokered a deal between the two factions in 2012 called the Erbil Declaration, which created a Supreme Kurdish Council (SKC) consisting of members of both the PYD and KNC and included a power-sharing agreement meant to avoid continued conflict between the factions.

Barzani's intervention into Syrian Kurdish politics extended beyond institutionalizing power sharing to the military arena. The PYD had, in 2012, repatriated many of its fighters from Turkey and had begun to engage in active combat in Kurdish populated areas. The PYD was the primary military force within the Kurdish areas when, in July 2012, Barzani announced that the Kurdish Regional Government (KRG) in Iraq would train and equip Syrian Kurdish fighters. This military force has never swelled to the point of seriously competing with the PYD forces (more below) but is nevertheless present in the Syrian Kurdish areas and under the control and influence of the Iraqi Kurdish groups. While there has been some evidence of military cooperation with the PYD, the two armed wings have generally operated independently of one another.

The PYD has established a rather sophisticated military apparatus in the northeast. Local People's Protection Committees (PPC) serve as a surrogate police force in Kurdish areas to maintain order. The PYD also has a militia that predates the uprising called the People's Defense Corps (YPG) that currently functions as the armed wing of the PYD and the de facto army of the Syrian Kurds. The YPG is deployed throughout the Kurdish areas; they are concentrated in the boundary areas where fighting with ISIS and other armed groups is most intense.

Despite the lack of military coordination among Kurdish groups and the persistence of mistrust among them, the PYD has actually been highly successful in creating an administrative structure that is exercising autonomy beyond the state. The Rojava (meaning Western Kurdistan) Project (discussed in Chapter Five) has not been fully supported by all of the Kurdish parties but is nevertheless an ambitious project to provide administration to the Kurdish-dominated areas. This has strengthened the PYD and the YPG's strength in those areas even though there has been a lack of consensus among Kurdish parties with regard to the authority and legitimacy of the Rojava administration. The PYD's strength within the Kurdish community, however, has allowed it to pursue the project despite opposition among some groups. Although this opposition has been politically relevant and has led to the collapse of intra-Kurdish projects aimed at unifying the Kurdish parties, such as the SKC, it has not descended into sustained violence between opposing Kurdish factions. The YPG's military strength relative to that of the other parties has largely discouraged such violence. Within this context of PYD strength, relations between the Syrian regime and the Kurdish parties are extremely complicated, and vacillate between direct conflict to the pursuit of mutual interests. On the one hand, the YPG has been very successful militarily in battles with ISIS and has prevented the expansion of ISIS-held territories in the northeast. Such battles have placed military pressure on ISIS and other armed groups and in some cases have directly affected their access to supplies. On the other hand, the PYD has taken over many of the government buildings in the northeast and through the Rovaja Project the Kurdish parties are governing the territory as the de facto authorities. It is unclear why the regime would have allowed the emergence of an autonomous Kurdish region without any political or military action whatsoever. However, the accusations that the PYD is working closely with the regime may provide some insight into a secret alliance between the two.

Such accusations of covert Kurdish–regime alliances are not entirely plausible, given both the history of the regime's treatment of Syrian Kurds and the legacy of mistrust this has bred. The withering of the regime's security apparatus has likely led to the calculation that security forces cannot engage Kurdish YPG fighters as this would deflect from other, more strategic areas of the country. The inability to engage militarily with the YPG should not be confused with the regime's tacit acceptance of Kurdish moves toward autonomy. Moreover, for the moment, the regime and the PYD have a common enemy in ISIS, and this has fostered cooperation. In this way, the same factors that shape intrarebel conflict and coopera- tion—pragmatism, capacity, and the need for military alli- ances—have shaped Kurdish–regime relations through 2015. The regime, however, is unlikely to allow the unchecked growth of the PYD and the YPG without some form of inter- vention into Kurdish affairs. For now, the regime tolerates the Rojava Project out of political necessity, and not out of some commitment to Kurdish autonomy or larger political calculation in favor of decentralizing power to the governor- ates in the post-conflict phase. Such Kurdish advances are as much a product of the PYD's ability to organize Kurdish areas in the context of the uprising, relatively unabated by the Assad regime, which has been militarily and politically focused on developments in other parts of the country. The convenience of a common enemy in ISIS has given the appear- ance of Kurdish-regime coherence, when this is in fact much more precarious than it appears, and subject to changing conditions on the ground. Should the regime make further military gains, or opposition dynamics shift toward greater military coordination, Kurdish-regime relations may very quickly shift from being cooperative to being conflictual.

The Islamic State of Iraq and as-Sham (ISIS)

The roots of the ISIS phenomenon in Iraq and Syria lie in the collapse of the Iraqi state, the subsequent U.S.-led occupa- tion, the rise of extremist movements in Iraq as a response both to occupation and political exclusion, and the rise and fall of the Sahwa (Awakening) movements in Iraq. The latter factor was central to ISIS's constellation in the late 2000s. The Sahwa movement began around 2006–2007 and was a central component of the U.S.'s surge strategy in Iraq. The strategy relied on cultivating Iraqi Sunni tribal leaders, ini- tially in the al-Anbar province, to take up arms against al- Qaeda fighters in Iraq. In September 2006, Arab tribes from Ramadi formed an alliance called the Majlis inqadh al-Anbar (al-Anbar Salvation Council) in order to cooperate with occupation troops in order to force al-Qaeda fighters out of the province. At the time, tribal leaders had become weary of al-Qaeda's presence and had opposed their ambitions in Iraq. Initial success of the al-Anbar Council led to its replication in other parts of the country and the creation of other Salvation Councils. Many Arab Sunni fighters had flocked to the councils for many reasons: tribal affiliation, a genuine desire to remove al-Qaeda from Iraq, or financial reasons. Regardless, the mobilization of fighters under the banner of the Salvation Councils proved military successful and by late 2007 many of the areas where al-Qaeda forces had been embedded were effectively pacified.

By 2009, however, al-Qaeda fighters had returned to areas such as Ramadi and began to wage attacks against Sahwa members and leaders. Although this occurred scarcely two years after the initial Sahwa mobilization, the counterattack forced the collapse of the movement, as members were not as quick to organize and take up arms, for a number of reasons. First, many had believed that the mobilization would have enhanced Sunni participation in the political system—but this proved not to be the case. Second, the drawback of U.S. forces left Sahwa leaders without direct access to resources and funding with which to maintain a counteroffensive against al-Qaeda. Third, the economic grievances that drove Sahwa mobilization—frustration over the loss of key economic resources and reconstruction contracts—were never fully addressed after 2007. The movement to expel al-Qaeda was largely motivated by economic needs and desires to capture both reconstruction contracts and the benefits of illicit activity rampant in the tribal areas, such as smuggling. By mid-2000, many tribes had ceded authority in the illicit economy to al-Qaeda and had used the Sahwa movement to regain it (Benraad, 2011). Furthermore, Sahwa fighters had been promised opportunities in the formal economy such as jobs in the public sector and security services, but the central state failed to deliver and left many of the fighters out of work. Under such conditions the former Sahwa fighters were not capable of reorganizing and mobilizing against the al-Qaeda attacks in the late 2000s, nor did many desire to. Finally, the central Iraqi state led by Nouri al-Maliki had opposed Sahwa from the beginning. The major Arab Sunni parliamentary bloc, the Iraq Accord Front, similarly bore hostility toward the movement for fear that it could grow to rival the Front's authority within the Arab Sunni community (Benraad, 2011). Such fears meant that the government failed to integrate the movement into the state and continued to deprive the movement and its core areas of economic resources.

The weakening of the Sahwa provided the opportunity for the reemergence of al-Qaeda fighters in Iraq. In the mid-2000s, as the Sahwa were organizing, al-Qaeda and other insurgent groups had been forming alliances out of which ISIS grew. In 2006, al-Qaeda in Iraq (AQI) declared a merger with five other groups to form the Majlis Shura al-Mujahideen (MSM). Later in 2006 amid the Sahwa movement the MSM announced the creation of the Islamic State in Iraq (ISI), an altogether new movement that was intended to be subordinate to the main al-Qaeda leadership. The ISI model and its supporters survived the period of the Sahwa and had begun a resurgence in the late 2000s, a period in which Abu Mohmmaed al-Julani, the current leader of JAN in Syria, assumed a leadership role within the organization. Despite the Sahwa effect and the death or capture of many of its top leaders, ISI survived in Iraq and was able to maintain local support for their operations because of widespread frustration with the failures of the central Iraqi government. By the time the Syrian conflict began, ISI was embroiled in continued battles with the Iraqi army. The conflict provided an opportunity for expansion.

In early 2012, less than a year after the uprising began, Jabhat an-Nusra (JAN), led by al-Julani, declared its presence in Syria and quickly became one of the strongest brigades, successfully engaging in battles with regime forces in both the northern and southern battlefields. By the end of the year, JAN was widely considered to be one of the most effective brigades in Syria. The expansion of JAN and its success in Syria prompted the leader of ISI, abu Bakr al-Baghdadi, to publicly reaffirm JAN's relationship with ISI and its subordination under the newly formed organization, The Islamic

State in Iraq and al-Sham (ISIS). The attempt to subordinate JAN to the new ISIS structure led to a power struggle between the two groups that resulted in the fracturing of JAN into two factions: mostly Syrian fighters remained in the JAN structure while the foreign fighters largely defected to ISIS. Moreover, the split between the groups and the subsequent refusal of ISIS leaders to accept subordination to al-Qaeda's central leadership prompted al-Qaeda leader Ayman Zawahiri to publicly denounce ISIS and declare them outside of the organizational structure of al-Qaeda. Henceforth, ISIS would be an independent entity operating in both Iraq and Syria.

The advances of ISIS in Syria and Iraq have fundamentally changed the course of the Syrian conflict and the international response to the crisis (discussed in the next chapter). At the beginning of 2014 ISIS controlled large swathes of Syrian and Iraqi territory stretching from Anbar in Iraq to the regions immediately east of Aleppo in Syria. By June of 2014, ISIS took control of Mosul in Iraq: the largest city under its control up to that time. Since then, ISIS advances have been limited but the territory under their control has not contracted, despite U.S.-led coalition air strikes, anti-ISIS coalitions in Syria consisting of various rebel groups, and operations by the Iraqi army and Kurdish and Shi'a militias against ISIS positions.

In addition to ISIS's ability to maintain multiple active fronts, they have demonstrated an ability to engage in counteroffensives. Repeated attacks in Syrian Kurdish areas, and the group's expansion against regime and rebel forces in the central parts of the country, serve not only to expand ISIS's territory but to increase their control over the economic levers of conflict. Much attention has been paid to ISIS control of oil and gas fields (Macias and Bender, 2014) but their control of supply routes and major corridors linking rebel reinforcement routes has also been a major economic and military gain for ISIS. As territorial expansion is the raison d'être of ISIS and is a main source of its own legitimation, the group has developed sophisticated military capabilities without which expansion and territorial control would have been impossible.

While ISIS shares many of the networked characteristics of other armed groups, they are distinct in their transnational character, their rejection of sovereign borders, and the almost entirely foreign composition of their leadership and fighters. ISIS thus stands out in distinct ways from the other networks of violence. The Assad regime's networks of violence, on the other hand, share some features with the rebel groups. The proliferation of different armed groups operating independently of each other, the presence of foreign fighters, and the absence of a central command structure are all features of the regime's network of violence, as well as of the rebel groups.

Regime Violence: The NDF, Shabiha, and Regional Actors

Independent armed actors have played an increasingly prominent role in perpetuating violence to further the Assad regime's strategic political and military objectives. The regime's reliance on these actors poses a serious dilemma: on the one hand, these actors, especially Lebanon's Hizbollah, have played a central role in preventing a military defeat of the Syrian Arab Army (SAA) while also inflicting terror and violence on communities outside of the SAA's reach, such as in the rural areas. On the other hand, reliance on these privatized actors moves strategic decision-making concerning military and battlefield issues more and more outside of the control of any centralized regime leadership. As such, the regime's leadership and the SAA itself is becoming increasingly peripheral to the execution of violence. Thus, while these independent groups are certainly fighting alongside the regime and in pursuit of their objectives, they are not doing so through coordinated leadership or planning. Regime violence, much like the violence of the rebel groups, is privatized, decentralized, and increasingly civilianized.

By 2015 it was difficult to determine exactly how much territory was under regime control or, because of internal displacement and refugee flows, what percentage of the Syrian population was located in these areas. The regime has consolidated its control over key corridors of Syria, mainly the Damascus-Homs-Aleppo axis as well as Hama, the coastal areas of Tartous and Latakia, and even some areas in the northeast that remain outside of ISIS or PYD control. The contiguous areas under regime control stretching from Damascus up to the north and west of the country to the Mediterranean contain the largest population concentrations in the country. Paradoxically, the SAA is largely absent from these areas, with local and regional militias largely responsible for security and control of checkpoints and the main highways. Thus, while the regime retains nominal control over large areas of the country and the majority of the remaining population, the networks of violence that maintain this control are largely outside of the regime's traditional security apparatuses—the army and the security service—and are instead reliant on privatized, civilianized forms of violence.

Aron Lund has called the process that brought this about "militiafication," to describe the evolution of the regime's reliance on militia groups for violence and security. From the beginning of the protests, the regime relied on the SAA, and not local police forces, to attack protesters. The SAA was aided by small groups of armed individuals known as the *shabiha* (thugs) who used knives, bats, guns, and other light weapons to attack protesters. The *shabiha* were quickly organized in *lijan shaabiyya* (popular committees) who assumed the dual role of providing violence in support of the regime and securing their neighborhoods from opposition violence. Despite this security role, they became feared within Syria, as they acted with impunity and enjoyed the support and sponsorship of the intelligence apparatus and key business leaders who funded them and provided salaries. Early on in the uprising, it was largely assumed that the *shabiha* consisted exclusively of poor Alawite men. This was not the case. Instead the *shabiha* should be understood as a genuine expression of regime support from different segments of Syrian society. While many of the members of the popular committees may have been Alawite, membership was by no means exclusive to the sect. Rather, the fostering of the *shabiha* by the regime should be understood as a means of militarizing civilian support for the regime on a cross-sectarian basis.

The cross-sectarian roots of the popular committees did not prevent their evolution into more institutionalized forms of civilianized violence. *Shabiha* recruits came from all corners of Syria's social mosaic—Baathists, Sunni tribes, religious minorities, and semi-urban dwellers—who had more commonalities in their socioeconomic backgrounds than they did in their religious affiliations. The main determining factor in the participation of youth with the popular committees was their geographic locale, as groups were composed of people from the same neighborhood or region and were not united by sect. In Jaramana, for example, popular committees were made up overwhelmingly of Druze members, while in Wadi al-Nasara they were predominantly Christian. In Aleppo, most of the Popular Committees were composed of Sunnis, while those in Homs and Latakia were mainly Alawites (Khaddour, 2014).

Although they began as informal, armed groups that sought to quell protesters, they quickly rose in importance, as the SAA contracted and the regime was forced to rely on privatized violence as the opposition become more militarized. The militarization of the opposition eventually led to the institutionalization and formalization of the *shabiha*. The popular committees morphed and grew into what is now the National Defense Forces (NDF). The NDF originally appeared in Homs and was involved in fighting alongside the SAA. Rather quickly, the NDF model spread throughout the country and different units fought alongside the SAA. Their loyalty to the regime has never seriously been in question, despite the cross-sectarian membership of NDF fighters. By early 2013, the NDF had emerged as a potential alternative center of power within Syria and a possible threat to the regime's power.

Such fears hastened the institutionalization of the NDF and their slow incorporation into the regime's security apparatus to guarantee their loyalty and codependence on the regime. In early 2013, the NDF had been granted government buildings for its leadership, was offered training facilities, an official government stamp and logo, standardized uniforms, and monthly government salaries (Khaddour, 2014). Most NDF leaders and many fighters have received extensive training and financial support from Iran and have developed strong military ties with non-Syrian militias and other localized fighting units. Yet, despite their institutionalization and their importance to the regime's war strategy, the NDF remains a largely autonomous network of local units very loosely organized under central command from Damascus. Much like the localized rebel units, the NDF units were created in specific neighborhoods in which they remain entrenched. Coordination between NDF units is limited and, while the network has a hierarchy with provincial commanders that report to Damascus, any forms of integration between the units across provinces is limited. Consequently, many of the NDF units operate with a high degree of autonomy and are less cohesive then their institutionalization would suggest (Lund, 2012).

The NDF are by far the most sophisticated and powerful pro-regime Syrian militias, but there are many other units operating throughout the country that perform similar military functions (Khaddour, 2014). The Ba'ath Battalions are the official armed wing of the Ba'ath Party and are the only other militia in Syria with a national structure. They have branches in Aleppo, Damascus, Latakia, Tartous, and other parts of the country. The remaining pro-government militias are mostly local groups concentrated in particular areas of the country. For example, the Jerusalem Brigade consists of Palestinian fighters from the Neirab refugee camp in Northwest Syria; it is active in Aleppo fighting alongside other pro-regime militias. Other militias are more sectarian, including Syrian Resistance, which is made up almost exclusively of Alawite fighters, and a militia controlled by the Syrian Social Nationalist Party (SSNP), an armed wing of the SSNP political party which operates mainly in Christian areas around Homs.

The social and religious backgrounds of the pro-regime militias vary considerably. There are other Palestinian factions as well as more sectarian militias active in specific locales. Syrian Sunni tribal militias are active in the Qamishli and Hassakeh region while there are known to be multiple secular militias operating under the title of the Arab Nationalist Guards. Beyond these groups, there are also other smaller conglomerations of fighters that have no official or formal affiliation but who are organized into small units and who receive weapons and resources from the regime.

The local Syrian militias have played a pivotal role during the conflict. Although they operate with relative autonomy from the regime their participation in fighting rebel units has reduced the burden on the increasingly emasculated SAA. Indeed, four years after the conflict began, it is clear that the regime would not have survived and maintained control over large parts of the country without the active participation of militias. Yet the presence and reliance on militias obfuscates the regime's actual control over the country. The presence of militias throughout the country and the absence of rebel groups in those territories actually reflects the regime's weaknesses, for its reliance on decentralized, privatized violence has dispersed decision-making power to centers potentially outside of the regime's control. As the SAA contracts further the army is forced to engage in military attacks alongside local and regional militias. Such reliance on militias that are outside of the immediate command and control of the regime implies a withering and not a strengthening of the regime.

While the local militias have been central to the regime's defensive strategies and its ability to withstand rebel advances in key areas, Hizbollah's participation in the Syrian conflict has been the decisive battlefield factor allowing the regime to regain control of territory and key transportation routes. There is no doubt that the regime's forces would not have been able to regain territory and make military advances against rebel groups without Hizbollah's participation in the conflict. The participation of Hizbollah's forces in Syria on such a large scale was not due to sectarian calculations, as some have argued (Phillips, 2015), but rather to the threat posed by the disruption of the arms pipeline from Iran. Rebel control of key distribution routes, especially along the borderlands between Syria and Lebanon, seriously compromised

Hizbollah's ability to maintain the steady weapons flow from Iran and Syria. Any interference of this distribution network could have serious consequences for Hizbollah's military capacity to withstand future Israeli attacks.

Hizbollah's combat involvement in Syria was thus motivated more by concerns over access to material resources than it was for sectarian considerations. This is not to suggest that sectarianism was not an important factor motivating Hizbollah to enter Syria. By 2013, more radical Sunni jihadist groups had entered the Syrian arena and a series of car bombs in areas populated predominantly by Shi'a in Lebanon raised the threat of a spillover of the Syrian conflict into Lebanon. Although it was believed that Hizbollah operatives were active in Syria in some capacity from the onset of the uprising, it was not until May 2013 that Hizbollah's involvement expanded significantly in the form of a ground assault on the Syrian town of al-Qusayr, a small town close to the Lebanese border that was controlled by rebel groups. Hizbollah forces were directly responsible for retaking the town and had done so with involvement of the SAA and other regime-affiliated militias. Al-Qusayr was strategically important for Hizbollah because it cut through their communication and distribution networks. If these had been disrupted the group's military readiness in the event of an Israeli attack on Lebanon would have been compromised. The assault on al-Qusayr began in mid-May and lasted only a few weeks before rebel forces retreated and then eventually withdrew entirely from the town. Less than a month after the al-Qusayr battle began, it was over.

Hizbollah's participation was not restricted to al-Qusayr. In fact, the success of the al-Qusayr operation led to a major commitment on the part of Hizbollah's leadership to preserving the Syrian regime, something that had been previously absent from their public comments about the Syrian conflict. Initially, at the outset of the conflict, Hizbollah's leadership was committed to not intervening in the Syrian conflict despite its strong relationship with the Syrian regime. This was motivated by many factors, among them a desire not to upset the delicate sectarian balance in Lebanon and anger other, mainly Sunni, religious communities, as well as a desire to avoid accusations of sectarianism. Thus, Sayyed Hassan Nasrallah, Hizbollah's Secretary-General, conducted many interviews in the first months of the conflict laying out the party's position toward the Syrian protests. Distinguishing the Syrian regime from the "stale" regimes being overthrown in Egypt and elsewhere during the Arab uprisings, Sayyed Nasrallah argued that, unlike them, the Syrian regime was capable of reform and of initiating a process of political dialogue and negotiation with nonviolent protesters (Abboud and Muller, 2012). Hizbollah's desire to steer clear of direct, large-scale involvement in the Syrian conflict was untenable, however, as the regime's hold on territory contracted and threatened Hizbollah's strategic interests.

The victory at al-Qusayr thus also involved a shift in the leadership's framing of the Syrian conflict and its involvement therein. The hesitancy exhibited in the early months was quickly gone and Hizbollah's leadership adopted a policy of regime preservation, effectively committing itself to securing the Syrian regime. Subsequently, Hizbollah's participation in Syria increased beyond al-Qusayr and the border areas that were of immediate strategic interest to include fighting in major areas around Homs and Aleppo, particularly around key strategic highways and routes that effectively cut off rebel groups from supplies. Over the next few months, Hizbollah's participation in combat operations proved crucial to the regime's offensive strategies. While battles in Aleppo did not allow the SAA to retake the city from rebel groups, they made significant enough advances to force rebel retreats and to strangle many of their supply lines. Battles in and around Homs and Damascus had similar outcomes. Contrary to what some believed after the quick victory in al-Qusayr, Hizbollah's participation in combat with the SAA, NDF, and other militia groups did not decisively tip the military balance in favor of the regime, although it did allow for more offensive combat operations.

It is impossible to determine how many Hizbollah fighters are active in Syria or the extent to which their participation in the conflict has depleted their human and material capacities to engage Israel in the event of an attack on Lebanon. What is known, however, is that Hizbollah fighters have been active throughout the major combat zones in Syria, including the northern areas, borderlands between Syria and Lebanon, Damascus, and even in the southern parts of the country. The size and importance of the units fighting in these areas varies widely; it is believed that in some parts of the country, especially the borderlands, Hizbollah fighters assume the lead in combat operations and actually command SAA troops while in other parts, such as Aleppo, they play a complementary role to support the SAA, NDF, and other militias.

The increasing importance of Hizbollah's combat operations in the conflict demonstrates the regime's weakness and increasing dependence on external armed groups for military gains. As the conflict has dragged on, Hizbollah and Iranian leaders have taken on greater roles on the battlefield and while they may coordinate with Syrian commanders, tactical and strategic decisions are increasingly out of the hands of Syrians. Moreover, Hizbollah is not the only non-Syrian armed group operating in Syria on the side of the regime. Militias from Iraq and Afghanistan, as well as fighters from other regional countries, have flocked to Syria and are also fighting alongside the SAA, NDF, and Hizbollah.

Iraqi militia fighters are extremely active in Syria and have entered the country in larger numbers after the ISIS threat. Many of these militia groups have military ties to the Iranian Revolutionary Guards and, in some cases, are under their indirect control. Indeed, many of the units that are participating in Syria, such as Asaib ahl al-Haq (League of the Righteous), were formed as militias by Iranian authorities after the U.S.-led invasion of Iraq in 2003. Other groups, such as Kataib Hizbollah (Hizbollah Forces) were also active in fighting U.S. occupation forces and have now moved many fighters into Syria to counter ISIS (Slavin, 2015). These are only two of the larger militias represented on the Syrian battlefield.

Other non-Syrian fighters fighting alongside the regime have flocked to Syria for largely sectarian reasons. Many Shi'a fighters have joined the battlefield from around the world for reasons that include the defense of religious shrines and as a counterweight to the growth of ISIS and spread of Sunni radicalism (more on this in Chapter Five). It is nearly impossible to determine how many foreign Shi'a fighters are active in Syria or to evaluate their impact on the battlefield. What is known, however, is that they are quite active fighting alongside Syrian and Hizbollah fighters throughout the country. Foreign fighters have not concentrated in specific areas but are rather distributed throughout the country and are engaged in active battles on the side of the regime.

The Syrian regime has been forced to rely on privatized and civilianized forms of violence to maintain its military capabilities and its ability to hold contested territory. The SAA has been gutted of personnel, with defections rampant and many Syrians avoiding being conscripted at all costs. During the conflict, more than 40,000 SAA fighters are believed to have lost their lives and many regime loyalists from across Syria's sectarian mosaic have begun to openly question and challenge the utility of sending soldiers to their deaths. Such discord among loyalists has been a sensitive issue in Syria and has placed tremendous pressure on the regime. The combination of low military morale, rampant defections, loyalist discord about rising deaths, disintegration within its ranks, and mistrust among SAA soldiers have all forced the regime to turn to civilian or non-Syrian violent actors. Without the involvement of fighters from outside of the SAA, the regime would likely have been unable to maintain control over large swathes of Syrian territory.

As the conflict drags on and the militias become more central to the regime's survival they are exercising more autonomy from any central regime command. Throughout Syria, the NDF elite are emerging as a conglomeration of warlords with their own agendas and interests that may not coincide with those of the Assad regime in the future. Similarly, non-Syrian militias active in the country are deeply embedded in the war economy and are especially active in looting and extortion. Such activities not only breed fear among Syrians but are a source of potential instability in the future. As regime violence has become more widespread, groups such as the NDF and regional militias are gaining a stake in the continuity of conflict. Warlords are benefitting handsomely from the persistence of violence and conflict and thus can serve as obstacles to any potential political solution. The phenomenon of warlords is not exclusive to nonregime areas. The emergence of warlords and this particular architecture of violence in Syria has contributed to the regime's withering and their loss of decision-making power during the course of the conflict.

The Expansion of Violence

By 2015 Syria was slowly fragmenting into four distinct regions: areas controlled by the Assad regime (from Damascus and then northwest to the coastal areas), areas controlled by the PYD (northeastern Syria around al-Hassakeh and Qamishli), areas controlled by ISIS (eastern Syria around Raqqa and Deir ez-Zor), and areas controlled by FSA-affiliated factions (in southern Syria around Dar'a and Sweida). The control of these territories, however, is precarious and constantly shifting. In April 2015, for example, Idlib had fallen to JAN fighters and most of Dar'a to FSA-affiliated brigades. The capture of these major cities is an important development in the conflict but likely a temporary one, as all armed groups have had difficulty holding territory. In the course of the Syrian conflict, armed groups have proven strong enough to make limited advances and hold some territory but have not been strong enough to expand and control larger areas. Such is the ebb and flow of violence and territorial control in Syria.

As I discuss in Chapter Five, violence and the military stalemate is contributing to the slow fragmentation of the country into different administrative centers of power. Yet these centers of power are not consolidated. The contraction of regime authority has not led to the growth of alternative or coherent state institutions but rather to a patchwork of administrative authorities that are backed up by violent networks. None of these networks are fixed. Fluidity and the constant shifting of alliances means that violence is widespread and will be extremely difficult to contain. As this chapter has demonstrated, the emergence of networks of violence that are often in competition with each other has been determined by many factors, including ideology, military strategy, and pragmatic calculations around the utility of alliances that serve economic and military interests in a particular moment. As these factors are not stable, neither are the networks of violence that make up the militarized landscape of the Syrian opposition.

With this in mind, it is easy to conclude that there is nothing resembling central control of the armed groups. The nodes and networks of violence in Syria are present in both regime and nonregime areas. The regime has been forced to rely on actors outside of the SAA and the security apparatus for military support. These privatized actors include regional militias, unorganized armed supporters, the NDF, and Hizbollah among others, who are exercising power and violence in regime-dominated areas. The exercise of this power is largely decentralized and outside of central regime control. The institutionalization of the NDF, for example, was meant to curb this power, but the continued growth and strength of the NDF and other militias has meant that they exercise authority and make decisions outside of central regime control. These militias, like the armed groups fighting against the regime, have the ability to perpetuate violence even in the event of a peace agreement.

A central factor explaining the proliferation of armed groups inside of Syria is the role of the international community, which is the focus of the next chapter. Throughout the conflict regional states have played an essential role in the cultivation, financing, and support of different armed groups in Syria. This is especially true of the main regional players: Iran, Saudi Arabia, Qatar, and Turkey. In many ways, the proliferation of armed groups and their division into competing networks of violence is a function of the role of the international community and the desire of regional states to assume control and stewardship of the militarized opposition. Regional conflicts over influence among the armed groups have certainly played a large role in the conflict but this was not the only way in which the international community has intervened (or not) in the Syrian conflict. As I discuss in the following chapter, the tensions and competing interests among the different regional actors have played a profound role in shaping the Syrian conflict. The absence of an international consensus on how to solve the Syrian conflict, and the lack of a political process that all parties are committed to, has fostered a situation in which most states have rejected international mechanisms and institutions as channels to end the conflict. With the exception of the American and Russian agreement over the dismantling of Syria's chemical weapons program, most international attempts at solving the conflict have failed. There is also a lack of international consensus about how to deal with key questions, such as whether and which armed groups to support, whether or not to intervene, and what a political transition process should entail. This lack of consensus has meant that regional and Western states have adopted radically different policies toward the Syrian conflict. The intervention of these states into the Syrian conflict has not, however, helped to de-escalate the violence or move the country toward a resolution. Instead intervention has propelled violence, solidified the stalemate, and embedded the Syrian conflict into wider regional geopolitics. In this context, the Syrian conflict has taken on an ever-more-important international dimension that will determine the prospects for de-escalation and the long-term resolution of the conflict.

4 | When the World Wades In

The internationalization of the Syrian conflict was an almost immediate aftereffect of the inability of regime forces to quell protests in 2011. The continued spread of protests and the repeated violence inflicted on protesters by regime forces had forced the international community to pursue different forms of diplomatic and military intervention to halt the violence. International concern with Syria increased as the uprising become more militarized and regional actors adopted radically different and opposing solutions to the conflict. On the one hand, powerful regional states, such as Qatar, Turkey, and Saudi Arabia, adopted a policy of regime change after initially pursuing diplomatic efforts and have marshaled considerable resources in support of opposition groups. On the other hand, the regime's allies, mainly Iran, Russia, and Hizbollah, have adopted a policy of regime preservation at all costs. As the conflict has progressed, the role of international actors in militarily, financially, and politically backing their respective allies in Syria is perhaps the single largest factor explaining the continuity of the conflict, the fragmentation of political and military forces, the failure of reconciliation efforts, and the existing stalemate that is slowly fragmenting the country.

In this chapter, we explore the international dimensions of the Syrian conflict through two main approaches. The first is to highlight and outline key state and regional actors and their policy approaches to the Syrian conflict. For example, although states such as Qatar and Saudi Arabia share a common goal of regime change, they have pursued this policy often in conflict with one another and at great detriment to the political opposition. The second approach is to highlight the key international issues and forms of involvement of the international community, including questions around intervention, arming the rebels, and defeating ISIS, to political processes aimed at ending the conflict.

The Arab World

The response of Arab states to the Syrian conflict must be understood within the overlapping contexts of the Arab uprisings sweeping through the region and the geopolitical rivalries between Iran and Saudi Arabia and their respective regional allies. Both contexts have shaped Arab states' response to the Syrian conflict. In the initial phases of the uprising, Arab states adopted a largely conciliatory and diplomatic approach to the conflict and attempted through League of Arab States (LAS) diplomatic efforts to bring about a resolution in the summer of 2011. The failure of LAS efforts and the lack of an Arab consensus on how to deal with Syria forced divergent policy paths among Arab states, especially Gulf states and Syria's geographic neighbors.

In October 2011 the LAS adopted a resolution condemning violence in Syria and advocating for immediate dialogue. This was on the heels of the Arab League's successful foray into the Libyan war, which resulted in a NATO-led intervention to topple Gaddafi, who had ruled Libya from 1969 until 2011. Egypt, traditionally a major actor in Arab affairs, could not contribute to Syrian diplomatic efforts due to its own internal political transition. This left Saudi Arabia and Qatar to lead diplomatic efforts in Syria.

Both states initially worked through the LAS on diplomatic efforts when there existed general consensus that the solution to the conflict lay in political dialogue. At the behest of Saudi Arabia and Qatar, LAS officials made overtures to the newly formed Syrian National Coalition and effectively legitimized the body as a participant in any political talks. The Syrian regime was unwilling to support the LAS-led talks or abide by the terms of a peace plan, which was put forth by the LAS in early November 2011 and was initially accepted by the regime. The plan consisted of the following main points: the withdrawal of the army from cities and towns, political dialogue with the SNC, the release of political prisoners, and the entry of an observer mission to Syria to monitor the regime's compliance. Within days of the proposed peace plan, the regime had not withdrawn the army from the conflict areas. Army attacks against protesters continued despite LAS threats.

The regime had signaled its unwillingness to accept the LAS plan. Nevertheless, a new peace plan was agreed upon the following month that was identical to the one agreed upon a month earlier. The regime's strategy in this period was simply to buy time and attempt to pacify the protests in the process. After the agreement on the second plan, however, an observer mission was allowed entry into Syria in late December 2011. The presence of the observer mission had no effect on regime violence and the lack of cooperation among government officials made it very clear that the observer mission was going to be unable to perform any of its mandated tasks or to have any impact in resolving the conflict. By late January 2012, the LAS suspended its observer mission, thus acknowledging the failure of its efforts to resolve the Syrian conflict through diplomatic measures.

The lack of cooperation led the LAS to take two important decisions: first, to suspend Syria's membership from the LAS in November 2011, and, second, to impose economic sanctions against Syria, including a freezing of government assets. The first decision was highly symbolic and isolated the Syrian regime from the regional arena. The second decision to impose sanctions would contribute to the slow collapse of the Syrian economy. The majority of Syria's non-oil trade was with Gulf countries and the closure of these markets would have a destructive effect on Syrian enterprises that were reliant on Gulf markets. The sanctions stipulated that contracts would be honored but could not be renewed; thus over a few months no new agreements were signed between Syrian and Gulf businesses, effectively destroying many Syrian businesses, especially in textiles (Abboud, 2013). The economic effect of the sanctions was lessened to some degree by the refusal of Iraq and Lebanon, two other key trading partners, to honor the sanctions. Nevertheless, the closure of the Gulf markets was a major blow to Syrian enterprises. In addition, all Gulf investments in Syria ceased and billions of dollars were withdrawn from the country. The withdrawal of Gulf funding led to the closure of many public and private investment projects, including key projects in infrastructure and public services. In the absence of public funds to complete the projects, many of them remained unfinished.

Such measures did not represent a consensus among Arab states. There were disagreements between states as some, such as Algeria and Iraq, were wary of increasing LAS involvement in Syria and of military intervention in the country. Moreover, Arab states were divided over the legitimacy of the Syrian political opposition, whose officials had actually advocated for military intervention over the LAS peace plan in late 2011. Such disputes among the LAS and the futile attempts at a diplomatic solution through the organization quickly foreclosed the possibility of a regionally negotiated solution or any substantial role for the LAS in the Syrian conflict. Henceforth, the LAS would not play any significant role in Syria: diplomatic efforts were now pursued by the UN and Arab states began to pursue separate policies toward Syria. Out of the rubble of the LAS efforts emerged Qatar and Saudi Arabia, the two most important Arab actors in the Syrian conflict.

Qatar has been an extremely important regional actor during the conflict, particularly in the formation of the political opposition and in the financing of key armed groups. Qatar's policy has shifted considerably since 2011. Its then leader, Hamad bin Khalifa al-Thani, charted a policy that began as accommodating and reconciliatory toward the Syrian regime and then quickly shifted toward confrontation. In 2013, power was handed over to his son Tamim bin

Hamad al-Thani, who has since slowly moved Qatar to a more neutral and less direct role in the conflict.

Although both are Sunni-dominated Arab Gulf monarchies, Qatar and Saudi Arabia have adopted divergent policies regarding the Arab uprisings that have put the two countries in regular conflict. Qatar's policies have often clashed with those of Saudi Arabia, leading to a war by proxy in Egypt, Libya, and Syria, among other states. These proxy wars have occurred in both the military and political arenas, with Qatari and Saudi interests supporting rival armed and political factions throughout the Arab world. In Egypt, for example, Qatar had supported the Muslim Brotherhood after Hosni Mubarak's resignation in January 2012, while the Saudis had supported the military officers and remnants of Mubarak's regime. The first presidential elections after Mubarak's resignation brought Mohammed Morsi to power, a Brotherhood official supported by Qatar, who defeated Ahmad Shafik, Mubarak's previous Prime Minister who was supported by Saudi Arabia. The Qatari-Saudi dispute in Egypt continued thereafter, with Saudi Arabia supporting a military coup d'etat against Morsi's presidency, leading to the assumption of power by the Saudi-supported Field Marshall Abdel Fattah al-Sisi.

Similar jockeying for political influence in the aftermath of the Arab uprisings would shape Qatari and Saudi involvement in the Syrian conflict. Qatar's leadership was initially keen on positioning the country at the forefront of the uprisings by supporting the overthrow of regimes. Although pursuing a diplomatic approach through the LAS at first, Qatar quickly shifted toward a more confrontational policy with the regime. Qatari officials began cultivating stronger relationships with different factions of the Syrian National Coalition (SNC), especially the Muslim Brotherhood, in an attempt to exert influence over the direction of the SNC. Similar efforts by Saudi Arabia have effectively split the SNC into Qatari, Saudi, and nonaligned factions that are in regular conflict with one another over policy and political strategy. Moreover, while the Saudis and Qataris have been keen to meddle in the SNC's affairs and cultivate conflict and mistrust among members, they have failed to sufficiently legitimize the body, in part out of fear of the other state exerting undue influence and control. For example, despite supporting efforts to remove Syria from the LAS, both Qatar and Saudi Arabia have resisted requests from the SNC to hand over the seat to the opposition. The political weaknesses and fragmentation of the SNC and the political opposition in general is in some measure the outcome of the Qatari-Saudi dispute over policy on the Syrian conflict.

As the two countries were cultivating their respective factions in the SNC, Qatar was simultaneously, in mid-2012, shipping light weapons to the militarized opposition which were acquired from Libya and Eastern Europe, flown to Turkey, and then distributed by Turkish and Qatari intelligence officers to the armed groups (Wezeman, 2013). The slow arming of rebels in 2012 brought about coherence in Saudi and Qatari policies. The largest and most effective brigades at the time, including Liwa al-Tawhid, were believed to have received light arms from both states. The policy on arming rebel groups at the time was characterized by confusion. Qatar, Saudi Arabia, and Turkey facilitated the inflow of light weapons that were dispersed to multiple armed groups, preventing the concentration of weapons in any particular group. Such strategies contributed to the proliferation of violent groups but also ensured that there would be military balance among them. This environment was not conducive to cultivating cohesion or solidarity among the armed groups; instead, it fostered mistrust and competition between them over scarce resources.

The factionalization of the opposition mirrored that of the Supreme Military Command (SMC) under General Salim Idriss. A key demand of Western states was the formation of the SMC to coordinate opposition military and political activities. However, while publicly supporting the formation of the SMC, Qatar and Saudi Arabia renewed their competition over the appointment of key Provincial Military Council leaders and, much to the detriment of the SMC's legitimacy, bypassed SMC structures to provide resources to armed groups. Rather than coordinating policies through the SMC structure, both countries actively undermined the SMC and pursued parallel policies that delinked brigades from the broader SMC structure and made them more dependent on foreign patronage than on the SMC leadership.

Russia

Russia has been the Syrian regime's most ardent supporter in the international community, having blocked efforts at the UNSCR to place political pressure on the regime to initiate a political transition or to pass UN-supported sanctions. Moreover, Russia has been a major arms supplier to the Assad regime and has continued to trade with Syria amid blockades and sanctions imposed by other states. Russia's support, however, has very little to do with any shared affinity with the Syrian regime or any ideological or political commitment to the survival of Ba'athism. Nor is Russian support determined by a reactionary impulse to "protect" an ally or its arms market (Strategic Comments, 2012). Instead, Russian support of the Syrian regime has been determined by the interplay of geopolitical, domestic, and economic factors. The major drivers of Russian policy toward Syria include skepticism and concern over the threat of Western military intervention, particularly after the NATO-led intervention into Libya; the threat posed by the spread of Salafist-jihadist extremism in the region and the Caucasus in particular; and Russian geo-economic interests.

Russian concern with Western intervention predates the Arab uprisings and goes far back into the early 2000s during the colored revolutions in Georgia, Ukraine, and Kyrgyzstan. At the time, the Russian political establishment largely viewed the revolutions as Western-led uprisings to promote regime change (Strategic Comments, 2012), a strategy that might eventually be exported to Russia itself. Such fears of foreign-led attempts at regime change through ostensibly grassroots national movements would shape Russian framings of the Arab uprisings only a few years later. By the time that the Syrian conflict had evolved into a crisis that would warrant international attention and give rise to discussions of intervention, Western interventions had already taken place in Afghanistan (2002), Iraq (2003), and Libya (2011), in addition to the unrest in the former Soviet bloc that was viewed by the Russian political establishment as being Western-led. Such interventions were extremely threatening to the Russian establishment, which viewed the continued instability wrought by interventions as a threat to both the international system and to their own geopolitical interests and to stability in their former spheres of influence (Charap, 2013).

The Russian political establishment was particularly shocked and alarmed by the Libyan intervention. In March 2011 the UNSC adopted Resolution 1973 authorizing a no-fly zone over Libya. Although Russia abstained from the vote, its representatives were active in articulating concerns over the meaning of the mandate and the potential use of military force for humanitarian reasons. Almost immediately after the passing of the resolution, Russia's position became critical of the implementation of Resolution 1973 as it became increasingly clear that the coalition was using the mandate not only to enforce a no-fly zone but to use force to overthrow the Libyan regime (Allison, 2013). The Russian establishment was jolted (Aras and Falk, 2015) not only because of the manipulation of the resolution by the coalition to engage in direct military intervention in the conflict on the side of one party, but also by the unilateral expansion of the mandate with UNSC approval and the implicit judgment of Western states about the political legitimacy of the Libyan regime (Aras and Falk, 2015).

The Libyan intervention would thus have profound effects on Russia's shielding of the Syrian regime. This, along with unrest in the 2000s leading up to and after the Arab uprisings, has decidedly shaped Russian views on the Syrian conflict. Russian skepticism concerning Western intentions and deep mistrust of any Western efforts to resolve the Syrian conflict, whether through military or political means, has been the most decisive factor in explaining Russia's intransigence toward any international efforts to resolve the crisis.

Informing the Russian mistrust of international efforts are the ongoing rivalries with the United States over key regional issues, including the Iranian nuclear issue. As Russia increasingly views the regional developments through the prism of its own simmering conflict with the United States, Russian policymakers have adopted positions in direct contradiction to the U.S. Such is the reason behind the continued use of the Russian veto at the UNSCR to block any efforts to impose economic sanctions against the Syrian regime. In all three cases of the use of the Russian veto to date, they have framed their opposition in terms of the principle of non-intervention into the sovereign affairs of Syria (Strategic Comments, 2012), a principle that reflects both the belief in the threat of continued intervention and their skepticism about Western intentions.

Dannreuther (2015) has argued that there has emerged a distinctively "Russian idea" about the nature of political order that is grounded in a critique of Western interventions to promote democracy in non-Western countries. While the immediate Russian concern has been with Western intervention into neighboring states, this idea has been extended to the Russian establishment's framing of the Arab uprisings. The Libyan case has merely affirmed Russian perceptions that Western states would use humanitarian motives to impose regime change. The Russian position on shielding Syria from diplomatic or international intervention efforts must be understood within this larger context.

Other geopolitical factors are important as well, including Russia's relations with Iran, Syria's major regional ally. Both countries border the Caspian Sea and have common interests in maintaining their naval superiority there as well as opposing the construction of oil and gas pipelines on the Caspian Sea bed (Strategic Comments, 2012). Iran is also a major purchaser of Russian arms and has relied extensively on Russian support for the development of its nuclear technologies. Finally, both states share a common fear of the spread of Salafist-jihadist fighters throughout the region and into the Caucasus. The spread of such fighters could be severely destabilizing for both states. For now, common economic and geopolitical interests have shaped the convergence of Russian and Iranian perspectives on the Syrian conflict. Such convergence is also exemplified in the cooling of Russian relations with Gulf countries, who have used the Russian stance on Syria as an impetus toward realignment away from Russia. This movement has included the canceling of lucrative economic agreements between both countries. In contrast, despite Turkish and Russian divergence on the Syrian conflict and the insistence by the Turkish leadership that Russia is partly to blame for the resiliency of the regime, there have been no noticeable negative economic effects of the conflict on Russian-Turkish relations (Dannreuther, 2015). Trade between the two countries has remained stable and, unlike relations with Arab Gulf states, economic agreements have not been threatened by their political disagreements over the Syrian conflict.

Finally, there are domestic reasons for Russia's support for the Syrian regime, including an arms market, a naval base in Tartous, and economic investments and commercial trade deals with which Russian companies are involved. Although it is impossible to determine the exact amount, it is estimated that Syria has around $4 billion in unpaid military contracts with Russian military companies (O'Toole, 2012). Russian companies have also made extensive investments throughout the economy, especially in oil and gas exploration (Gorenburg, 2012). Russian manufacturing companies have also been active in Syria, with many contracts signed in the late 2000s and in the early stages of the uprising for the creation of joint Syrian-Russian projects or for the Russian provision of goods. While many of these contracts have been affected by the conflict, Russian traders and the arms establishments are concerned that any regime change would mean a loss of existing contracts and their peripheralization in any post-conflict reconstruction. The arms establishment is particularly concerned that the Libyan scenario could be repeated. In that country, more than $2 billion in contracts that were agreed upon by the Gaddafi regime were invalidated after the new government took over. The new Libyan government subsequently signed weapons agreements with French military companies, effectively closing off a once robust market for the Russian arms establishment.

The interplay of these geopolitical, domestic, and economic factors have made it difficult for the Russian political establishment to abandon the Syrian regime. While support for the regime is clearly not based on any ideological considerations or commitments, there are very strong reasons behind Russian support of the regime. Geopolitical fears of Western intervention, coupled with the threat of Salafist-jihadist expansion into Russian spheres of influence, as well as a wide range of economic interests, have all contributed to the sustained Russian support of the Syrian regime.

Iran

Iran has the largest geopolitical stake in the survival of the Syrian regime. Iran has exercised a tremendous amount of control over regime decision-making up until this point, and is likely to continue to do so, as the regime is financially and militarily dependent on Iran for its survival. However, its staunch support of the regime has brought the country into proxy conflict with Saudi Arabia and has inflamed sectarian tensions in the region. For the time being, Iran seems willing to assume the short- and long-term burden of its support of the Syrian regime.

There is a long history of strong Syrian-Iranian relations that predates the uprising and goes well back into the 1970s (Goodarzi, 2009; von Maltzhan, 2013). For the Iranian establishment, the survival of the Syrian regime is not merely a necessity born out of this historical relationship, however, but a policy goal that is viewed within a larger regional and geopolitical context. One of the central prisms through which the conflict is refracted is the regional conflict with Saudi Arabia and other Arab states. While it has become commonplace and convenient to frame this as a Sunni-Shi'a rivalry with the two states at opposite poles, this is simplistic. It ignores how political and economic ambitions and interests, and not merely amorphous sectarian expansionary goals, shape geopolitical rivalries (Hokayem, 2013). With this in mind, it is difficult to unravel Iran's role in the Syrian conflict without reference to its regional geopolitical situation.

Iran has had to balance its regional rivalry with Saudi Arabia and its support of the Syrian regime alongside the negotiations over its nuclear program, which culminated in 2015 with a long-term deal called the Comprehensive Agreement on the Iranian Nuclear Programme. The effect of sanctions on Iran and the decline in oil prices had been major drivers of the Iranian establishment's desire to break its international isolation and submit its nuclear program to international inspection. Prior to the deal negotiated between Iran, the United States, Russia, China, France, the United Kingdom, and Germany, there was a belief that any nuclear deal should be embedded into a larger regional grand bargain that would also contain agreements concerning Iran's role in Syria. However, such a grand bargain does not seem to have been achieved. All indicators are that the negotiations occurred independently of any reference to Iran's role in the Syrian conflict. There were suggestions that any nuclear deal would involve pressuring Iran to lessen its support of the Syrian regime and its other allies, including Hizbollah, but the nuclear deal is unlikely to yield a shift in Iran's regional alliances.

Primary to Iran's regional alliances is its relationship with Hizbollah in Lebanon. This relation has evolved since the 1980s when Hizbollah was first formed (Shaery-Eisenlohr, 2008; Abboud and Muller, 2012; Alagha, 2006). Today, Hizbollah cannot be said to be in a subservient relationship with the Iranian regime, whereby the latter dictates the former's goals, interests, and policy choices. The Iranian leadership does not control Hizbollah; rather, there is an alliance and relationship based on mutual interests and coordination within the region (el-Hokayem, 2007). Thus, Iran's involvement in the Syrian conflict goes well beyond what some commentators suggest is the control of Hizbollah and the use of Hizbollah's weapons to serve Iranian interests (Daoud, 2014).

While Hizbollah has indeed been active in the Syrian arena, Iranian involvement has gone well beyond this. Iran has provided military supplies to the Syrian regime and training to thousands of *shabiha* who eventually formed the core membership of the NDF. Iranian military officials and fighters have been active in Syria and some Iranian strategists have died in fighting between regime and rebel forces (Evans and Karouny, 2013). Moreover, Iran has likely financially supported the movement of Iraqi and Afghani militias into Syria and provided them with training. Thus Iran's military involvement in Syria is extensive, so much so that it is believed that Iranian officials are making key battlefield decisions in place of Syrian officials (Hashem, 2015).

Although Iranian support for the Syrian regime has been sustained and unyielding, there is no reason to believe that Iran wants a continuation of the conflict. Over the long term, the Syrian conflict directly threatens Iranian interests in the region (Goodarzi, 2013). The stalemate has forced a readjustment of the Iranian strategy and what appears to be a gradual move away from a military solution to the conflict. For example, Iran has played a large role in the local ceasefires and the Iranian leadership is believed to have floated the idea that a deal for a political transition could be reached if key Iranian conditions were met. At this point, the Iranian calculation may be to contain the damage of the conflict and attempt to reach a gradual solution, as the instability wrought by the conflict directly affects the Iraqi government and Hizbollah, both key Iranian allies (Goodarzi, 2013). In addition to this, the military and financial dependence of the Syrian regime on Iran is unsustainable over the long term (Sadjadpour, 2013). With sanctions and low international oil prices severely crippling the Iranian economy, it is likely that the Iranian establishment will eventually question its support for the Syrian regime.

Turkey

Turkey plays a major role in the Syrian conflict, first as a supporter of the opposition and as a facilitator of the flow of weapons and fighters into Syria, and, second as a host of hundreds of thousands of Syrian refugees and as the main corridor for humanitarian aid work. After initially urging President Bashar al-Assad to enact meaningful political reforms, Turkey abandoned its Syrian ally and declared the overthrow of the President to be its foreign policy objective. The Turkish position on the Syrian conflict has evolved considerably over the last few years but the one constant has been the commitment to removing Assad from power. Under this broader policy objective of removing al-Assad, Turkey faces a number of challenges regarding the Syrian conflict which have shaped its policies.

Turkey had initially adopted a nonconfrontational policy toward the Syrian regime in the early stages of the conflict, advocating for reform and seeing the protests as an opportunity to push for the inclusion of marginalized Syrian political forces. When this strategy failed, Turkey adopted a three-pronged policy toward the conflict (Stein, 2015). First, the Turkish government allowed for the transit of army defectors who would later form the nucleus of the FSA. They were given shelter by Turkey and permitted to operate from inside the country. Second, Turkey worked to organize the external opposition and to legitimize the opposition as the representative of the Syrian uprising. Finally, Turkey adopted a policy of advocating intervention in Syria and the creation of a no-fly zone in the northern parts of the country. The goal of this strategy was to organize an opposition and provide them a geographic base from which to conduct operations and govern Syria.

By 2012 this strategy was in tatters and the consolidation of rebel groups under the command of an external opposition never materialized. This forced a rethinking of Turkish strategy and a partial abandonment of its earlier allies. Increasingly, Turkish intelligence had provided covert and overt support to other armed groups, including Jabhat an-Nusra, which had been making substantial military gains against the regime. The Turkish government tried to reorganize the external opposition and to rally the international community into supporting it through the creation of the Friends of Syria initiative, a coalition of states supporting the Syrian uprising.

These policies have had a major impact on the course of the conflict and the shaping of both the political and military opposition.

One explanation for the failure of Turkish policy to bring about regime change is that policy has occurred largely within the context of multiple balancing acts between Turkey and regional powers. On the one hand, Turkey's regional relations have stunted Turkish ambitions and interests vis-à-vis the conflict. Turkish policies have placed the country in direct confrontation with Iraq, Iran, and Russia, all important political and economic partners prior to the uprising. While there has been minimal economic fallout from the conflict on relations between Turkey and these countries, the threat of regional tensions or, at worst, conflict, has likely tempered Turkish activities in Syria. Not all that dissimilar are Turkey's relations with erstwhile allies Qatar and Saudi Arabia. As I have detailed throughout the book, disagreements between the three states over which armed groups to support and how to structure the external political opposition have been important factors in explaining the rebel and opposition weaknesses during the conflict. On the other hand, the Turkish government's policies in Syria do not enjoy the full support of Turkish citizens. Indeed, Turkish policies in Syria have caused considerable national discord (Yilmaz, 2013).

The Turkish government's need to balance its regional alliances alongside domestic opposition to the conflict is further compounded by the challenges posed by the conflict itself. The first challenge concerns the threat of civil violence and the spillover effects of the war. There have been a number of bombings and attacks in the southern borderlands that have led to dozens of Turkish deaths. The second challenge concerns Turkey's military involvement in the Syrian conflict. In 2015, Turkish forces, working in coordination with the YPG, entered Syria to remove the tomb of Süleyman Şah (the grandfather of Osman I, the founder of the Ottoman Empire). This was the first direct Turkish troop intervention into the Syrian conflict despite multiple border clashes and the downing of two Turkish planes by Syrian forces in 2012. As the conflict worsens and spillover occurs there is the potential of deeper Turkish military intervention. The third challenge is represented by the presence of Salafist-jihadists in the opposition's ranks and the concern that some groups, especially ISIS, could begin to target Turkey if the government adopts restrictive policies on the movement of fighters and supplies. Fourth, there is the challenge of ensuring humanitarian assistance for the increasing number of refugees in the country.

The West

Western states have not adopted similar positions and strategies toward the Syrian conflict. The lack of a Western consensus on Syria, coupled with Russian obstruction of UNSC intervention, has meant that many Western states have adopted largely ineffectual and insignificant policies in relation to the conflict. From the conflict's outset, Western states were unanimous in imposing sanctions against the Syrian regime and state institutions in an attempt to induce high-level defections and paralyze the regime into a political compromise. However, as the conflict developed and there was paralysis within the UNSC, the range of policy options available to Western states shrunk. This has led to the perception of Western inaction and ambivalence on Syria.

From the perspective of many Syrians who had pinned hopes on Western political or military intervention, the European Union's policy toward Syria has appeared inconsistent and ambiguous (Trombetta, 2014). Indeed, such sentiments reflect a major problem of Western policy toward Syria in general, mainly, that the disconnect between actual policy and official positions has not translated into any meaningful policies to effect change. Across the EU, North American, Australia, and New Zealand, Western states have been unanimous in their condemnation of the Syrian regime and their expressed desire for regime change and a political transition. Yet very few political resources have been brought to bear to realize this. Russian obstruction of UNSC efforts has been met largely with head-scratching in Western capitals while the failure of sanctions to bring about regime change has simply led to more extensive and deeper sanctions that are having profound effects on average Syrians (Moret, 2015).

For the European Union, sanctions have been the main policy tool. Seeberg (2014) has identified four phases of sanctions imposed by the EU on Syrian officials and state institutions. The first three phases were between 2011 and early 2013 and were defined by the imposition and extension of sanctions. This included sanctions against a range of officials, state institutions, and trade, such as the banning of all Syrian oil exports (this was significant because the European Union was the main market for Syrian oil). The fourth phase, which began around April 2013, represented a shift in European Union policy toward the conflict and was defined by the easing of some sanctions with the intention of supporting the political and military opposition by, for example, allowing them to sell oil from nonregime areas. This easing suggested a reinvigorated policy toward Syria which has never materialized. Since 2013, there have been few sanctions and the European Union has even shifted positions on the major issue of whether the Syrian regime can be a party to any political negotiations.

What explains the European Union's sanctions regime and the shift toward acceptance of the Syrian regime as a negotiating partner? One explanation is that European Union officials had come to the realization that sanctions were mostly ineffective (Seeberg, 2014: 10). The sanctions had not induced defections of the political or economic elite or led to a collapse of the security apparatus. Moreover, the failure of the political opposition to marshal European sanctions toward regime change forced a rethinking of the role of sanctions as a strategy and as a tool to support the opposition. Most important, however, were the disagreements among European Union states about how to deal with the situation (Trombetta, 2014). The divisions between member states manifested in multiple ways, including disagreements over the oil embargo (which threatened certain domestic interests) and a general unwillingness to use the weight and power of the Union in a conflict concerning which many member states were on the periphery. Such disagreements and ambivalence mirrored the ineffectiveness of European Union institutions in coordinating a response to the humanitarian crisis caused by the conflict. Four years into the conflict, there has been very little coordination between European institutions around it and many member states have retreated into policies that privilege their domestic interests over those of the larger regional body (Trombetta, 2014).

Similarly, within the United States there has been little agreement over how to deal with the Syrian conflict. On the one hand, the Obama administration can rightly be accused of saying one thing on Syria and doing another. Much like the European Union, the Obama administration has not been willing to marshal political resources and capital toward achieving its stated goals of regime change and a political transition. On the other hand, the administration's hands have been tied by the lack of an international, let alone Western, consensus on Syria, Russian and Chinese blocking of UNSC efforts, and internal disagreements over what policies the administration should adopt, including whether to intervene militarily or not. Without a doubt, the Obama administration's calculations have been shaped by the legacies and fatigue of the Afghanistan and Iraq wars that have reduced American and Western appetites for long-term commitments to overseas military occupations.

For the most part, Western policy toward the Syrian conflict has been reactionary, with the European Union and United States exercising much less influence then the other regional states involved in the conflict, such as Turkey, Iran, Qatar, and Saudi Arabia. In many instances (elaborated throughout the book), Western allies in the region adopted policies that directly contradicted or undermined stated Western goals. In such cases, Western states have not been able, or willing, to adopt policies that radically alter the course of the conflict.

Western disunity and disagreement about how to deal with the Syrian regime has perhaps best been highlighted by the response to the rise of ISIS in Syria. The presence of ISIS has actually initiated a slow retreat in Western capitals toward a position of greater neutrality to the regime and to the larger conflict. Increasingly, discourse in Western states is presenting the problem as one of the regime or ISIS. Such framing of the conflict has given the regime allies within Western states who believe that the regime should be supported in order to eliminate the ISIS threat (Dreyfuss, 2014). Such framing of the conflict presents false choices, however, as the battle is not between the regime and ISIS. In any case, the ISIS threat has begun to shape Western thinking of the conflict and is leading to a relegitimization of the Syrian regime as a proxy partner in the fight against ISIS. The Western shift on the regime brought about by the presence of ISIS highlights Western paralysis around Syria. As the next section will detail, disagreements among Western states on key issues persist despite agreement on the need to confront ISIS.

Arming the Rebels

Syrian armed groups have received weapons from three main sources: weapons provided by regional patrons, weapons captured from government supplies, and the black market trade in light weapons, mainly from Iraq and Lebanon. These weapons have been insufficient, and their supply inconsistent enough to preclude larger military gains against regime forces. As a result, one of the key demands of the political opposition and the armed groups inside of Syria has been to provide weapons for the armed groups. However, there is no consensus in the international community and the Friends of Syria Group—a coalition of more than seventy countries that support a political transition in Syria—has failed to develop a common policy on arming rebel groups. Qatar, Saudi Arabia, and Turkey (discussed below) have taken the lead in providing weapons to armed groups but have largely avoided providing heavier weaponry such as anti-aircraft equipment. Western states, on the other hand, have been less willing to provide weapons to rebel groups. The Obama Administration in particular has been hesitant to provide anything other than nonlethal equipment to armed groups. France and Britain have advocated for a more active EU policy involving direct arming of the rebels but have thus far been rebuked by most other EU states.

For Western states, the issue of arming Syrian rebels is complicated by the widely held belief that the weapons could eventually be turned against Western soldiers in Iraq, Afghanistan, or elsewhere in the region. The "blowback" fear is widely held in Western capitals. Yet this does not entirely explain the reluctance of Western states to provide military backing to the rebels. Notwithstanding public declarations to the contrary, there is Western ambivalence about the Syrian conflict. The major Western policy toward the conflict thus far was to impose sanctions on regime officials and state institutions. Such sanctions did not induce major defections or have any demonstrable effect on the cohesion of the regime and its security apparatus. Diplomatic attempts at ending the conflict have similarly produced few results. For supporters of the Syrian opposition, the only remaining strategy is to arm the rebels.

As the Friends of Syria group debated whether and how to arm the opposition, jihadist groups quickly gained in strength on the ground and began to shift the military balance away from the FSA–aligned brigades. The speed at which more extremist fighting units overtook FSA positions made the issue of rebel armament both more urgent and more complicated to disentangle. Western states were alarmed at the rapid military gains of more extremist groups and thus became even more reluctant to arm the rebels for fear of weapons ending up in the hands of these extremist groups. Yet, at the same time, the failure to support and provide military resources to the FSA brigades was placing them at a military disadvantage to their better equipped and increasing larger extremist counterparts in the rebellion.

The reality is that the dichotomy between what have been called "moderate" or "secular" rebels in the West and the extremist or Islamist rebels has been a false one from the beginning. Many FSA brigades had a distinctly Syrian character to them, having mostly adopted nationalist symbols and figures into their names as and brigade flags (Lund, 2012). By 2012, however, this had begun to change and the symbolism and discourse of the brigades slowly shifted away from nationalism to more Islamist rhetoric. The rise of more extremist groups, such as JAN and the Syrian Islamic Front (SIF), drew fighters away from FSA brigades who were themselves becoming increasingly Islamized in their rank and file.

The split, however, between moderate and extremist or national and jihadist groups is extremely ambiguous on the ground. Many of the major battles during 2012 involved FSA and Islamist brigades fighting alongside one another against regime forces. This was the case when Raqqa, the first major city in Syria, came under rebel control. Moreover, larger and more powerful brigades, such as Ahrar as-Sham, and larger organizations such as JAN, have consistently emphasized the Syrian character of their leadership, rank and file, and of their struggle. Eschewing the transnational jihad of their ISIS and al-Qaeda counterparts who see the Syrian conflict as part of a broader global struggle, JAN, Ahrar as-Sham, and other Islamist groups have emphasized the distinctly national (Syrian) nature of their goals and struggle. Many of their fighters and their leadership are Syrian and are socially rooted in the towns, cities, and villages in which they have been active. This distinguishes them sharply from ISIS, who have relied mainly on non-Syrian fighters and Iraqi leaders. While they are distinguishable from FSA brigades in many respects, the Syrian character of their struggle has complicated the Western view of the rebel landscape.

The question of whether to arm rebels has been in the West a question of ensuring that weapons are controlled by "moderate" rather than "extremist" forces. Yet, as the rebel landscape beyond ISIS demonstrates, such distinctions are false ones and do not accurately reflect realities and the fluidity of alliances on the ground and the levels of cooperation between rebel groups. The dispersed and fragmented structure of the armed opposition is such that no brigades or units exercise autonomy from one another. Groups are deeply interconnected, whether through alliances or battles over territorial control. Confusion and misunderstanding in the West concerning the fluidity of the rebel landscape has complicated the question of arming rebel groups. At various times in the conflict, different Fronts, brigades, and units that are Islamist have either pledged allegiance, fought alongside, or maintained some affiliation with the FSA. In 2012, for example, the Islamic Front for the Liberation of Syria fought alongside FSA brigades and had closely cooperated with them. Later iterations of different Islamist Fronts, such as the morphing of the Syrian Islamic Front into the Islamic Front (IF) have complicated alliances on the ground. The IF, for example, has rejected the SNC and is largely funded by private donors (more below), but has also cooperated with FSA brigades on the battlefield. One of the principal brigades of the IF, Liwa al-Tawhid, had once been a part of a broader Islamist Front under the FSA umbrella but had removed itself and eventually joined the IF.

The fluidity of alliances and the flexibility of FSA affiliation has meant that rebel brigades are interconnected in networks of violence that make unraveling their ideological and political affinities and interests virtually impossible. In 2012, for example, southern Syria was experiencing an inflow of weapons from Jordan to brigades affiliated with the FSA. The rebel landscape at the time was dominated by four groups— FSA-affiliated Maghawir Forces, the Sufi al-Habib al-Mustafa Brigade, the Salafi al-Islam Brigade, and the Shuhada al-Islam Brigade— which shared no common ideological affinities and each of which actually belonged to larger networks of violence (the Salafi al-Islam Brigade, for example, was a member of the Islamic Front for the Liberation of Syria) (Pierret, 2013). Cooperation between the four brigades and other military units allowed them to withstand regime advances. The interconnectedness of these groups who have fought alongside each other and cooperated in the shared administration of southern areas belies dichotomies of "moderates" and "extremists."

Moreover, brigades have been known to stress or deemphasize their ideological commitments based on funding opportunities. Private donors in the Gulf were reported to have funded more Islamist-oriented units based on the quality of their propaganda videos (Windrem, 2014). Other brigades have shifted alliances for financial and material, not ideological, reasons. The Dur al-Din Zanki Battalions, for example, was established as a unit of the radical al-Fajr movement (which eventually became part of Ahrar as-Sham), then shifted to Liwa al-Tawhid, and then the Front for Authenticity and Development (FAD), which was a Saudi-funded coalition that has no distinctly Islamist features (Pierret, 2013). Beyond the JAN and ISIS networks of violence then lies a complex, interconnected web of violent networks whose ideological affinities, allegiances, and military commitments are consistently shifting, rendering the attempt to classify groups into "moderates" and "extremists" an exercise in futility.

For Qatar and Saudi Arabia, the calculations have been quite different and have been informed by more pragmatic calculations and a different understanding of the rebel landscape. Distinctions between "moderate" and "extremist" groups were not major factors in the calculations except in reference to specific jihadist groups believed to be affiliated with al-Qaeda. Instead, three major approaches were adopted concerning arming the rebels. First, the rebel groups that were strongest and were believed to have made the most substantial gains were provided with resources. Qatar and Saudi Arabia were very interested in supporting those who were successful and had battlefield momentum. This approach had the effect of drowning out many of the smaller brigades and units and eventually forcing their absorption into larger networks of violence. The intervening variable here is that Saudi Arabia had eschewed support of many Islamist, especially Salafist, brigades and had thrown most of their support behind FSA-affiliated groups. Qatar, on the other hand, had no reservations about supporting Islamist groups. However, as discussed below, many of the more hardline groups have received their support from private donors. Second, the rivalries between the two states for control of the opposition manifested on the battlefield with both states arming rival brigades (Byman, 2014: 91). This was especially the case after the creation of the Supreme Military Command, as different provincial councils were wholly supported by one state or another. Differing international alliances among the provincial military councils led to sustained conflict between them, mistrust, and a failure to share resources. Thus, Qatar and Saudi Arabia (and by extension Turkey, which largely facilitated the transfer of weapons to rebels) made radically different calculations in approaching the question of whether to arm the rebels. For these states, playing out their regional rivalry and supporting the most military successful groups took precedence over ideological calculations.

In addition to the differences between Arab and Turkish and Western approaches to the question of arming the rebels, the role of private donors needs to be sufficiently understood. In 2012, the majority of financing directed at more radical, jihadist groups had been provided by private donors from Gulf countries, including Syrian exiles (Windrem, 2014). The private financing of these jihadist groups gave them superior military resources and allowed them to make significant battlefield gains at the expense of FSA brigades. Moreover, the flow of private donations allowed the jihadist groups to avoid the criminality and illegality that was rampant in FSA brigades who were increasingly infiltrated by opportunists and criminals hoping to gain economically from violence.

In sum, then, there has been no consensus between Arab and Western states over the question of arming rebels. Moreover, private donors from mostly Gulf countries have played an instrumental role in arming the more radical, extremist elements of the rebels, much to the frustration of both Saudi Arabia and Western states who have actively attempted to prevent the growth of more extremist groups.

Intervention and Non-Intervention

The NATO-led intervention in Libya during that country's civil conflict brought hope for some that Western countries would similarly intervene in Syria to aid the opposition in overthrowing the regime. Given the military stalemate, many supporters of intervention argued that Western involvement could tip the balance in favor of the rebels (Kleinfeld, 2013) and lead to the collapse of the al-Assad regime. In this view, intervention would be a definitive solution to the stalemate and would allow the rebels to take Damascus.

To date, there has been very little Western appetite for intervention in the country. Similarly, Arab states have not directly intervened against regime forces, relying instead on proxies. Nevertheless, there has been outside military intervention in Syria by Israel, Turkey, and a U.S.-led coalition of Arab states, all of which occurred for very different geopolitical reasons. Israel has intervened a number of times during the conflict by bombing key regime sites and transport convoys believed to be delivering weapons to Hizbollah. Turkey's military intervened in 2015 to rescue a mausoleum but then quickly retreated back into Turkey, while the U.S.-led coalition began aerial bombing of ISIS targets in Syria in August 2014. In all three cases, outside military intervention targeted specific targets and did not directly engage regime forces. Outside powers have proven willing to directly intervene when there are specific reasons and have shied away from pursuing policies of intervention aimed at regime change.

Chemical Weapons

In a press conference on 20 August 2012, American President Barack Obama stated the following in response to a journalist's query into American policy toward Syria's chemical weapons: "We have been very clear to the Assad regime, but also to other players on the ground, that a red line for us is we start seeing a whole bunch of chemical weapons moving around or being utilized. That would change my calculus. That would change my equation." President Obama's so-called red line was violated one year and one day later on 21 August 2013 when the Ayn Tarma, Muadamiyah, and Zalmalka areas of Ghouta, an agriculturally rich area in the Damascene countryside that was under opposition control, was struck with rockets carrying the nerve agent sarin. The estimates of the number of deaths resulting from the incident range from several hundred to at least two thousand. The Ghouta attacks had come on the heels of unverified opposition claims that the SAA had been using nerve agents in other parts of the country in similarly opposition-controlled areas. Thus, on the eve of the attacks there was concern among opposition groups and the international community that the regime could utilize nerve agents on the battlefield. Almost immediately after the Ghouta attacks occurred, the United Nations requested access to the sites, which was not granted until 25 August. Over the next week, UN inspectors inspected the site and confirmed that the agent sarin had indeed been used in Ghouta.

Syrian and international attention immediately turned to the United States, whose President had declared the use of chemical weapons a "red line" that would likely invite American intervention into the conflict. This was not an altogether unwelcome possibility, as many in the Syrian opposition, particularly those in exile, and regional supporters of the opposition, such as Saudi Arabia, Qatar, the United Arab Emirates, and Turkey, had been advocating for American intervention for some time. Indeed, the prevailing assumption in opposition circles at the time was that, in addition to supporting the UN's inspection efforts, the United States was preparing its military to strike against the regime. At that point in 2013, Hizbollah had already intervened in the Syrian conflict with its mobilization of fighters in the al-Qusayr area in May, 2013. The capture of al-Qusayr from rebel groups was a strategic boost to the regime as it cut off rebel supply lines from Lebanon and from the northern city of Homs, and it expanded Hizbollah's role in the conflict. Thus, at the time of the Ghouta attacks, the military balance in the conflict was shifting in favor of the regime.

Rather than follow through on its intervention threats, however, the Obama administration negotiated an agreement with Russia that would ensure the removal and destruction of the regime's chemical weapons by June 2014. By forcing the chemical weapons issue into a political track, the Obama administration made it clear that it had no intention to intervene in the Syrian conflict militarily and that its main objective was to contain the conflict, avoid contagion effects outside of Syria, and to immobilize the regime's chemical, as opposed to conventional, weapons capacity. While the decision to realize chemical weapons disarmament through a political process that spared American lives and billions of dollars in military spending could be hailed as an achievement for the administration, it was an overwhelming disaster for the opposition groups that had advocated for Western intervention. Indeed, by mid-2013, the Supreme Military Council (SMC) had been unable to make significant advances against the regime, with the exception of small victories in noncontiguous territories. As such, the SMC's leadership and its supporters believed that the only way to break the stalemate and allow the SMC-affiliated brigades to make national and territorially contiguous military advances was to undertake battles under Western intervention. Some combination of a Western enforced no-fly zone or direct Western attacks against regime targets became the central goal of the SMC and the National Coalition, as this was considered the only way to break the stalemate. Thus, when the administration committed itself to a political process and effectively rejected intervention as a strategy, the SMC and National Coalition were faced with no concrete strategies to support.

With the prospect of military intervention off the table, the Syrian opposition was thrown into political disarray and forced to contemplate the possibility of a negotiated political solution with the regime. With intervention an after thought, and the Western states increasingly advocating for a second round of Geneva talks, it was clear that Western states had no desire to intervene, despite their stated desire to have al-Assad removed. Such a shift in the Western position would have severe consequences on the Syrian opposition landscape.

As part of the agreement between Russia and the United States, Syria became a signatory to the Convention on the Disarmament and Destruction of Chemical Weapons on 14 September, 2013. Almost two weeks later, on 27 September 2013, UNSCR 2118 was passed, which included a clause (in section 21) that authorizes the Security Council to invoke Chapter VII clauses regarding intervention in the event of the use of chemical weapons by the Syrian government. The clause had given Syrians temporary reprieve from the horrors of the chemical attacks and had at least maintained the prospect of intervention should further attacks occur.

However, this particular clause invoking intervention has never been invoked, although as many as seventy-eight breaches of the Convention have been documented and referred to the UNSCR (SNHR, 2015a). In March 2015 the UNSC acknowledged the continued use of chemical weapons in Syria and passed Resolution 2209 condemning the use of chlorine gas against civilians and again invoked Chapter VII raising the threat of intervention. At least six chlorine gas attacks were recorded in the two weeks after the passing of the resolution (SNHR, 2015a).

Many of these attacks were delivered through barrel bombs, an especially horrific method of indiscriminately bombarding besieged areas. Barrel bombs have been used throughout the conflict with total impunity by regime forces. They typically contain all forms of explosives and are randomly tossed on populated areas. More recently, the regime forces have begun using barrel bombs to deliver chlorine gas. One witness to the chlorine gas attacks on Sirmen told the Syrian Network for Human Rights (SNHR) that "one of the two barrels fell over a house and caused the death of a whole family which suffocated due to the gas attack. We noticed that those barrel bombs weren't destructive as usual" (SNHR, 2015a: 6).

UNSCR 2139 in 2013 dealt directly with the use of barrel bombs and called on the Syrian regime to cease using them in civilian areas. However, since then, the SNHR documented almost 2,000 barrel bomb attacks, raising the total from the beginning of the conflict to more than 5,150 attacks (SNHR, 2015b). These attacks led to over 12,000 Syrian deaths, the overwhelming majority of which were civilians and more than 50 percent of which were women and children.

International efforts to halt the use of chemical weapons attacks against civilians have not been successful, as the Syrian regime has consistently flaunted UNSCRs that demand they fulfill their obligations under the Convention on the Disarmament and Destruction of Chemical Weapons. The regime's disregard of these resolutions is consistent with their approach to the UN since the beginning of the conflict. With the Russian (and Chinese) veto at the UNSCR playing a major role in preventing harsher rebukes and any real, legitimate threat of UN-sanctioned intervention occurring, the regime has repeatedly ignored resolutions that demand the cessation of violence and chemical attacks. The inability of the UNSCR to act cohesively on Syria or to place political pressure on the regime to abide by the resolutions has meant the continuation of horrific chemical attacks against Syrian civilians. At the time of writing, YPG officials were also accusing ISIS fighters of using chlorine gas against Syrian Kurds in Kobani (Coles, 2015). Thus, while the passage of UNSCR 2118 was successful in reducing Syria's stockpiles of chemical weapons and preventing the use of sarin, it has failed to prevent the use of other chemicals and has not prevented the proliferation and spread of those banned weapons to other parties to the conflict.

The United Nations Security Council

The United Nations Security Council (UNSC) has been in permanent paralysis regarding the Syrian conflict. The five permanent members—Great Britain, the United States, France, China, and Russia—have pursued their policies outside of the UNSC in large part because of the conflicting interests represented by China and Russia, who are generally supportive of the Syrian regime on the one hand, and the U.S., Great Britain, and France, who have declared policies of regime change on the other. The paralysis of the UNSC has meant that the United Nations has played a rather limited role in the conflict, being increasingly confined to humanitarian aid work with little progress made by UN-sponsored mediation talks. Since the outset of the conflict, the UNSC has passed a number of resolutions in regards to Syria. Because of disagreements and conflict between the permanent members these resolutions have largely ignored the security situation and have focused predominantly on humanitarian issues.

The UNSC has passed three resolutions that form the pillars of the humanitarian response: resolutions 2139, 2165, and 2191. These resolutions were consistent in their demands for a cessation of violence, demilitarization, the protection of civilians. Resolution 2139 even went so far as to demand the comprehensive implementation of the Geneva Communique of June 2012 calling for a political transition. Without any significant political pressure exerted by the UN on any of the warring sides, the security and political elements of the resolutions rang hollow. The more substantive aspects of the resolutions—the ones where the international community could actually affect the conflict—had to do with humanitarian assistance. More specifically, the resolutions called for the lifting of sieges on populated areas and the safe passage of UN humanitarian agencies to conflict zones while calling on member states to increase funding for humanitarian efforts.

While such resolutions were never seriously going to bring about a political transition, they held out the greatest prospect for a collective, international response to the humanitarian catastrophe. Yet the number of Syrians living in areas that were outside of the reach of aid agencies doubled from 2.5 million in 2013 to 4.8 million at the start of 2015 (Norwegian Refugee Council, 2015: 13). In 2014, UN humanitarian convoys had reached just over 1 million Syrians, which was 1.8 million fewer than the year before. Further aggravating the situation is the dramatic reductions from member states to UN aid agencies, who received a 96 percent reduction in food aid in 2014 (Norwegian Refugee Council, 2015). Such reductions in food aid parallel reductions in money and other resources channeled to international nongovernmental organizations (INGOs). According to the *Syria Response Plan* and the *Refugee Response and Resilience Plan* (United Nations High Commission for Refugees, 2014) the estimated aid costs to address Syria's humanitarian crisis is over $8 billion USD. The trend in addressing the humanitarian situation is a negative one: as humanitarian needs increase, access to the most affected populations is decreasing while aid resources dwindle.

Deliberations at the UNSC about Syria did not take place until early 2012, almost one year after the uprising began, after the failure of a League of Arab States initiative to end the conflict. A resolution calling for an end to violence and a political transition process that involved Assad handing power to his vice-president was drafted but eventually vetoed by China and Russia. Supporters of the resolution easily had it passed in the General Assembly but the vote was of no consequence because it was nonbinding and could not actually commit the UN and its member states to any action on Syria. With stalemate at the UNSC level, the UN initiated mediation talks. Since 2012, there have been three different Special Representatives for Syria—Kofi Annan, Lakhdar Brahimi, and, since July 2014, Staffan de Mistura—who have been dedicated to bringing about a political settlement to the conflict.

Geneva I

Kofi Annan began his tenure as special envoy by proposing a six-point peace plan that built on the Arab League initiative and was intended to serve as a transitional plan. Annan was successful in ensuring the deployment of a UN observer mission to Syria, which began in April 2012 and was eventually suspended because of violence and a lack of cooperation by the regime in August. While this was occurring, Annan was also able to gather representatives of the UN and Arab League, and the foreign ministers of the major regional and international acting nations, including the U.S., U.K., France, Russia, Turkey, China, Kuwait, Iraq, and Qatar, in Geneva to negotiate and adopt a plan for mediation and political transition. In the absence of a UNSC resolution, the Geneva process became the focus of international efforts to end the Syrian conflict.

On 30 June 2012, Annan presided over an Action Group on Syria and thus initiated the first process to bring together the international community to solve the Syrian conflict. Curiously, there were no Syrian representatives from the regime or opposition present at the conference aimed at deciding Syria's future. The intent, rather, was to bring together supporters of the regime and opposition to negotiate and agree upon principles that would guide a solution. Among the principles that the parties agreed to were an end to violence, humanitarian aid access, the release of all political prisoners, the resignation of President al-Assad, and a Syrian-led transition that would lead to a multiparty democratic system. The final communique called for the transition to include regime and opposition members in government; the participation of all major Syrian parties in a national dialogue; a reform of the constitutional and judicial systems; and free, democratic elections.

Not surprisingly, the Syrian regime and the main opposition group, the National Coalition, accepted these ideals and pledged support for the Geneva process. Such support did not, however, come without conditions and caveats. The regime, for example, rejected participation of "terrorists" in the political process, while opposition groups demanded that Assad resign as a precondition for the implementation of the plan (Asseburg and Wimmen, 2014: 3). While regime and opposition rejection of Geneva was an important factor in derailing the process, the actual commitment of the international community to the implementation of the plan was also seriously in doubt. Many regional states, including Saudi Arabia and Iran, have never been fully committed to an international process to solve the Syrian conflict and have instead viewed the conflict through their narrow geopolitical prisms. The process was thus never given the full political support of the major regional powers who had the ability and opportunity to invest the political resources in the Geneva process and bring about a resolution to the conflict. The military solution—and not the international process started in Geneva—was the preferred method of conflict resolution for the regional parties.

International actors were also not fully committed to the process. Western states had placed a tremendous amount of faith in a process that they were reluctant to support with political pressure on regional actors or Syrian opposition groups. Although many Western states had shunned the arming of Syrian rebels, they similarly failed to support the development of the Syrian grassroots and develop the administrative and governance capacity of groups attempting to establish alternative institutions in nonregime areas. Meanwhile, the Russian and Chinese delegations were highly skeptical of the process and eventually contributed to its collapse because of their opposition to the plan's insistence on a transition that involved the resignation of Assad and other preconditions that had been insisted upon by Arab and Western states. The collapse of the Geneva process eventually led to Annan's resignation and his scathing criticism of the Syrian regime and the international community, noting in a press conference announcing his resignation that "without serious, purposeful and united international pressure, including from the powers of the region, it is impossible for me, or anyone, to compel the Syrian government in the first place, and also the opposition, to take the steps necessary to begin a political process" (NYT, 2012). When asked what the future of the peace process he started would be, Annan claimed that "the world is full of crazy people like me, so don't be surprised if someone else decides to take it on" (NYT, 2012). A few weeks later, Algerian diplomat Lakhdar Brahimi took Annan's place as the UN Special Representative on Syria.

Geneva II

Brahimi's appointment as Special Representative brought some initial optimism that an international peace process could be revived. Facts on the ground had changed and it was believed that the regional climate was perhaps more conducive to a collaborative peace process. The advent of ISIS and other radical jihadist groups had created a greater urgency for Western and Arab states to resolve the conflict and the military option preferred by regional players was leading to nothing but stalemate. In this context, Brahimi attempted to restart the Geneva process.

Unlike the first round, there would be Syrian representation at the talks, held in Montreux in January 2014, with both regime and opposition representatives committed to attending. By this stage of the conflict it was clear that the main opposition group, the National Coalition, no longer enjoyed any legitimacy on the ground in Syria and could not serve as the representative of the armed groups or the internal political opposition. The Coalition was wholly unable to generate consensus among Syrian opposition and armed groups around the need for a political solution. Nor could it ensure the support of various opposition factions for the negotiations. Immediately after accepting the invitation to the talks, the Syrian National Council withdrew from the National Coalition in protest. The leaders of the major armed Fronts, including Ahrar as-Sham and the Islamic Front, immediately rejected the talks, while others, including the now-defunct Syrian Revolutionaries Front (SRF) supported the talks and had even requested the right to send representatives. The Kurdish PYD had similarly asked to send a delegation, which was rejected by the organizers. Although Geneva II was heralded as being more inclusive of Syrian representatives, the mosaic of opposition groups was not sufficiently represented.

Such incoherence and conflict between the different opposition and armed groups reflect how precarious the situation is on the ground. The armed groups were outside the influence of the external opposition, and the overwhelming majority of armed groups rejected the talks as pointless political theatre, effectively pledging commitment to a military solution. The Coalition and its various political factions were left with an inescapable dilemma: how to engage in a political process with an entrenched regime that was unwilling to meet the basic demand of the resignation of President Assad. For all the talk of transition and democracy that had permeated the first round of Geneva talks, the opposition was unable to realize this core demand of the opposition groups.

The failure of the Geneva Process to bring about any substantive changes in the conflict, let alone to move the various parties toward a resolution, is indicative of the inability of the international community to bring to bear political pressures on the regime, rebels, and opposition groups to resolve the conflict. There is no doubt that the regime and its state supporters had never taken the Geneva platform seriously as a forum for political transition that would remove Bashar al-Assad. In the second round of talks in January 2014, for example, the regime's negotiators framed the conference as a "counter-terrorism" effort in an attempt to reframe the conflict within the broader global war on terror. Such intransigence, however, was not the sole reason for the collapse of the Geneva Process. Although most parties to the conflict did attend, they did not do so in good faith. Most participants from the regime and opposition camps did not demonstrate a commitment to a political solution. The National Coalition suffered from the defection of key allies and a strong perception of illegitimacy that undermined their ability to seriously negotiate a political solution. For the regime, it was clear that their commitments led instead in maintaining a military solution to the conflict and not an internationally driven process largely outside of their control. International actors, such as the United States, were mostly ambivalent and unwilling to offer much by way of political incentives to bring the parties closer to a political solution. At the same time, the two rounds highlighted the failures of the Syrian opposition to shape events on the ground. Many of the groups fighting inside of Syria, and many of the nonviolent groups, rejected the very premise of the Geneva Process and the prospects of negotiating with the regime. As the external opposition lacks legitimacy both inside of Syria and in the international community, its participation can be seen as an effort to assert itself as a legitimate actor in the Syrian conflict and to present itself as not only a partner in peace, but as an alternative to the regime. Their participation in the talks did not increase the opposition's legitimacy and did very little to unify opposition groups, but instead highlighted the fissures and detachments between them. The total rejection of Geneva II by the armed groups who at that point were exercising the most influence on the ground in nonregime areas was a further nail in the Geneva Process coffin.

It is thus a mischaracterization to suggest that the Syrian opposition landscape was split over the question of whether to participate in Geneva II. It is more accurate to suggest that the overwhelming majority of violent and nonviolent groups rejected dialogue with the regime, especially if that dialogue did not carry a precondition of al-Assad's immediate removal. Groups such as Jabhat an-Nusra and ISIS, who at this point were the strongest actors in the nonregime areas, categorically rejected Geneva II, as did many of the other armed groups, including the powerful and relatively organized Islamic Front. Of the armed groups inside Syria, only the FSA pledged support to the Geneva Process. This, however, should be understood within the general framework of the FSA's general political and military fragmentation and decentralized leadership. Such a decision then cannot be said to apply to all brigades associated with the FSA but rather with the representatives of the central command. Whether fighters on the ground would have obeyed any ceasefires or demilitarization measures associated with the Geneva process is unlikely.

The political opposition was equally in favor of rejecting the talks. On the eve of the Geneva II talks, the National Coalition itself was not unanimous in its support of the talks. The decision to participate in the talks—which was taken days before they would start—was not approved until the Syrian National Council, a third of the Coalition delegates, had withdrawn from the body in protest against the prospects of negotiations and the failure to secure al-Assad's resignation as a prerequisite for talks. By the time of approval, only 58 of the original 121 Coalition delegates had voted to support attending Geneva negotiations.

Leading up to the Geneva negotiations, the influence of regional and international actors on Syria's opposition groups was becoming more and more obvious. Decisions taken by these groups were no longer autonomous or independent, but heavily influenced by the main international players in the conflict. However, throughout the conflict, the interests and political goals of these external actors have not coalesced and are more conflictual than cooperative. Such discord among the international parties to the conflict was quite evident around the Geneva II negotiations. Western states have gradually grown to frame the conflict in counter-terrorism terms and to regard the rise of ISIS, Jabhat an-Nusra, and other Islamist groups as more threatening to security than the conflict itself. To this central geopolitical concern over expanding Islamist influence we can add the continued flow of refugees, the ongoing negotiations with Iran over its nuclear weapons program, and the potential violent spillover effects of the Syrian conflict, as the main interests of the Western powers. The Geneva process has thus morphed into a sideshow for larger geopolitical issues.

The regime itself has been under very little pressure from its main international backers to offer concessions through the Geneva Process. Iran and Russia have very little appetite for ceding political ground to Qatari- and Saudi-backed groups, let alone supporting a political transition process that would remove al-Assad and, potentially, the main pillars of the security apparatus. Thus while all parties involved, from the UN to the major international players, through to the regime and the National Coalition, pledged support for the Geneva process, it ultimately failed because of a lack of political will, a poor negotiating framework, and the commitment to a military solution by most of the regional powers.

Local freezes?

Kofi Annan and Lakhdar Brahimi eventually resigned from their positions because of an unwillingness on the part of warring sides and their regional patrons to take seriously a political settlement. Brahimi's resignation in May 2014 led to the appointment of Staffan de Mistura as the new Special Representative. De Mistura's strategy has been fundamentally different from that of his predecessors. Instead of focusing on larger peace plans for Syria, he has devoted energy toward local "freezes" in Aleppo. These freezes are essentially short-term ceasefires negotiated in specific areas where fighting is most intense and aimed at accomplishing two key goals: first, to allow for humanitarian aid to reach the most affected areas, and, second, to build momentum and confidence to spread the freezes and move toward a larger political settlement.

The plan was drawn from a report prepared by the Center for Humanitarian Dialogue in Geneva and was adopted after secretive consultations between regime and opposition figures. Rather than focusing on the formation of a transitional government, the plan envisions a series of steps to be undertaken over a two-year period, beginning with local freezes and the expansion of local administrative capacity and then followed by parliamentary and local elections. A new parliamentary system would be established that devolves powers from the President to the Prime Minister. Unlike the Geneva process that imagined a transitional government and new elections as the beginning of the transition process, de Mistura's plan calls for a series of steps prior to a transitional government being established.

This bottom-up approach to a political settlement is radically different from the Geneva process model developed by de Mistura's predecessors. The Geneva process relied on a political model that aimed at a grand bargain between Syrian parties and regional players. Increasingly, however, the talks were disconnected from events on the ground and were not inclusive of the main parties to the conflict, raising serious doubts about whether an agreement would actually lead to a cessation of violence. The strategy pursued by de Mistura instead relies on engaging local actors involved in fighting and encouraging the reduction and freezing of violence to facilitate the delivery of humanitarian aid. Aleppo, Syria's most devastated city, would be de Mistura's test lab.

Although this strategy is a unique deviation from the strategy of his predecessors, it is not without problems and its potential for success is unclear. de Mistura has yet to prove that the regime will honor the freezes and cease air raids and barrel bombing in Aleppo, which are the primary cause of casualties in that city. For any freeze to be successful the regime's forces must be committed to honoring any agreements, and as past ceasefires demonstrate this is very unlikely (*The Guardian*, 2012). The possibility of "frozen" areas becoming cleansed of fighters and leaving civilian areas entirely unprotected and at the mercy of regime bombardment risks turning these areas into killing fields rather than safe havens. Moreover, the plan does not have any clearly defined incentives for fighters to lay down their weapons and it is unclear how local freezes would not simply encourage fighters to move from one district to another. While regime officials have met the suggested plans with caution and public optimism, some Fronts have already rejected the plans as unrealistic.

The Moscow Process

The local freeze plans have had a lukewarm response in many Western capitals where doubt over the regime's commitment to a ceasefire is strong. For Russian officials, however, the local freeze plans have emerged as a parallel track to a recent Russian political initiative to end the conflict. Both de Mistura's plan and the Russian plan reflect alternatives to the Geneva process. Both were born out of the stagnation of the Geneva process and the recognition that it was not moving the parties any closer to a political solution.

In late 2014 the Russian Foreign Ministry proposed hosting a series of talks between regime officials and the Syrian opposition. Deputy Foreign Minister Mikhail Bogdanov was placed in charge of organizing the talks, which were to take place in early 2015. The attendees from the opposition consisted entirely of individuals and groups that were part of the internal loyal opposition and not a serious threat to the regime. The five opposition parties represented at the talks were never serious actors in the uprising and have only survived as parties because of their loyalty to the regime, or, as one observer put it, they are "nothing more than the other face of the regime" (Pizzi, 2015).

Although the Russian Foreign Ministry declared that the basis of the Moscow process was the initial Geneva Communique, it is clear that they never took seriously the responsibility to address many of the deficiencies and problems of the Geneva process. Rather, the Moscow process merely reproduces the regime's narratives of the conflict and does not represent a serious attempt at reconciliation. For this reason, all major opposition parties and armed groups rejected the talks as illegitimate because they do not satisfy any of the key demands of the opposition, such as the necessity of a political transition, or fundamentally alter the regime's control of the political system.

The extent to which the Moscow process reflects the regime's strategic interests is reflected in the 11 Principles (Barmin, 2015) of a resolution adopted at the talks:

1. Preservation of the sovereignty of Syria
2. Countering international terrorism and fighting terrorism and extremism in Syria
3. Resolution of the Syrian crisis through peaceful political means on the basis of the Geneva Communique of 30 June 2012
4. Syria's future will be determined by the free and democratic expression of its people
5. Rejection of outside interference in Syria's affairs
6. Ensuring the preservation and continuity of state institutions, including the army
7. Ensuring civic peace through equality of all Syrians
8. Equality of all citizens before the law
9. Rejection of all foreign forces on Syrian territory without the consent of the Syrian government
10. An end to the occupation of the Golan Heights
11. Lifting of sanctions against Syria

Declarations that followed the adoption of the principles focused mainly on urging the international community to alleviate the humanitarian catastrophe and to support the regime's efforts to eradicate terrorism in Syria. As such, the negotiations avoided serious discussion of any of the substantive demands of the opposition and armed groups. In particular, the fate of President al-Assad was not a topic of discussion and fundamental changes to the distribution of power through constitutional, legal, or political reforms were not taken seriously. This even led one of the delegates from the Syrian Kurdish community to declare that all of the negotiations and the adoption of principles actually reflected the regime's lack of desire for political change and refusal to recognize Kurdish autonomy and self-rule in the northeast.

Not surprisingly, Iran has supported the talks as an alternative to the Geneva process. And while the United States initially dismissed the talks, Russian Foreign Minister Lavrov and Secretary of State John Kerry met in March 2015 to discuss the prospects of future talks and new diplomatic efforts to end the Syrian conflict. Ultimately, despite being competing alternatives and radically different visions of what a political solution in Syria could look like, the Geneva and Moscow processes suffer from major flaws that cast serious doubt on the prospects for diplomatic resolution to the conflict in the short term. First, the major international actors have not demonstrated a willingness to privilege a political solution over a military one, and neither have their proxies in Syria. The FSA has pledged lukewarm support to negotiations but it is unclear whether they would comply with any ceasefire or demilitarization measures. The remaining armed Fronts have all rejected international negotiations. Second, the negotiations have failed to demonstrate to the regime or opposition groups that negotiations are in their best interests. International mediation efforts have thus lacked incentives for parties to enter into serious political dialogue. This is in part an outcome of the regime's calculation that it has the military advantage but also a product of the opposition's fragmentation which has precluded the realization of a larger political solution to the problem that is inclusive of all major forces and which could guarantee a cessation of violence. Third, negotiations have not led to any tangible benefits for Syrians. It remains to be seen how de Mistura's plans for humanitarian aid will unfold but even on this issue of humanitarian access the regime has remained stubborn.

A Global Conflict

The internationalization of the Syrian conflict has failed to move the crisis closer to resolution. Rather, the internationalization of the conflict and the emergence of Syria as a battlefield for regional proxy wars has only served to prolong the conflict at the needless expense of Syrian lives and futures. In the first months of the conflict, the Syrian uprising was indeed a domestic issue that arose out of domestic sociopolitical discontent and the mobilization of that discontent throughout the country. As the uprising developed and morphed and assumed a much more militarized character, Syria was easily penetrated by regional states, thus giving the conflict a more international character. Today, the Syrian conflict has become about more than the demands for political rights and freedoms that were the basis of the early protests.

The internationalization of the conflict has added another layer of complexity to our understanding of events and to the prospects for resolution. There are a number of factors behind the internationalization of the conflict. First, there has never been anything resembling a political consensus among any of the regional actors regarding Syria, with key questions about the resignation of Assad, the role of the political opposition, and the question of arming rebels proving extremely divisive. Second, Syria's main international allies, Russia and Iran, have not placed enough pressure or leverage on the regime to engage in a real peace process. Similarly, Qatar, Saudi Arabia, and Turkey have pursued policies in favor of a military solution to the conflict, while the Western states and the UN have proven unable to offer alternative political paths. Despite the apparent failure of the military solution, all major sides continue to pursue it. Third, the opposition's fragmentation and the conflicts between armed groups on the ground have so dispersed power in the conflict that any international efforts toward resolution would inevitably exclude major parties and raise serious questions about the legitimacy of negotiations. Both the Geneva and Moscow processes were largely disconnected from the events and actors on the ground and were rejected by major armed groups. Fourth, the major foreign actors in the conflict have radically different geopolitical interests. For Iran and Saudi Arabia, the Syrian conflict is occurring within the broader context of a regional cold war in which all states seem happy to fight until Syria is destroyed.

5 | Fragmentation ──────────────

The Syrian regime, rebels, and their foreign supporters have adopted the military solution as the approach to ending the conflict. Yet it is unlikely, given the battlefield realities and dynamics, that such an approach will yield an end to the conflict. As all parties pursue the military option, large segments of Syrian territory have been divided among competing rebel groups. The country is now very loosely divided among four large, identifiable areas that are militarily and politically dominated by different groups: areas controlled by the regime (between Damascus and the coastal areas); areas controlled by the PYD in northeastern Syria near the Turkish-Syrian and Syrian-Iraqi borders; areas controlled by ISIS in eastern Syria, mainly Raqqa, and southern and northwestern areas controlled by various rebel factions. There has not been a monopolization of violence or authority in these areas, as intrarebel infighting, regime bombardment, and international intervention have rendered different authorities' control over areas tenuous at best. Thus while Syria has fragmented no single alternative to the regime has emerged. No viable alternative to the regime currently exists in Syria. Instead, outside the regime areas the country has been divided into a patchwork of administrative structures with competing politico-military groups vying for power throughout the country, and these competing administrative structures contribute to the fragmentation of the country.

What we are witnessing in Syria, then, is the emergence of new political authorities whose military power is being translated into different political-administrative structures: a rapid decentralization of authority into multiple, often competing networks of violence and power structures. Decentralization and dispersal of administrative authority has given the Syrian conflict two features which are contributing to its longevity. First, authorities are highly decentralized and lack vertical (with central or external authorities) and horizontal (with other administrative structures) integration. Administrative models differ radically. In the Kurdish areas, for example, the grounds are being laid for autonomous government in a post-conflict Syrian state while in ISIS areas there is a radical social engineering project underway to reimagine those territories as part of a new Caliphate. Second, the lack of integration between the authorities has led to the parallelization of administrative institutions and has prevented the monopolization of power and the establishment of alternative state institutions.

The normative view of conflicts suggests that the contraction of state authority leads to sovereign gaps, creating lawless and ungovernable spaces. Such a view is too simplistic, however, and fails to capture the organizational structure of violence and how armed groups do more than just commit violence but also attempt to govern and administer territory. In Syria, a form of alternative governance (Carpenter et al., 2013) is emerging. "Alternative governance" here refers to forms of governance in which constellations of actors exist in an architecture whose functionality is inconsistent and temporary. These are organized and administered by "non-state complexes" (Podder, 2014) whose power and agency in a conflict is constantly shifting and contested by other groups.

In this view, there can exist governance without sovereign government. This is precisely what has emerged in Syria, as different, competing projects of territorial control have led to the rise of different administrative models. Because of the constantly changing geography of the conflict and the fluidity of alliances, these administrative models are unstable and unsustainable over the long term. They are nevertheless having a major impact on the course of conflict and influence what a post-conflict Syrian state may look like. In this chapter, we consider how the conflict has led to the fragmentation of the country into competing administrative models, and we will examine the impacts that this division of the country along radically different lines are having on key questions of national identity, sectarianism, and the regional role of a fragmented Syria.

Rojava

In mid-2013 the PYD had declared its intention to carve out an autonomous region in Kurdish-populated areas in the northeast of Syria. Later that year, the PYD announced that an interim government would soon be formed that would include KNC parties and be inclusive of most Kurdish political currents in Syria. This led to the establishment of an Assembly that declared the three regions of Efrin, Cizre (Jazeera in Arabic), and Kobani (Ayn al-Arab in Arabic) as three autonomous administrative units linked to a central administration. By January 2014 the three cantons had declared their autonomy and began establishing a new administrative authority officially called the Canton Based Democratic Autonomy of Rojava (CBDAR). Militarily, the YPG has focused on securing the Rojava areas and in creating contiguous territory under Syrian Kurdish administration.

The emergence of the Rojava administration during the course of the conflict is remarkable given the history of Syrian Kurds' relationship with the central state and the regime. After the breakup of the Ottoman Empire, Syria's Kurds found themselves separated from social and familial networks in Turkey and Iraq. The borders drawn by the French authorities in the Kurdish populated areas had imposed on Syria's Kurds new forms of identity and belonging that had hitherto been nonexistent. In the population movements and political upheavals of the late Ottoman period, many Kurds had migrated back and forth across what would become the

Syrian-Turkish border. The French authorities' creation of a border and a state apparatus to enforce authority within that border meant that many Kurds found themselves locked in a political community that was ethnically, linguistically, and socially, new. The development of the new Syrian state's bureaucracy and its institutions were to service an Arabic-speaking population. The demands of Syria's political elites at the time for an Arabized state reflect their ideological gravitation toward Arab nationalism. As such, the Arabization of the Syrian state and the strength of the Arab national-ist movement had created the discursive and political conditions to define the Kurdish population as a minority community—despite many being co-religionists with the majority Sunni Arab population (White, 2012: 112).

French authorities in this period recognized how poten-tially destabilizing Kurdish unrest in the new Syria state could be for both Syria and Turkey, the latter of whom had placed pressure on French authorities to restrict Kurdish autonomy and political power in Syria. For this reason, the carving out of an autonomous, or even separate, Kurdish political entity was never taken too seriously by the French authorities who instead sought to integrate the Kurds into the new Syrian State. The Kurdish community's differential incorporation into both the new Turkish and Syrian states and the new post-Ottoman regional order in general, bred political resent-ment and hostility to the colonial and state authorities.

Subsequently, the threat of armed activities by Kurds in Turkey and Syria remained strong, and the urban Kurdish notables in Damascus had begun agitating for deeper Kurdish integration into the Syrian state (White, 2012: 112–16). Such agitation on behalf of the Kurds in the northeast was simul-taneously a reaction to emergent forms of Kurdish national-ism and a means of resurrecting patronage networks between the urban notables and rural communities, shoring up com-munity support for notables' power (White, 2012: 116). The assertion of Kurdish minority rights and demands by notables for greater access to the state was met with hostility from Arab nationalists who rejected the Kurdish claim to a sepa-rate identity within Syria and autonomy in the northeast. In the clash of identities and identity politics at the time, Syrian Kurdish interests ultimately were subordinated to the larger Arab nationalist interests.

The differential and unequal incorporation of Syria's Kurds into the Syrian state would be a key feature of Syrian politics up until the uprising. In the 1960s right before the Ba'athist coup, the state conducted a census that was then used to strip more than 100,000 Kurds of their Syrian citizenship and to effectively render them stateless. They have no rights to work, own property, travel, or benefit from social services, except through registration as foreign residents in the country. From the 1950s onwards, the Kurdish language was banned in all educational institutions in an attempt to eliminate its use in Syria. Simultaneously, Kurdish place names were increasingly Arabized.

The Syrian Kurdish population has been spread throughout Syria, with large numbers of Syrian Kurds in Damascus and Aleppo. The Rojava areas are themselves not ethnically homogeneous; they have large non-Kurdish populations, including Yazidis, Sunni Arabs, Armenians, and Turkmen. The diversity of Kurdish areas and the dispersion of Syrian Kurds has contributed to their relative political quietism during the Ba'ath period. The most important factor, however, has been Ba'athist cooptation of Kurdish parties and the suppression of all forms of political activity. Syria's regime had fostered strong relations with the PKK in the 1990s and had even harbored its leader Abdullah Öcalan. In 1998, Turkey had threatened to wage war against Syria over the issue. Succumbing to this threat, the Syrian regime forced Öcalan to leave the country. While the regime was willing to support Kurdish political and military activity in neighboring countries, the same was not tolerated in Syria. Instead, the Syrian Kurds lived under severe discrimination, with tens of thousands deprived of Syrian citizenship and basic rights.

When the uprising began, then, the Syrian Kurdish community was balancing regime cooptation, which afforded the areas certain benefits on the one hand, and political quietism that had been the result of decades of exclusion from access to the Syrian state. Indeed, the precariousness of Syrian

Kurdish politics was evident in the first months and year of the uprising. Many Kurds joined the protests and participated as activists and organizers. Yet many others were pacified by the regime's extension of citizenship to stateless Kurds and the release of some political prisoners. Major parties refused to throw their support behind the regime or the opposition, playing a waiting game that was as much about political expediency and strategy as it was about genuine distaste for both camps. While the opposition worked to court Kurdish officials into its ranks, the regime largely left the Kurdish areas alone militarily, despite some protests in these areas, in order to avoid opening another battlefront. Regime security forces had gradually redeployed during the uprising, creating an opportunity for the PYD to assert its authority in the northeast. Eventually, by 2012, with regime security forces largely absent from the area, the YPG removed government officials from state buildings and took them over, lowering the Syrian state flag and replacing it with PYD flags. The process of asserting Kurdish control and authority over the Rovaja areas had begun.

Despite the conflicts between Kurdish political parties and factions, especially the KNC and PYD, the northeast is slowly coming under the administrative control of the Rojava administration. The Rojava administration is not an ethnic-based authority but rather a body that has assumed responsibility for the administration of a particular geographic area. The distinction between an administrative versus an ethnic project is important; the basis of the Rojava claim to authority is not based on the name and interests of the Kurdish community. Kurds form a numerical minority in Rojava, and officials have been keen on including non-Kurds in the administration and in using the Kurdish, Arabic, and Syriac languages in all administrative proceedings. The de-emphasis on Kurdish identity and interests in the administration is further reflected in the Charter of the Social Contract of Democratic Autonomy: a sort of constitution governing the structure and work of the Rojava administration. In it, all ethnicities of the region are recognized as equal partners and the commitment to autonomous decision-making within a centralized state structure, not separatism and the creation of an entirely new state, is affirmed.

The central idea behind the administration is that of Democratic Autonomy, a notion developed by PKK leader Abdullah Öcalan to refer to the rejection of a separate Kurdish state and the desire to seek integration and participation into existing state structures, including respecting current borders and state authorities. Moreover, any ethnic identification is removed from the notion of Democratic Autonomy and instead "unity in diversity" is stressed. The multi-lingual, multi-ethnic, and multi-religious milieus in which Syrian Kurds reside are assumed as the basis of communal unity, rather than ethnicity.

Such public proclamations should not necessarily be taken at face value, however. The possibility of Kurdish separatism remains real. First, any declaration of independence by the Rojava administration would have radically altered the strategic calculations of all neighboring states and the regime itself. Demands for an autonomous administration within Syria remain politically unpalatable to most regional actors. Second, there is no monopoly on political authority in the region; intra-Kurdish disputes often lead to violence between different groups and consensus around major issues such as negotiations with the regime and relations with the political opposition is lacking. Such rivalry threatens to paralyze or even collapse the Rojava administrative project. Third, continued military threats from ISIS, JAN, and potentially the regime threaten the security monopoly that the YPG currently enjoys. In an environment of fluid strategic relationships and constantly shifting battlefield dynamics, the relative calm in Rojava areas remains precarious.

Nevertheless, the Charter of the Social Contract has established a sophisticated network of administrative institutions that have assumed the role of the contracted Syrian state. The three cantons are divided as shown in Table 5.1 (Kurdistan National Congress, 2014).

The structure of the Cezire Canton sheds some insight into the institutional architecture of the autonomous region. There are four main councils. The Legislative Council consists of

Table 5.1   Cantons of the Rojava Administration

Canton	Capital	Official Languages	Official Religions	Population
Cezire	Amude	Kurdish, Arabic, Syriac	Islam, Christianity, Yezidi	1.5 million
Kobane	Kobane	Kurdish	Islam	1 million
Efrin	Efrin	Kurdish	Islam, Alawi, Yezidi	1.3 million

101 members (at least 40 percent women), a President and two Deputies. The Legislative Council works directly with the main Executive Council, which serves as the central government for the canton. This body has 22 ministries, including environment, external relations, defense (YPG), and education, and is presided over by a Kurdish President and one Arab and one Syriac Deputy. The Judicial Council (composed of at least 40 percent women) constructs and regulates the application of the law. Finally, the Local Administration Council is the main body representing the ten cities within the Cezire Canton. A seven-person (at least 40 percent women) Constitutional Court oversees the application of law while the eighteen-member (at least 40 percent women) High Commission of Elections regulates electoral procedures. Below this larger structure are a series of other institutions, such as a police force, civil society groups, and neighborhood councils. Even the YPG units have begun to institutionalize through the establishment of a higher military council and military academies to recruit and train a new generation of fighters. Finally, the PYD established an umbrella organization called the Rojava Democratic Society Movement (TEV DEM) that coordinates all aspects of political and social life in the areas. Technically speaking, the PYD is one subentity among many of the TEV DEM.

The administrative structure of the cantons and their relationship to a centralized provincial government is not without problems. First, the territory under Rojava administrative authority is not contiguous, making relations between the cantons and the authorities extremely difficult. Second, the basic mechanisms of population management, such as a census, are unavailable to the administration. Third, the institutional architecture within and between the cantons is subject to PYD influence and control. Notwithstanding the official and public rhetoric of diversity and cohabitation among all, the PYD exercises tremendous influence within the administration. Local councils, for example, have very little decision-making authority and have been relegated to carrying out PYD directives. Other bodies are largely emasculated and the theoretical responsibility of governance and administration that lies in the different integrated units actually lies with the PYD, who largely make major decisions outside of the administrative structure. Finally, the largest problem is not necessarily administrative, but political. The Rojava project is essentially an entirely PYD project as the KNC, the major political alternative to the PYD, withdrew its support for the project before its inception. The split between the PYD and KNC was largely about which group has the authority to speak and act on Kurdish political interests, but it also reflected the rivalries between the PYD and KNC's patrons and their desire to similarly exercise leadership in regional Kurdish politics. The creation of the Supreme Kurdish Committee aimed at creating committees made up of PYD and KNC members but the agreement has never materialized into any concrete cooperation.

In establishing the Rojava administration, Kurdish leaders have taken full advantage of the political opportunity presented by the collapse of the Syrian state and the withering of the regime. Although it is unclear whether collective Kurdish political aspirations will result in a separation from the Syrian state, it is certain that any post-conflict Syrian political architecture must absorb or contend with Kurdish autonomous administration and the demands of the leaders and many community members for institutionalizing and recognizing decentralization and Kurdish autonomy. However, the success of the Rojava project and its potential integration into a post-conflict Syria will be shaped by many factors moving forward, the least of which are intra-Kurdish disputes and radically different visions for how Syrian Kurdish areas should be governed and administered and by whom. Kurdish parties, much like the Syrian opposition and rebel groups, have international patrons who exercise a tremendous amount of influence on them. Thus, the future of Rojava will be subject to regional geopolitics and any grand bargain made by regional actors to resolve the Syrian conflict. The main question moving forward is how a post-conflict Syrian authority can incorporate Kurdish autonomy into the larger political body in ways that satisfy Kurdish political demands and entrench Syrian Kurdish rights and aspirations into the political system. In the absence of such recognition and institutionalization of Kurdish autonomy and rights, the likelihood of Kurdish separatist aspirations may increase.

At this stage of the conflict, the Rojava project is an ambitious attempt to organize a segment of society embedded in a larger conflict. The ability to establish an administrative structure that will outlive the conflict remains to be seen. The Rojava administration is already being contested by the KNC and for all intents and purposes, the project remains dominated and controlled by the PYD. Pacifying or coopting Kurdish competitors and gaining legitimacy among the Kurdish population and diffusing political power throughout the region is a major challenge facing the PYD.

ISIS Areas

Central to ISIS's legitimacy among its supporters is its territorial control and expansion over parts of western Iraq and eastern Syria. The control and administration of territory is central to ISIS's claims of representing the new Caliphate and distinguishes the group from JAN, al-Qaeda, and indeed all other rebel groups in Syria in that its claim is to function as a state. The projection of ISIS power and authority across these lands represents a dramatic attempt at radical social change. Unlike the other armed movements in Syria, ISIS does not profess or have pretensions toward political integration into a post-conflict Syrian order. Nor does ISIS aspire, as does the PYD through the Rojava administration, to accept the nation-state system and some form of communal or geographic autonomy institutionalized in the Syrian state. ISIS's control over large swathes of territory that transcends the borders of two states represents an altogether different form of fragmentation. Whereas the Rojava areas are attempting to establish a structure of autonomous government that intends to be incorporated into a larger centralized structure, ISIS's administrative structure and political goals leave no room for such integration into a post-conflict order. The ISIS project represents an objective threat to the Syrian state and Syria's territorial contiguity and integrity.

Some caution should be exercised when discussing the goals and structure of ISIS's administrative project in particular because information from these areas is severely limited. The Western world knows very little about daily life in ISIS territory beyond anecdotal stories emerging from individuals who have fled from it. The secrecy of the organization, the lack of adequate reporting from ISIS areas, and the rapid growth of the group within Syria and Iraq have made key questions around its social base of support, economic management, and bureaucratic capacities difficult to determine. What follows, then, is an attempt to outline the broad contours of the administrative structure of ISIS in the areas under its control, the background of its leadership (and to the extent possible, its supporters), and its overall organizational and bureaucratic capacities.

Unlike the Syrian Kurdish project, ISIS's raison d'être is the establishment of a state, or an alternative political authority in the form of the Caliphate, out of lands extracted from Syria and Iraq. The state ISIS purports to govern is headed by Abu Bakr al-Baghdadi, who has recently taken on the title of Caliph. Personal advisors and assistants surround al-Baghdadi, while the larger administrative structure includes deputies, a cabinet, and a military council (these councils are relatively small). While al-Baghdadi has attempted to project legitimacy through his clerical background, many of his deputies and other officers lack any forms of Islamic legitimacy.

Two of al-Baghdadi's known deputies were actually formerly high-ranking officers in the Iraqi military under Saddam Hussein: Abu Ali al-Anbari was a major general in the Army while Abdullah al-Hiyali was a lieutenant colonel in the Iraqi Military Intelligence and a former Iraqi Special Forces officer (Gorman et al., 2014). Below these deputies are hundreds or thousands of military commanders who similarly have no religious training or background but have expertise in bureaucratic and security affairs.

A central factor in explaining the expansion and consolidation of territorial control is ISIS's embeddedness in the Syrian and Iraqi war economies and the ability to generate and distribute wealth in its territory. However, this income is not generated through productive activities but rather through wartime economic activity—extortion, kidnapping, taxation, resource extraction, and looting—that is not sustainable. Under such conditions, populations develop dependencies on the authorities for the distribution of goods, as jobs and other means of productive economic activity are severely limited, particularly as trade occurs through black markets or smuggling channels. The productive activity that does occur in ISIS areas is limited. There has been a great deal of attention paid to the oil resources controlled by ISIS and the belief that the group accrues handsome profits from the extraction and sale of oil to neighboring countries and to the regime itself (Hubbard et al., 2014). However, many of the figures offered in popular accounts are presumptive and it is more likely that ISIS production is limited and that the revenues are not in the daily millions of dollars. While it may indeed be the case that ISIS is the "richest terrorist group in history," it may also be that their wealth is severely exaggerated. The only other products produced in ISIS territory are agricultural and are mainly distributed within the territories and thus have not generated sufficient income to financially support their administration.

Electricity provision is severely limited and has forced ISIS to enter into barter deals with regime forces to exchange electricity for oil (Taylor, 2015), further limiting the extent to which oil and agricultural production can serve as the financial backbone of the ISIS administration. The issue of electricity provision also highlights the co-dependence ISIS has on the Syrian regime. After ISIS seized control of dams and gas plants in Syria, agreements were made with the Syrian regime to exchange gas for electricity. Since ISIS does not have the engineering capacity to operate the plants, the Syrian regime also continues to provide salaries for the workers at the dams and plants (FT, 2015). The same situation has occurred in Iraqi areas where ISIS controls key production plants while the employees are paid their salaries from the central Iraqi government. Control of these plants has not meant that ISIS can provide the actual service; it has forced them into agreements with the Syrian and Iraqi states.

Beyond agricultural production and oil extraction, ISIS is economically dependent on illegality and wartime activities for its finances. Extortion is a major source of income and ISIS networks of extortion operate throughout Syria and Iraq. Transport and customs taxes are regularly imposed on goods traveling between Jordan, Syria, Iraq, and Turkey, reflecting ISIS's control over key transport routes in the region. Finally, the looting and sale of antiquities has provided ISIS with another substantial source of revenue, at the expense of Syrian and Iraqi cultural heritage.

The control of key economic levers and the ability to acquire finances through wartime economic activities is not a sufficient basis for the ISIS administration. Indeed, throughout most of its territory, services are virtually nonexistent. This is especially true in the rural areas, where brute force and fear are as important to their ruling strategies as distribution of goods and services. In major cities, such as Raqqa, ISIS has a fairly developed administrative presence and the residents are provided some limited services, as schools and medical facilities are most developed in the more densely populated areas.

Ultimately, however, the ISIS project in Syria is subject to the same economic logics and restraints of all wartime orders. As discussed in Chapter Three, a conflict war economy is important in structuring how armed groups relate to one another and how they finance their military activities. Despite its claims to statehood and to being a Caliphate, ISIS has not been immune from these logics. Warlords within the ISIS structure operate throughout Syria and Iraq, taxing populations and extracting wealth from them. In this way, ISIS operates similarly to other warlords and armed groups in Syria. Like many of these groups as well, ISIS's economic activities and attempt to impose a separate administration on these areas is contributing to deepening fragmentation in the Syrian context.

Jabhat an-Nusra and the Salafist-Jihadist Network of Violence

The split between ISIS and JAN in 2013 was an important development in the Syrian conflict, as it diffused Salafi-jihadist loyalties between the two groups, who were already in conflict with other armed Islamist groups on the battlefield. The split between the two reflects the pluralism of the Salafi-jihadist landscape in Syria and demonstrates the ideological and political distinctions among the different groups which have prevented cooperation, despite a presumably shared ideology and worldview. Despite its association with al-Qaeda, JAN's leadership and its fighters have a remarkably Syrian character. The roots of JAN's leadership in Syria's social mosaic are an extremely important factor in explaining their military success and their adoption of particular strategies. This is an important point of distinction between JAN and ISIS: whereas the latter is mostly made up of foreign fighters and leaders who see the Syrian conflict as part of a larger struggle to expand the Caliphate and are thus less focused directly on the overthrow of the Syrian regime, JAN's leaders and fighters have adopted rhetoric and political strategies that are consistent with the original goals of the uprising.

Since its entry into the Syrian conflict in 2011, JAN has become one of the major alliances fighting the regime. Alongside its military activities has grown an administrative apparatus that is quite distinct from that developed in other nonregime areas in Syria. The alliance has acquired a tremendous amount of administrative influence within the nonregime areas through their cooperation with other rebel groups, even in areas where they may be militarily weak. For example, in the southern and northwestern areas of the country, JAN has fought alongside many FSA-affiliated brigades and other alliances against regime forces. In other areas, JAN has proved to be capable of military advances on its own without support from other brigades. The ability and willingness to enter into larger networks of violence has expanded JAN's influence within the nonregime areas considerably.

Moreover, JAN has demonstrated a larger geographic reach than other rebel groups and has been active in most major battle areas in the country. Upon entering the Syrian conflict, JAN fighters had adopted more guerrilla tactics targeting regime security forces, including car bombs and attacks on security installations. These occurred throughout the country and were not confined to one governorate or city, which allowed fighters a degree of mobility and also allowed them to evade besiegement from regime forces. The success of JAN's operations coupled with gradual regime retreat due to FSA military advances allowed JAN's leadership to recruit more Syrian fighters, especially from the rural areas that were increasingly outside of regime control. This allowed JAN's fighters to grow and coalesce into larger units and brigades, which encouraged more strategic military activity that was focused less on attacking regime security forces and more on acquiring and controlling territory.

Its renewed military strategy and initial successes in defeating regime forces fostered greater cooperation with FSA brigades and allowed JAN fighters to more solidly root themselves in nonregime areas and begin social service provisions. This gave the organization a base to begin establishing their administrative authority in Syria. While the provision of social services has been an important area of JAN's activities, the group has also devoted considerable effort to the creation of Shari'a courts in nonregime areas.

Unlike ISIS- or PYD-controlled areas, JAN does not control contiguous territory. Moreover, JAN has relied extensively on cooperative relations with other armed rebel groups, as discussed in Chapter Three. Indeed, relations between JAN and many FSA brigades have been cooperative and have led to the sharing of resources and the formalization of governance structures. For example, JAN has been very active in water and food provision and has extended its efforts into areas that are not directly under their territorial control. The group has put great effort into fostering relations with certain rebel groups, especially in the northwest, in order to gain a foothold within the rebel movement. Such relationships give JAN a wider reach and enhance their military strength considerably. Typically, cooperative relations around social services provision have provided opportunities to establish more formal institutional structures, especially in regard to law.

The main administrative strategy pursued by JAN translates military operation into shared governance. For this reason, JAN has cultivated strong relations with other Salafist-jihadist groups and other armed groups. Their governance strategy has been to pursue mixed-authority institutions in which JAN shares responsibility with other groups. The main focus here has been on Shari'a courts. In 2013, for example, the Aleppo Shari'a Committee (ASC) was formed with JAN as one of the five founding members (four other brigades participated). Although the committee eventually expanded to fifteen members, JAN has exercised major influence because of the relative weakness of the other members and has devoted considerable resources to strengthening the courts. The ASC oversees the public administration of the areas under the control of its members and has offices dealing with education, services, aid, property, and so on. The ASC is the most powerful and largest Shari'a committee in Syria to date. The model has been replicated throughout the country in areas in which JAN is active, especially in Deir ez-Zour where a similar Committee has been established (called the Mujahideen Shura Council) with subordinate offices and departments.

Even in areas that have not formalized shared governance in the form of Committees of Councils, there are similar arrangements. The Kafr Nabel Shari'a Court is another example of the patchwork of authorities that underpin administrative structures. In mid-2014, the court was controlled by JAN, the Foursan al-Haq brigade (an FSA affiliate), and the Souqour al-Sham brigade (affiliated with the Islamic Front), which upheld the court's rulings. Similar courts have appeared throughout the country, especially in the areas where JAN has been most active: Dar'a, Eastern Ghouta (Damascus), Deir ez-Zor, and Aleppo.

JAN's governance strategy has been successful because they have relied on alliances to build stronger networks to provide social services, coordinate military activities, and implement Shari'a law. The fusion of social and military strategies has been important to JAN's ability to build these alliances. Moreover, unlike ISIS, which is mostly composed of foreign fighters and foreign leaders, JAN's base is predominantly Syrian. The group has demonstrated a remarkable flexibility in adapting to local conditions and not overly disrupting local traditions and power structures. Instead, they have integrated themselves into existing rebel networks and into the social bases of these networks.

Southern Syria: The FSA's Last Bastion?

The southern regions of Syria—the governorates of Dar'a, Qunaitra, and al-Swedia—have become the last major areas of FSA control in the country. A civic administration has been created in the south paralleling and shored up by FSA armed control of the area. Although the south remains under constant bombardment by regime and other rebel forces (especially JAN) and has not enjoyed the relative autonomy of the Rojava administration, various civic groups have organized an administrative structure that relies on shared governance by the various brigades.

The area under nonregime administrative control is not contiguous and control by FSA brigades is very tenuous, with JAN troops active in Qunaitra and in control of key areas in that province. The regime maintains a presence through military bases in Qunaitra and Dar'a as well and, in later 2014, many of the regime's proxy forces have begun to mobilize in the three southern provinces. Even in Dar'a, a major southern city, territorial control is divided between regime, FSA, and JAN forces, all of whom control various key intersecting transport routes, such as border crossings and highways. The spread of the three opposing forces has meant that the southern front of the war, much like the northern front, has remained extremely active throughout the conflict.

Thus, unlike the ISIS or Rojava areas, southern Syria remains highly contested with territorial control shifting between different groups. However, unlike other areas of the country where intrarebel conflicts have occurred amid regime bombardments and military advances, the southern areas have not been characterized by the same intra-FSA conflicts as other areas. Instead, FSA brigades have displayed a high level of cooperation and coordination there. Such cooperation has allowed the brigades to maintain the south as a stronghold while territorial advances in the rest of the country were rolled back after regime, JAN, ISIS and other rebel advances against FSA forces. More important, the FSA brigades in the south have been successful in avoiding splits into different administrative structures (Oweis, 2015). The majority of municipal services in the south are administered by the Civic Defense Council, a body that has close relations to the National Coordination Body for Democratic Change, a Syria-based opposition group. Other administrative bodies, such as the Supervision and Follow-up Council, have been effective in establishing health care facilities and school services for children (Oweis, 2015).

Although these different bodies have remained active, and have a regular turnover of members, they are mostly limited to providing social services and distributing aid and other forms of support to families and towns. The intense fighting in the south and the fracturing of territorial control has made the establishment of alternative state institutions virtually impossible. Much like the Syrian civil-society organizations who have been forced to devote their energies to humanitarian relief and aid efforts and not to building alternative state institutions, the various administrative bodies in the southern areas are similarly focused on providing services and alleviating hardship. Moreover, these bodies do not have sustainable funding. Many find their primary funding in donations or sponsorships from wealthy Syrians abroad. While this has allowed them to pursue neutral positions toward the armed groups, or at the very least to maintain some autonomy from them, this has limited their capacity. Moreover, decreased capacity has prevented the development of any interlinkages with councils in the rest of the country. In Aleppo, for example, similar structures exist but because of the degree of violence, many of the councils operate independently of each other in that city. Linkages between councils in other parts of the country is simply impossible under such circumstances.

What makes the southern areas unique is that the problems of centralized leadership and control that have plagued the FSA and the opposition throughout the conflict are not as pronounced in the south. While it is the case that interlinkages with other councils are impossible, the intra-FSA infighting that occurs in other parts of the country is largely absent here. The merger of different FSA-affiliated brigades provided some degree of military cohesion and allowed the brigades to resist the advances of ISIS, JAN, and the regime forces. The strength of the brigades has translated into tangible military gains in other ways. Local agreements with regime forces have spared FSA-controlled areas from shelling and guaranteed the provision of water and electricity to these areas as well. Nevertheless, the FSA brigades and the councils themselves are active in an area of intense fighting and fragmentation, making any administrative projects or military alliances tenuous at best.

The Interim Government: Failed Transition

Any government's legitimate claim to authority must be based on its ability to govern territory under its control. A major

dilemma that the Syrian opposition has faced from its inception is its lack of legitimacy inside of Syria. The perceived
illegitimacy of the opposition arose from their absence on the
ground and the inability of opposition forces to bring about
political change or to positively affect the dire humanitarian
situation in the country. For many Syrians, watching opposition members aimlessly shuttle between Western capitals to
advocate for empty policies was both alienating and insulting.
The legitimacy deficit grew even more when armed groups
took greater control of the country and became the security
and political reference points for residents. All of the things
that became important to Syrians—food, security, and so
on—were provided by other groups, many of which were
openly hostile to the political opposition.

In an attempt to close the legitimacy deficit, the Syrian
Interim Government (SIG) was formed by the National Coalition. The SIG proclaimed itself the sole legitimate government
of Syria and assumed control for governing areas outside of
regime control. Financially speaking, the SIG would be wholly
supported by Saudi Arabia, which had initially agreed to
provide a budget of around $300 million USD per month
(Abushakra, 2013) to finance the SIG's activities. The logic
of establishing the SIG was simple: to bridge the legitimacy
gap, provide an opposition presence on the ground, and
demonstrate an ability to govern.

In March 2013, the National Coalition elected its first
interim Prime Minister, Ghassan Hitto, who subsequently
sought to create a cabinet of ministers. None of the Coalition
meetings and none of the ministers were actually based inside
of Syria. This not only contributed to the legitimacy deficit
but meant that they had no organizational base in Syria from
which to govern and administer the territories and, what was
very important, no social basis of support from which to
derive the legitimate authority to govern the areas under its
control. Moreover, it was unclear what territories the SIG
actually sought to govern. The fluidity of the situation on the
ground and the constant changing of alliances and territorial
control meant that the SIG could not claim authority over

contiguous territory or have definitive borders within which to govern. A relationship with the FSA was institutionalized through the creation of a Minister of Defense appointed by the FSA but, beyond this, the SIG had no relationship to the military situation.

The SIG was beset with so many problems from its inception that is has been completely ineffectual and is unlikely to withstand the conflict. The decision to locate SIG offices outside of Syria throughout Turkey completely undermined their claim to govern. While the SIG paid salaries to employees inside of Syria, the overwhelming majority of money spent was to cover expenses in Turkey for officers, staffers, ministers, and other projects. Besides paying salaries to Syrians, there was no discernible material benefit inside of Syria from the SIG. Between its creation in 2013 and 2015, the SIG slowly slipped into near-bankruptcy, with Saudi funding slowly withdrawn and the Western countries pledging very few resources. Yet corruption and mismanagement of funds also contributed to the financial collapse of the SIG. Many employees inside and outside of Syria reported not being paid wages for months and there was growing disillusionment within opposition circles about the SIG's ability to administer Syrian territories. The irony of attempting to govern Syria from outside of the country seems to have been lost on the SIG.

Despite the opposition's desire to present itself as a legitimate alternative to the regime, its one attempt at governance and administration has failed spectacularly. The disconnections between the opposition and Syrians have grown substantially during the conflict and nothing has highlighted the opposition's absence and ineffectiveness in the conflict more then the creation of an alternative government outside the country and the subsequent collapse of that government. Although the SIG's goals may have been modest—pay salaries, initiate some humanitarian projects, establish a bureaucracy, and so on—the stakes were very high. The collapse of the opposition's main administrative project in Syria has further highlighted its political weaknesses and legitimacy deficit inside the country.

Sectarianism

As Syria fragments and new centers of power emerge through-out the country, sectarianism has become a prominent feature of the conflict. Many have argued that it was one of the conflict's driving causes (Byman, 2014). The evidence of this, however, is weak (Phillips, 2015; Farouk-Alli, 2014). In fact, the opposite is quite true: that many of the early protesters had sought to articulate a nonsectarian vision of a new Syria that was inclusive of all its communities (Ismail, 2013). Yet, as the conflict evolved, sectarianism played an extremely important role in how it was framed by both regime and rebel supporters. What began as an uprising against authoritarian-ism and socioeconomic decline has morphed considerably and has now assumed a sectarian dimension that was not so salient in March 2011 when the protests began.

Sectarian affiliations are not new in Syria, nor are the politicization of those identities. From the late Ottoman period through to the Mandate era, sectarian identities and the creation of minorities/majorities in Syria (White, 2012) played a major role in distributing political power and in shaping citizens' relations with the central state. When the Ba'ath Party came to power its leadership was dominated by Alawi leaders, but the party never ruled in the name of the Alawi community. The Ba'ath's sectarian policies cer-tainly favored Alawis in positions of political and security power but this had not come at the complete exclusion of other communities. Sectarianism then during the period of the Ba'ath had contradictory features: on the one hand, the party attempted to rule in the name of Syrians as a national community but had actually adopted policies that high-lighted and aggravated subnational identities, especially reli-gious ones.

With this in mind, it is important to remind ourselves that Syria's social and political identities are not only tethered to sect and religion. Regional differences as well as urban/ rural divides and class divisions have similarly contributed to Syria's social mosaic. The stratification of society along sectarian, geographic, and class lines further complicates reducing Syrian identity to sect. Moreover, the assumption that sectarianism is a major driver of the conflict is premised on false assumptions about communal cohesion and homogeneity that simply do not exist in a place such as Syria.

How then can we understand the role of sectarianism in the Syrian conflict? The uprisings began without an explicit sectarian dimension or the articulation of sectarian identities and interests. There was certainly some element of it expressed in the protests and on social media supportive of the protests, but the LCCs and the majority of protesters were clear to present the movement as a national one inclusive of all sects. The regime's response to the protests was to reaffirm its nationalist symbolism as well and to paint the protesters as sectarian agitators. Sectarianism began to play a larger role in the rhetoric of both the regime and the opposition during the process of militarization. The regime was increasingly engaging in overt policies of fearmongering by framing the protesters and armed opposition as sectarian agitators. Meanwhile, the regime fostered the *shabiha* and then the NDF, which were largely, although not exclusively, drawn from Alawi communities.

The militarization of the opposition eventually led to the rise and fall of the FSA and the entry into the Syrian conflict of armed groups with explicitly sectarian or ethno-sectarian agendas. The introduction of groups such as the YPG, JAN, ISIS, Hizbollah, regional militias, and the various other Salafist-jihadist brigades injected the conflict with a sectarian identity that was previously absent. The presence of these groups started to reframe the nature of violence in Syria as sectarian. Kidnappings, looting, population cleansing, and rapes were increasingly understood as occurring for sectarian reasons and perpetrated by members of one sect against members of another. The increasing presence of foreign actors with presumably sectarian agendas—Saudi Arabia, Qatar, and Iran—gave further meaning to the sectarian logic of the war.

Most important, however, for many Syrians sectarianism has become a facet of everyday life during the conflict and has begun to reshape relationships on the personal level.

Sectarian identity is increasingly associated with loyalist or opposition identities even though the two do not directly correspond. The process of communal cleansing that has been central to the strategies of violence by all groups, regime and rebel, has further fueled sectarianism, as many Syrians experience violence and displacement as an outcome of their own sectarian affiliation.

While many Syrians have experienced sectarianism and sectarianism may certainly have been a motivating factor for some armed groups, it does not explain the trajectory or evolution of the conflict. Many minorities supported the opposition and many Sunnis have supported the regime and actually participated in violence on behalf of the regime, whether in the SAA or NDF. Nevertheless, sectarian identities have been politicized and mobilized. Rhetoric from ISIS, JAN, and even the regime's supporters is increasingly sectarian and suggests that this logic is increasingly drawn upon to mobilize violent actors. This reality has diluted the nationalist goals of the uprising and contributed to the retreat of Syrian identities into narrow allegiances to sect.

The rise of sectarianism has also been a by-product of the larger regional rivalry between Saudi Arabia and Iran. The assumption that the Syrian conflict should be understood through an amorphous Sunni-Shi'a war is problematic because it does not accurately reflect the complexity of the conflict and places undue weight on sectarianism as a driver of the conflict. Nevertheless, regional rivalry is indeed one dimension of the conflict. Fragmentation and sectarianism are fueled by the regional geopolitical conflict and are having multiple effects on neighboring countries and their policies toward Syria. The fragmentation of the armed groups and the regime's networks of violence have given different actors proxy clients inside of Syria from which to influence the trajectory of the conflict. Qatar and Saudi Arabia have ties within the political and armed opposition; Iran strongly supports the NDF, Hizbollah, and other militias; the PKK supports the PYD and the KRG supports the KNC; and so on. The web of alliances that link domestic actors to regional ones is increasingly defined by ethnic or sectarian ties. This increases the opportunities for regional actors to play spoilers to any peace deal.

Social and Political Collapse

Syria's fragmentation into competing centers of territorial control is reshaping the social and administrative landscape of the country. The administrative picture outside of regime areas is extremely complicated, as groups exchange control over territory and attempt to expand their administrations. The administrative structures identified in this chapter have radically different structures. In the Rojava areas, an autonomous government is emerging which is establishing the basis for integration into a postconflict state or even for independence. The Caliphate established by ISIS is an altogether new form of administration that rejects the very idea of a nation-state and which seeks territorial expansion across the region. In southern and northwestern Syria, forms of shared governance between FSA and Salafist-jihadist groups have emerged, and these relationships of convenience are giving rise to patchwork forms of administration that are constantly shifting. Finally, the political opposition's attempt to administer nonregime areas has failed miserably because of corruption and a lack of resources.

Fragmentation and the consolidation of centers of control have increased sectarian mobilization throughout the conflict. What initially began as a movement demanding civil, national rights for all Syrians has slowly morphed and taken on increasingly sectarian dimensions. For many Syrians, sectarianism has become a reality of daily life and previous social and familial bonds have been placed under great strain as the conflict is increasingly framed and experienced in sectarian terms. The realities of the conflict are more complicated, however, and cross-sectarian allegiances and support can be claimed by both regime and opposition forces. Syria's complicated social mosaic, in which sect, geographic, and class intersect to give political identities salience and meaning, is being reconfigured.

Syria's social mosaic is being transformed also by the horrific and unprecedented humanitarian crisis that has affected all Syrians regardless of class, sect, gender, or geographic locale. The pace at which the humanitarian crisis has accelerated has not been matched by efforts by the international community or various armed actors within Syria to mitigate or buttress the descent into humanitarian catastrophe. At the time of writing, more than half of all Syrians have either been killed, maimed, or forced out of their homes in less than five years. Such a humanitarian tragedy will take decades, if not generations, to unravel, and for Syrian society to heal from the infliction of such widespread destruction, displacement, and emotional and physical trauma.

Unfortunately, while some commentators have celebrated the political and administrative achievements of some areas outside of regime control (International Crisis Group, 2014), the realities of daily life for most Syrians have deteriorated considerably. The geographic fragmentation of the country into different centers of power makes distribution of aid difficult. Syrians find it difficult or impossible to move from one governorate to another or to leave the country, to access goods and services, and to maintain basic daily patterns to work, school, or social gatherings. The risk of death, kidnapping, arrest, or even the lengthy commutes around checkpoints have severely affected the ability of Syrians to attend to their basic needs. The restriction of movement of people and goods and the constant violence throughout the country has placed tremendous pressure on Syrian families, whose main coping mechanisms—divestment of assets, migration, and so on—have been exhausted during the first four years of the conflict.

6 | The Humanitarian Crisis

The humanitarian costs of the Syrian conflict have been staggering. The depth and scale of human suffering and loss of life has led many, including officials at the United Nations, to identify this as "the worst humanitarian crisis of our time." Unfortunately, this crisis worsens each month, and as the prospects for a political solution wither and humanitarian aid decreases, the coming years will not relieve it. The human cost of the conflict cannot be overstated: more than 200,000 Syrians killed, more than 4 million refugees, approximately 8 million displaced inside Syria, close to 650,000 Syrians living in areas under regime besiegement and completely cut off from humanitarian access, and 12 million Syrians inside of the country in need of humanitarian assistance.

The gravity of the humanitarian catastrophe in Syria cannot possibly be captured in the numbers and figures that follow in this chapter. Nigel Fisher perhaps summarizes the problem of telling the story of human calamity through numbers best:

> "Displaced." Such an innocuous word. But with its now-commonplace usage, accompanied by mind-numbing and ever-increasing numbers, have we become inured to the human drama behind the devastating facts of displacement in Syria today? Tucked away behind that rather bland term are, for millions, repeated stories of family separation; the loss of

children, parents, friends, homes, entire neighbourhoods; and the terror of raining barrel bombs, of extremist depredations, of reprisals against family members imprisoned, tortured, raped, disappeared or killed. Displacement not once, twice or three times but multiple uprooting—to the homes of neighbours or into shells of buildings in their own neighborhoods, displacement within their own districts and governorates or, ultimately, fleeing across borders to an unknown future. Few responses today are taking into account the trauma that the displaced have suffered. (Fisher, 2014: 4)

The scale of the humanitarian crisis is directly related to the levels of violence experienced over the period of the conflict. As violence has increased, the humanitarian crisis has worsened. Thus, the widening of the violent landscape and the proliferation of armed groups has not increased the security of average Syrians but actually decreased it. In this chapter, we will trace the dramatic rise in displaced peoples and physical damage to the country's infrastructure alongside the expansion and proliferation of violence. The chapter will begin with a discussion of the economic impacts of the conflict on Syria's economy and infrastructure. From here, we will explore the displacement crisis and address the reasons behind the massive movement of Syrians inside and outside of the country during the conflict. Syrian displacement will have impacts for generations to come as the rupture of Syria's social fabric has created serious generational needs around health care and education. Such issues are further explored later in the chapter when the major humanitarian issues facing Syrians are explored.

Economic Impacts of the Conflict

The formal Syrian economy has severely contracted over the course of the conflict. In the four years of conflict, formal economic patterns have all but collapsed and production within the country has ground to a standstill. Internal and external trade has been strongly affected by the conflict, with virtually no goods being exported from Syria to neighboring markets. Violence and fragmentation have carved up the Syrian lands into a mosaic of cantons where exchange and movement within Syria has become nearly impossible because of the control of key distribution routes by warring armed groups. Instead, the borderlands have assumed strategic economic importance for the various armed groups as the sources and conduits of supplies and goods.

As discussed in Chapter Three, war economies have played a major role in the Syrian conflict. Under such conditions, goods are acquired and distributed with reference to the means of violence and, thus, armed groups assume a central role in the economy as the guarantors of products, goods, and the means of economic livelihood. The contraction of the formal economy and the rise of war economies has brought with it the rapid expansion of illegality, informality, and black markets. As unemployment has increased sharply and average Syrians deplete their savings and other resources to acquire basic goods, armed groups take on a more powerful role as the guarantor of goods.

Every major economic sector in Syria has contracted since 2011. The Syrian Center for Policy Research has provided conservative estimates of real Gross Domestic Product (GDP) loss by sector from 2010 until the end of 2014 (Table 6.1).

Table 6.1   Real GDP Loss by Sector, 2010–2014

Sector	Percentage of Real GDP Loss 2010–2014
Agriculture	145
Construction	183
Government Services	201
Social Services	220
Utilities	243
Mining	251
Internal Trade	252
Finance and Real Estate	254
Transport and Communication	271
Manufacturing	310

(SCPR, 2015: 16)

Beyond the rapid decline of all sectors of economic activity lies the collapse of household income. The conflict has generated a number of pressures on individuals and households that have been difficult to sustain. Unemployment and underemployment are rampant in Syria and the most affected group of Syrians are young people who were already disproportionately represented in the total unemployed. Wages have not kept up with the price of goods and inflation has significantly devalued Syrian savings and purchasing power. In this context, many Syrians have resorted to selling off assets in order to survive or to relying on remittances from abroad. Quite simply, for the overwhelming majority of Syrians, the conflict has been economically unsustainable.

This is also true of the Syrian business community, which has suffered from the physical losses inflicted by the conflict as well as the losses of markets, labor, and capital. Many Syrian businesses have sold their assets and moved outside of the country, dramatically reducing national production and fueling the demands of the war economy. In Lebanon, Turkey, Iraq, Egypt, and Jordan, Syrian businesses have been reestablished but more often than not the Syrian businesspeople have been forced to rely on their wealth to survive outside of the country. This represents a dramatic depletion of Syrian business assets and will have serious consequences for the ability of the domestic business community to participate in reconstruction.

Refugees and Internally Displaced Persons

The Syrian refugee crisis is completely reconfiguring the social landscape. The tragedy of the Syrian conflict is best captured in the staggering numbers of Syrians who have died, been maimed or disfigured, or been forced to leave their homes, a figure which in 2015 represented at least half of all Syrians. Men, women, and children have been forced to leave their homes by foot, car, bus, and, most dangerously, on boats, as they traverse dangerous roads and seas in search of security and safety from violence. The gravity of the humanitarian crisis has, unfortunately, been lost on the international community. As the years pass, fewer refugees are resettled, borders become more restrictive, and less aid is reaching Syrian refugees. Under such circumstances, it is almost impossible to accurately convey the extent to which the Syrian refugee crisis is redefining Syria, now and in the future. What follows, then, is an attempt to map out the broader structural factors behind the crisis and then to ground the discussion in the different countries to which Syrian refugees have fled.

Syrian refugees are the second-largest refugee population in the entire world. The United Nations High Commission on Refugees (UNHCR) has declared the Syrian refugee crisis the largest operation in its history and have requested billions of dollars in immediate aid to provide services, aid, and shelter to more than four million Syrian refugees. In addition to the millions of Syrians outside of the country, there are millions more displaced within the country.

The Syrian refugee crisis is directly tethered to the escalation of violence and its attendant effects, including the contraction of the economy. As the conflict has dragged on, the displacement figures have risen on a yearly basis. The increasing displacement has corresponded to a tightening of entry restrictions in neighboring countries and a rapid deterioration in the availability of aid for many Syrians, so much so that the United Nations World Food Programme (WFP) was forced to suspend its voucher program for 1.7 million Syrian refugees because of a lack of funding (Miles, 2014). In addition to the pressures of increased violence, Syrians are facing a severe food, education, and housing crisis that is forcing hundreds to leave their homes each day.

More than nine million Syrians have been displaced either as refugees or IDPs, just less than half the population. Official figures provided by the UNHCR give some sense of the extent of the refugee crisis but do not capture the full picture, as they only account for registered refugees. Table 6.2 below provides a demographic breakdown of the registered Syrian refugee population in Iraq, North Africa, Lebanon, Turkey, Jordan, and Egypt.

Table 6.2 Demographic Profile of Registered Syrian Refugees

Age	Male (%)	Female (%)
0–4	9.2	8.8
5–11	10.9	10.3
12–17	6.6	6.3
18–59	20.6	24.2
60+	1.4	1.7
Total	48.7	51.3

The number of registered Syrian refugees has increased each year since the conflict began and only began to taper off in 2015 when neighboring countries imposed greater entry restrictions. In December 2012, for example, the UNHCR has registered less than 500,000 refugees, while a year later close to 2.5 million had been registered. In 2013, the number of registered refugees rose considerably in all the host countries and then has slowly tapered off. Jordan, for example, registered more than four times the number of refugees in 2013 than in 2012 or 2014.

All Syrian governorates have experienced significant population displacements so it is difficult to determine what areas have been the most affected. Geographic location, familial and social networks, and ease of entry have determined the movement of Syrians outside of the country. In Jordan, for example, the majority of registered refugees come from Dar'a governorate, which borders Jordan (46 percent) but sizeable portions of the refugee population come from Aleppo and Homs, which are much further north and closer to Turkey or Lebanon (UNHCR, Registered Syrians in Jordan 24 January 2015). Lebanon has received Syrians from all governorates, including in the far northeast, but the majority of registered Syrians come from Homs, Aleppo, rural Damascus, and Idlib, all governorates where fighting has been the most intense. In Turkey, the majority of refugees come from the northern governorates of Syria.

In addition to geographical factors and proximity to neighboring countries, many refugees fled to countries where they had established familial and social networks. This was particularly true during successive waves of displacement, when refugees would follow other family members or friends to refuge. Such familial and social networks have helped sustain refugees, especially in countries such as Lebanon where there are strong ties with Syrians. Finally, there are issues of mobility and accessibility that determine an individual or family decision where to relocate or take refuge. In some cases, moving inside of the country is more dangerous than moving outside to a neighboring country. The threat of violence and the presence of dozens, if not hundreds, of checkpoints along major highways make travelling through the country extremely dangerous. Even moving within governorates is extremely dangerous in areas where different armed groups control checkpoints. For example, someone in Damascus may find it easier to relocate to the northwest of the country along the coast, Lebanon, or Jordan, instead of Turkey, because of the danger of highways and checkpoints.

The evolution of the refugee crisis was gradual. In the early stages of the conflict, very few refugees fled into neighboring countries, with Jordan registering barely 2,000 refugees at the end of 2011. Typically, major military offensives would lead to movement of the residents to other parts of the country, or in the case of the northern areas, into Turkey. For many Syrians who fled to Lebanon, the move was not intended to be permanent. Individuals and families had begun to rent homes or enroll their children in school but would often travel back and forth to Syria for work. This reflected the temporary nature, or at least the assumption many refugees held, of their stay in Lebanon and neighboring countries. Host governments shared such assumptions; in Lebanon, refugees were not even registered until early 2013.

However, by late 2011 and into 2012 Turkey and Iraq began establishing refugee camps as the massive influx of Syrians was creating pressure on the governments to provide services. In 2012, the flow of refugees was small, with 2,500 registered refugees in Turkey in April representing the largest daily number up until that point. While many refugees were fleeing violence, others were also leaving because of the deteriorating economic situation or because of the threat and fear of violence in their areas. This was also a period in which many businesspeople began to sell their assets and to move to nearby countries. Between 2011 and most of 2012 the refugee situation was worsening but became much more aggravated in the summer of 2012 when violence began in Aleppo and more than 200,000 Syrians left almost immediately.

The situation in Aleppo in 2012 reflected the emerging order of violence in Syria. Armed groups would force the regime's retreat in certain parts of a city and then take up positions. These cities, such as Hama, Homs, and Aleppo, would effectively be divided between rebel and armed groups who would assume entrenched positions and continue attacks against the other forces. Residents of these cities were caught in the middle of this violence.

The entrenchment of the armed groups and the division of major population centers into regime and nonregime areas would have profound impacts on the refugee crisis. From mid-2012 until the end of the year, there were thousands, rather than hundreds, of Syrians at border crossings each day. Such figures only increased into 2013 when, by the summer, there were at least 6,000 Syrians fleeing each day to neighboring countries and thousands more displaced internally. It is during this period that the military stalemate in the country began to take root and the various armed groups retreated into their areas of territorial control. The YPG had begun to carve out the Kurdish areas, while ISIS continued to expand into the northeast and further west into Aleppo, and Salafist-jihadist groups in cooperation with FSA brigades continued their attacks against regime forces in the north and south of the country. The proliferation of networks of violence and the carving out of areas of control, and thus the establishment of battlefield frontiers, accelerated the violence and displacement of Syrians.

Life did not prove to be much easier for Syrians in refugee camps. Host countries had increasingly turned hostile to them, especially in Lebanon and Jordan, who began to adopt restrictive policies on Syrian entry. As early as 2012, Syrians were already not receiving adequate medical care, with some suffering from a range of treatable conditions, including tuberculosis. Spillover of the conflict into Lebanon invited harsh social responses from Lebanese, with many incidents of harassment, violence, and even murders being reported to the authorities and the UNHCR. Bombings in Beirut, which had nothing to do with the refugees themselves, invited further revenge from Lebanese, who set fire to makeshift camps, attacked Syrian workers, and continuously harassed people, scaring many Syrians into immobility.

By far the largest problem facing refugees is the lack of adequate food and services. In all the regional camps, malnutrition has become a major problem. There are acute problems around health care and educational provision, and many refugees are suffering from treatable diseases and conditions because aid agencies do not have the resources to provide them the services they are denied in their host countries. The denial of services in host countries is compounded by the inability of international organizations to reach many of the most vulnerable Syrians. A lack of resources, capacity, and political will in Western states has meant that many of the needs of Syrian refugees are going unfulfilled by local and international humanitarian organizations. Such neglect of the health and education needs of Syrians will have profound impacts on generations to come.

Health Care

The health care crisis in Syria has reached catastrophic proportions, with an estimated 6 percent of the total population killed, injured, or maimed since the conflict began (SCPR, 2015: 52). The United Nations Children's Fund (UNICEF) has declared Syria's children a "lost generation" (UNICEF, 2013). In addition to this, a majority of Syrians live in impoverished conditions without recourse to basic health services. Such conditions have not only deprived them of health care access but have led to the spread of communicable diseases, including polio, which had been previously eradicated. The public health calamity in Syria is total: basic access is limited, medicines are severely limited, people are dying from preventable ailments, disease is spreading, water is increasingly contaminated, doctors and health care workers are in extreme shortage, and hospitals are being destroyed.

Violence in Syria has left more than half of all major hospitals in Syria destroyed or significantly damaged, with around twenty-three hospitals (out of ninety) completely nonfunctioning. Attacks on hospitals and other health care facilities have been widespread throughout the conflict, both indirectly through sporadic violence and through direct targeting by regime forces as collective punishment against rebel-held areas. The destruction of hospitals and other health care facilities has been worse in areas experiencing the most violence: Aleppo, Raqqa, Deir ez-Zor, and Idlib.

Many aid agencies have begun to address this problem by establishing mobile health clinics or re-establishing hospital operations (more below). However, even when these facilities acquire resources they are severely understaffed. Many Syrian doctors fled the country after the conflict began, leaving the Syrian health system in a severe personnel crisis. An astonishing number of hospitals in major population centers report not having any emergency physicians, including eight of eleven hospitals in Aleppo, four of five in Deir ez-Zor, seven of eight in rural Damascus, and three of four in al-Hassakeh (SCPR, 2015: 52). Hospitals in regime and nonregime areas report shortages of health workers in all areas. Such personnel shortages have a major impact on the treatment of conflict- and nonconflict-related conditions and have severely exacerbated the health care crisis. Treatments for basic conditions, or for different forms of cancer, for example, have become extremely difficult throughout the country.

The destruction of health care facilities and the depletion of medical care staff is compounded by the effects of the conflict on Syria's once-strong pharmaceutical industry. Prior to the conflict, Syria produced more than 90 percent of all medicines consumed within the country. Violence has led to the destruction of much of this capacity and pharmaceutical production has plummeted. The besiegement of many areas and the division of the country has further prohibited the delivery of medicines to areas that are most in need. Medicines produced in regime areas only make it to other parts of the country through the black market (IRIN, 2012) and aid supplies are often redirected by regime forces away from vulnerable and desperate regions to loyalist areas. The prevalence of diseases such as measles, polio, tuberculosis, and typhoid is merely one of the outcomes of the deprivation of medicines and vaccines. Medicinal shortages have fueled black market activity and increased the dependence of Syrians on criminal networks for access to goods. Medicinal products have become a quite lucrative enterprise for smugglers and criminals, for everything from Tylenol to cancer-fighting medication. Under such conditions, hundreds of thousands of lives are negatively affected each day because of the lack of access.

Nowhere is this more acute than in the nonregime areas under besiegement, which are largely inaccessible to humanitarian aid agencies. This segment of the population, mostly in the northern areas controlled by rebel groups, ISIS, and JAN, have suffered tremendously over the last four years and have been almost entirely reliant on the humanitarian efforts of Syrian, Turkish, and international NGOs. The Union of Syrian Medical Relief Organizations (UOSSM), for example, is a coalition of Syrian relief organizations that have attempted to alleviate the gaps in the health care system through the provision of aid and the reestablishment of health care services in affected areas. Yet, despite the efforts of UOSSM and other relief groups, the health care crisis remains severely acute.

Education

Syrian children have suffered tremendously throughout the conflict. As children, they are far removed from the disputes that breed violence—of which they are among the first victims. For many aid workers, the Syrian conflict is a generational one and will require support from the international community for decades to come. Unfortunately, this generation of Syrians is the first of the "lost generations" who will bear the greatest burden of the conflict.

Syria's educational crisis is dire. While many schools remained accessible and operating in the first months of the uprising, the escalation of violence set in motion processes that would slowly destroy the educational system throughout the country. One of the key factors in the educational crisis is the destruction of actual schools and other educational infrastructure. According to the SCPR, by the end of 2014, 25 percent of Syrian schools had fully ceased to function, more than 600 were being used as IDP shelters, and more than 4,600 schools were totally or partially damaged (SCPR, 2015: 49).

The use of schools and playgrounds by armed groups invited violence and destruction and forced many schools to close. Many teachers, administrators, and students fled the country as well, leaving the schools that were accessible without adequate staff and resources to teach. Violence, damage to physical infrastructure, and the displacement of students and teachers were the initial causes of the educational crisis. By 2015, it was estimated that over 50 percent of all school-aged children in Syria were not attending school (SCPR, 2015: 48). This figure does not account for the number of school-aged children who are refugees and have limited access to educational opportunities in neighboring countries.

The geography of educational access and deprivation mirror the fragmentation of the country. In areas where the violence is most pronounced, especially in the north, nonattendance is as high as 74 percent in Aleppo and 64 percent in Raqqa (SCPR, 2015: 48). Paradoxically, while attendance declined in these areas and others most hit by violence, including Deir Ezzor, Idlib, and the Damascene countryside, attendance increased in areas that were under nominal regime control, such as Damascus, Homs, Tartous, and Latakia. Such figures indicate a direct correlation between the intensity of the fighting and educational access. They also suggest, as will be discussed later, that many IDPs have taken refuge in regime areas because violence is less intense and there is greater access to services such as education.

Despite the increase in student enrollment in parts of the country, the overwhelming majority of Syrian students lack adequate access to education. Internally displaced children are not always able to enroll immediately into schools. For many families, displacement has become a fact of everyday life and they have been unable to settle in one area after leaving their homes. In the north, for example, many families will flee one village to a neighboring village, only to be forced to flee again as fighting spreads. This permanent state of uncertainty and displacement discourages families from enrolling children in schools. Such a state of permanent movement is not unique to IDPs but has also been experienced by middle- and upper-class Syrians who "circulate" between different locations in order to avoid violence (Oesch, 2014). While many refugee children do not necessarily experience the same levels of continued displacement, they nevertheless are deprived of access to education in many camps.

Refugees in Lebanon

The presence of Syrian refugees in Lebanon is complicated by the legacies of overlapping factors that have shaped Syrian-Lebanese relations, including the presence of Syrian forces in Lebanon until 2005, political-economic factors that fostered a Syrian labor force in Lebanon, and sectarianism. There are currently an estimated 1.2 million registered Syrian refugees in Lebanon. More realistically, the total number of Syrians is likely closer to 2 million, as many refugees have not registered with the UNHCR. While this number is only slightly more than the total registered in Turkey, it represents around half of the total Lebanese population, which is estimated at 4 million. Unlike Turkey, which has received millions of dollars in aid from Western governments and is host to many aid agencies, Lebanon has received much less funding to support service provision to refugees. Complicating humanitarian assistance further has been the Lebanese policy not to establish refugee camps. While informal camps exist throughout the country, these are not sanctioned, managed, or protected by the Lebanese government or any NGOs. The majority of Syrians are thus forced to find housing on their own and are subject to very few protections in doing so.

There are four main factors that place a tremendous amount of stress and strain on Syrian refugees in Lebanon: first, a restrictive legal environment that makes employment, residency, and access to services extremely difficult; second, existing strain on the Lebanese service system that makes accessibility difficult; third, spillover effects of the Syrian conflict that have led to violence in Lebanon; and, finally, prejudice from some Lebanese who bear hostility toward Syrians for political, sectarian, or economic reasons and who fear another permanent refugee crisis in their country similar to that of the Palestinians in Lebanon.

The Lebanese legal system has undergone many changes since 2011 that have placed increasing restrictions on Syrian residency. In addition to this, many towns and villages in Lebanon have enacted unofficial curfews against Syrian residents, often distributing curfew restrictions via leaflets and enforcing them through violence and intimidation. Among many Syrians in Lebanon there is a tremendous amount of uncertainty and confusion about their collective status and rights. Compounding this uncertainty is the prevalence of rumors regarding Lebanese government actions toward refugees: stories circulate among Syrians and Lebanese that suggest larger changes in Lebanese law or policy toward Syrians. While these rumors tend not to be grounded in reality or in the actual experiences of refugees, they nevertheless spread fear and insecurity.

Like other neighboring countries, Lebanon had an open-door policy toward Syrians that was coded in law dating back to 1943. This policy allowed Syrians visa-free entry into Lebanon as well as rights of movement within the country. By 2015, this law had been cancelled and all Syrians entering Lebanon needed a visa to enter the country. Syrians in Lebanon who do not have a residency permit or proper travel documentation thus fall outside any legal protections and are subject to potential arrest and deportation if caught. Many Syrians who arrived in Lebanon prior to the legal changes have themselves imposed restrictions on their movement out of fear of checkpoints (Aranki and Kalis, 2014: 17). Even refugee status conferred on Syrians by the UNHCR affords them no protections in Lebanon, as the country is not a signatory to the 1951 Refugee Convention. Registration gives Syrians access to some UN aid but this is rarely enough to satisfy basic needs or services, such as health care or education. Ultimately, Syrian refugees without residency or visas do not have recourse to the international refugee rights regime or the Lebanese legal system in order to demand rights or legal protections.

The absence of refugee camps has meant that Syrians have had to rely on private rentals for accommodation. In the early phases of the conflict housing and accommodation was not very difficult to acquire and Lebanese law contained no restrictions on renting to Syrians. Lately, however, the law has changed and renting out accommodations to Syrians without proper residency documents has become a crime punishable by a substantial monetary fine. This has placed tremendous stress on the social networks that have sustained Syrians in Lebanon. For years, many of the refugees have relied on these social networks for employment, accommodation, and, in worst cases, food, aid, and other forms of daily support. Many Lebanese hosted Syrians in their homes or allowed them to take up residency in empty apartments. Muslim and Christian religious leaders facilitated the settlement of many Syrian families through donations and support from their communities. Such donations and generosity took on multiple forms beyond religious motivations, including financial help, and was important in helping Syrians settle in Lebanon.

All of this support was based on the dense social and familial networks linking Syrians and Lebanese. Individuals and religious institutions have received no funding from the Lebanese government or the international community for any of the forms of support offered to refugees. While there have indeed been many cases where Lebanese landlords or employers have taken advantage of Syrian refugees, this has not necessarily been the norm. Personal and social affiliations make up a large portion of the support that Syrians have received in Lebanon (Mackreath, 2014) and this has been an important factor in the survival of many Syrians. In addition, many Syrian civil society groups have been established to provide relief services to refugees in Lebanon. Such forms of aid and support, however, are by nature temporary and unstable and cannot replace long-term strategies for a sufficient response to the Syrian crisis by the government or aid community.

There are other factors that make the Syrian reliance on personal humanitarian efforts of Lebanese problematic and which engender fear and insecurity among many Syrians. The Syrian conflict has effectively spread into Lebanon, with rival political factions supporting different parties to the conflict. Such allegiances have further divided many Lebanese and jolted a political system that was already paralyzed by largely sectarian-based disputes between the main political parties. The Syrian conflict has ignited many of these sectarian prejudices and led to resentment and violence toward Syrians in Lebanon. In addition to the sectarian resentment toward Syrians, there are also various forms of socioeconomic resentment from many poor Lebanese, who believe that Syrians are accessing aid, support, and services that they are deprived of, and by more middle- and upper-class Lebanese who believe that Syrian professionals are being employed in professional positions at lower salaries.

An excellent example of how Lebanon has become enmeshed in the Syrian conflict are the events that have occurred in the town of Arsal. Located in the northeastern part of Lebanon, Arsal is a mostly Sunni town that is home to around 35,000 Lebanese residents and tens of thousands of Syrian refugees. During the conflict, Arsal became a safe haven for smugglers and fighters flowing back and forth between Lebanon and Syria. The residents prospered during the conflict and many began to politically support the Syrian revolution and the fighters. Many of the neighboring towns did not share Arsal's allegiance to the Syrian revolution and there was considerable resentment among people in the area, especially those who believed that the people of Arsal were unnecessarily inviting fighters, and thus the conflict, into Lebanon. Tensions between Lebanese residents and Syrian refugees deteriorated even further in August 2014 when thirty-four Lebanese soldiers were abducted by fighters loyal to Jabhat an-Nusra (JAN) and ISIS. Immediately, the residents of Arsal were accused of collaborating with them and of being responsible for the abductions. The Lebanese army surrounded Arsal and effectively placed a siege on the city for weeks as negotiations for the release of the abducted soldiers began. By March 2015 four of the soldiers had been killed, five had been released, the remaining twenty-five were still hostages, and the town was still encircled by the Lebanese army.

Many of the Syrian refugees in the town were physically caught between the Lebanese army, Syrian fighters who had taken refuge in Arsal, and Lebanese citizens who were increasingly directing their resentment at them. The blockade had effectively cut off the town. Eventually, the army lessened the siege and allowed for the movement of Syrian refugees outside Arsal. The situation in Arsal is certainly exceptional but nevertheless highlights some of the many complicated political and social challenges that Syrian refugees face and the terrain they are forced to navigate in order to survive in Lebanon. The presence of millions of Syrians has also placed a tremendous amount of stress on the Lebanese government's ability to provide services: many Syrians there, especially children, are deprived of access to schools, hospitals, and other basic services.

Refugees in Turkey

Turkey is host to the largest number of displaced Syrians, with more than 1.7 million registered refugees residing in Turkey. The unofficial figure is probably much closer to 2 million. Of this number, around 30 percent of Syrians live in one of the close to two dozen refugee camps spread across Turkey's southern border with Syria, from the south-central province of Mardin bordering the Rojava areas to the southwestern province of Icel along the Mediterranean coast. The majority of Syrians are concentrated in the border provinces closest to the northern areas experiencing the most fighting: Hatay, Gaziantep, Kilis, and Sanliurfa. The former two provinces have become central locations for aid agencies providing relief work. A significant number have also taken refuge in major cities, such as Istanbul and Ankara, where they have opened up businesses, enrolled in schools, found employment, or simply taken up residence. Since 2014, the trend has been toward Syrian refugees residing outside of camps. While many of them continue to register as refugees, the move outside the camps has made accessing relief services more challenging.

Turkey has thus far provided the most hospitable environment for Syrian refugees as compared to the other neighboring countries. Much like Jordan and Lebanon, Turkey adopted an open-door policy to the Syrian refugees, which it has maintained into 2015 (notwithstanding border restrictions placed on Syrian Kurds fleeing fighting in Kobane). Turkey's policy toward Syrian refugees has been complicated; it relies in part on the steady flow of humanitarian aid to Turkish and international nongovernmental organizations who have assumed growing management of the camps and provision of services to refugees. For Turkey, the open-door policy arose out of both a sense of responsibility to the refugees and a political opportunity for the government of Prime Minister Erdogan to project its power among the Syrian opposition and the wider Middle East (Kirisci and Salooja, 2014).

Turkish policy toward the Syrian refugees has evolved considerably since 2011, and, unlike Lebanon and Jordan, the authorities have adopted greater protections for refugees. The first influx of Syrians in 2011 were legally considered "guests," a designation that absolved Turkey of responsibility to protect them as refugees under international law. However, by late 2011, the Turkish authorities had instead granted Syrians refugee status and temporary protections. By 2013, with the Syrian refugee population increasing rapidly, the government passed a new refugee rights law that would offer greater protection to refugees and asylum seekers. Currently, Syrians are able to acquire either a residence permit or temporary protection status, both of which provide them social and economic rights and protections under Turkish law.

The presence of formal legal protections has not, however, guaranteed safety and security for many Syrians. The dispersion of Syrians throughout Turkey means that it is difficult for many aid agencies to access them to provide services. Moreover, many Syrians, despite enjoying the right to work, have become something of an exploited underclass in southern Turkey, where they have taken on wages much lower then their Turkish counterparts. This has provided a boon to local businesses but placed severe strains on Turkish citizens who have found themselves in competition for work with newly arrived Syrians. In certain areas of southern Turkey, the crowding of the labor market by Syrian refugees has indeed led to tensions between Syrians and Turkish citizens, particularly in areas with heavy reliance on agricultural and service employment, which are the main sectors of labor-market competition.

Economic realities in southern Turkey are slightly more complicated, however. Cities such as Reyhanli, Gazientep, and Antakya, and southern provinces in general, have experienced a significant economic boom since 2011. Turkish banks have been flooded with Syrian money, and, according to figures from late 2012, banks in the Hatay province reported foreign currency deposit increases of 101 percent (Abboud, 2013). Similar increases have been recorded throughout southern Turkish banks, suggesting that many of the Syrians who fled the country came with savings and were able to afford to live outside of the refugee camps. Moreover, many Syrian industrialists who had sold their assets in northern Syria had begun to reestablish themselves in Turkey, channeling their capital resources into the country to establish new operations or enter into partnerships with local Turkish businesspeople. Southern Turkey has also seen a massive inflow of aid money from international organizations. This has mitigated some of the impacts of the refugee crisis but is not a sustainable solution to the residency of so many Syrians in Turkey.

Refugees in Jordan

According to the UNHCR, there are over 620,000 Syrian refugees registered in Jordan. Unofficial figures are likely much higher, as many Syrians have not formally registered as refugees there. Like other neighboring countries, Jordan had an open-door policy toward refugees which has since been revoked in favor of a more restrictive policy that effectively forecloses entry into the country for many Syrians by requiring travel visas, which are difficult to acquire.

Jordan is not a signatory to the 1951 Refugee Convention and, therefore, Syrian refugees do not have recourse to the international refugee rights regime. Jordanian law has integrated many of the main tenets of the international refugee regime, including the principle of *non-refoulement* but does not allow for the integration of refugees into Jordan through naturalization. Unlike Lebanon, which has a similar policy forbidding refugee integration, Jordan has established five refugee camps for Syrians, although most live outside of the camps.

Refugees in Iraq

There are close to 250,000 Syrians who have taken refuge in Iraq, the overwhelming majority of whom (97 percent) in the regions of Iraq under the administration of the Kurdish Regional Government (KRG) (Sood and Seferis, 2014: 14). Overall, approximately 90 percent of all Syrian refugees to Iraq are Syrian Kurds. Unlike the cases of Lebanon, Jordan, and Turkey, where Syrians of varied class and social backgrounds took refuge, many of the refugees in Iraq have been impoverished and were not able to financially sustain themselves in Iraq for long periods of time without access to the labor market. Most indicators suggest that Syrian refugees had little access to income-generating activities and had few savings from which to meet household needs (Sood and Seferis, 2014). Around half of the refugees lived in major population centers such as Irbil and Dohuk, while the remaining refugees lived in ten camps located throughout the region.

There are three general categories of Syrian refugees who fled into Iraq (Saadullah, 2014). The first consists of those who were fleeing violence from areas such as Aleppo, Qamishli, and al-Hassakeh. The second are those from areas that experienced very little violence but who came as economic refugees in search of work. Finally, there are those refugees who have fled infighting between the Kurdish parties inside the Rojava areas.

Syrian refugees into Iraq came in two rather distinct stages. The first stage involved those prior to 2014 who were fleeing violence in the northern parts of the country or who were arriving for economic reasons. Many of these refugees had chosen Iraq over Turkey because of their social, cultural, and sometimes familial relationships with Kurds in Iraq and for the economic opportunities presented by the region. The smaller numbers of refugees prior to 2014 had placed relatively minor strains on the public service system in the region, which had been experiencing high levels of economic growth and had labor market gaps in low-paying service jobs that some refugees could fill. The majority of refugees had taken up residence in local housing and although rents and the cost of living increased in the years prior to 2014 it is unlikely that this was caused by the influx of refugees. It was likely due to other factors related to the economic growth of the Kurdish areas.

In 2014 a second wave of refugees crossed into Iraq because of the intense fighting in and around the Kobane area between ISIS and the YPG and other armed groups. The months-long besiegement of Kobane by ISIS forced upward of 170,000 Syrian Kurds to flee the area. However, Turkish authorities had restricted access to the border crossing between the two countries, effectively trapping many of the refugees on the Syrian side. As a result, the refugees made their way into other parts of Syria or into Iraq.

ISIS advances in other parts of Iraq and the siege of Mosul had forced many Iraqis to take refuge in the Kurdish areas as well, placing tremendous social and economic pressure on the region already attempting to cope with hundreds of thousands of refugees. As a result, many of the Syrian refugees fleeing Kobane were forced away from the cities and into the camps where aid agencies could provide services and residents could still work and access the labor market.

To date, the influx of Syrian refugees and Iraqi IDPs fleeing ISIS advances has not threatened the protection and opportunities afforded Syrian refugees. Although the KRG has handed over camp management to the Norwegian Refugee Council (NRC), the authorities have maintained a commitment to providing services and have allowed residents work permits. This has provided a semblance of stability for many refugees who find themselves caught between ISIS violence, Syrian regime bombardment, Turkish border restrictions, and Kurdish infighting in Syria.

Europe and the Refugee Crisis

The European Union's policy toward the Syrian humanitarian crisis has been contradictory. On the one hand, the EU has donated more than half of all humanitarian aid to Syrian refugees. On the other hand, EU countries have adopted very restrictive entry policies and have failed to resettle large numbers of Syrian refugees, with less than 4 percent of all Syrian refugees located in Europe. The EU policy toward Syrian refugees is to support humanitarian efforts at alleviating their hardship but to restrict them refugee or asylum status in EU countries.

The EU has provided more than 3.5 billion euros in humanitarian assistance to Syrian refugees. This is by far the largest single contribution to humanitarian efforts. Within the EU, however, there are vast differences in what countries provide support, with the United Kingdom, Germany, and Norway providing the majority of it. This support has been distributed between government and nongovernment agencies and has also provided financial support to host countries in their efforts to provide aid and services to refugees.

While the EU has been a leader in providing humanitarian support, the organization has failed to provide sufficient opportunities for Syrian refugees and asylum seekers to settle in the regional bloc. In 2015, barely 150,000 Syrian refugees have declared asylum in the EU. The top five states receiving Syrian refugees overall are Sweden, Germany, Bulgaria, Switzerland, and the Netherlands. Of these countries, more than half of all applications have been submitted in Sweden and Germany. The remaining EU countries have adopted extremely strict policies and have rejected many Syrian refugee applications. Countries in the Mediterranean, including Cyprus, Greece, and Malta, have resorted to detaining refugees before deporting them back, oftentimes to Turkey, as it is usually their point of departure. The Turkish Republic of Northern Cyprus (TRNC) authorities have also resorted to detaining and deporting refugees to Turkey.

Entry into Europe through Turkey is extremely difficult. As a result, most refugees risk their lives on boats travelling through the Mediterranean. There are tremendous risks associated with this sea travel and many thousands of Syrians have lost their lives crossing the waters to gain entry into Europe. In most cases, Syrians flee to Turkey, Egypt, or Libya, where they pay smugglers to take them to Europe. These boats are often unsafe and many capsize before reaching shore. Such dangers make the restrictive policies of the Greek, Cypriot, and Maltese governments even more appalling, as these are countries closest to the ports of departure for refugees. Greece's police patrol the Aegean Sea to apprehend and deport refugees before they arrive in Greece. Such fears for refugees have meant that many make longer, even more dangerous trips to more northern points of entry.

Syrians Respond: Humanitarianism in Action

Amid the Syrian tragedy a number of Syrians have come together to provide relief to their co-nationalists who have suffered tremendously over the last four years. In earlier chapters, I outlined some of the challenges facing the LCCs as they assumed greater governance roles throughout Syria. Today, many of the activists that were involved in the early stages of the uprising remain active in relief efforts and have literally risked their lives on a daily basis to provide Syrians with foods and basic services. Efforts inside of Syria by many of these activists have been supported and buttressed by efforts from Syrians in the diaspora, especially in Europe and the United States, and other recently displaced Syrians in Lebanon, Turkey, and neighboring countries.

Many relief groups operate inside Syria without any government or opposition support. They rely extensively on external networks of funding and, while they explicitly support the goals of the uprising, have focused their efforts almost exclusively on providing relief. Perhaps the best example of this today are the Syrian Civil Defense, also known as the White Helmets (Miller, 2014), who came together as a loose group of Syrians who simply wanted to identify ways in which they could help others affected by the conflict. The White Helmets are now an organized group of volunteers operating throughout nonregime areas who provide rescue operations to Syrians under regime bombardment. Many of their volunteers have received advanced medical training (very few were involved in the health-care field prior to the conflict) and have risked their lives on a daily basis. Their goal is simple: to provide rescue and relief efforts in the immediate aftermath of regime bombardment. Such work has saved many Syrian lives but has, unfortunately, caused the deaths of many volunteers.

Similar efforts by Syrians in the diaspora to provide relief efforts have been established. Umbrella organizations such as the Syrian American Medical Society (SAMS) and the Union of Syrian Medical Relief Organizations (UOSSM) have brought together international humanitarian organizations and Syrian NGOs, many of which did not exist prior to the conflict, in an effort to provide coordinated and widespread health services to Syrians inside and outside the country. These efforts have included everything from raising funds to pay doctors' salaries to the construction of underground hospitals (to avoid regime bombardment) and mobile health clinics. As the Syrian health situation has deteriorated so rapidly and the international community lags in its response, efforts by UOSSM and SAMS have buffered against further collapse of the health care system.

The humanitarian efforts of the White Helmets and Syrian diaspora organizations compliment the more sustained and widespread efforts of the local LCCs and other local organizations that have been ongoing since 2011. These organizations are often reliant on funding from Syrians abroad or from wealthy Arabs and Muslims keen on providing some relief efforts. Groups such as Najda Now (Assistance Now) provide food, clothing, and daily medicines to Syrians as well as psychological support to children suffering from trauma (de Elvira, 2013). Many of these organizations do not have a national reach and instead focus on efforts in particular locales and regions. Because many of these organizations lack funding and have capacity shortages they tend to concentrate on specific projects targeting specific communities. The group Jamiyyat Ghiras al-Nahda (Association of the Seeds of Resistance), for example, was, in 2012, providing relief efforts exclusively to the Damascene countryside (de Elvira, 2013). Organizations such as these have been extremely important in staving off even further humanitarian collapse. Unfortunately, they are mostly neglected in the headlines.

The absence of these organizations' efforts from the public eye should not obscure their importance in Syria and the role they play in the conflict. The LCCs have, from the outset, engaged in a wide range of humanitarian efforts that focused on addressing individual and household needs as well as providing emotional and psychological support to affected communities. The LCCs have referred to their collective relief efforts as Souriya Bil Alwan (Syria in Colors) to reflect the cross-sectarian and national efforts of the different groups operating under the LCC framework Among Syrians the LCC relief activists are known as the "unknown soldiers" because they work covertly and attempt to provide services beyond the control of regime and rebel forces (Abu Hamed, 2014).

These services range from youth-focused efforts to encourage play to relief efforts to provide clothing and housing to displaced Syrians. Most of their funding comes from Syrian expatriates who want to support relief efforts in the country with some support provided by international organizations. Regardless, LCC efforts have been focused on meeting Syrian needs and not addressing donor priorities or the needs of regime or rebel forces. The dependence on external support and their activities within rebel areas means that LCC efforts are not entirely autonomous and are subject to the physical and financial constraints imposed on them by the conflict. As the humanitarian crisis continues to worsen and relief efforts are stalled by the violence, the work of the LCCs and other groups inside of Syria will become increasingly important. The rise of a robust, committed, and active Syrian civil society has been one of the few foreseeable long-term positive impacts of the uprising.

The Syrian Tragedy

The Syrian conflict will have lasting impacts on generations of Syrians. The massive displacement of around half of the total population is a crisis that will not easily be undone or rectified even when the violence subsides. Syrians have suffered through an economically and physically devastating conflict that is redefining Syrian society. In addition to the generational impacts the conflict will have on Syrian families, many of which have been physically split up since 2011, there are long-term concerns about health care and education. Syrian access to health care inside the country and in neighboring countries has been dramatically reduced and Syrians are finding even the most basic health services to be increasingly inaccessible. At the same time, a majority of Syrian children are now outside of schools. The destruction of schools, migration of teachers, and the increasing levels of violence have restricted children's access to education. In refugee camps, a number of factors prohibit their enrollment in local schools as well.

The long-term consequences of Syria's "lost generation" will be impossible to predict. However, as the conflict persists the humanitarian crisis wrought by the violence will only deepen and compound.

Conclusion: Prospects for Resolution

In the preceding pages, I have attempted to outline what I see as the main factors behind the current political and military stalemate in Syria. Time will tell how long this stalemate persists and what long-term effects this has on the Syrian state and society. The goal of my analysis in this book has been to introduce readers to the main parties to the conflict and also to help the reader think analytically about why the Syrian conflict has taken on this particular trajectory. At this point, it is worth cautioning you, once again, about thinking that the conflict has a linear path. As I have tried to describe throughout the book, the conflict has many dynamics that are driving violence, the humanitarian crisis, and, ultimately, the prospects for a political resolution. With this in mind, it is difficult to chart what the future may hold for the millions of Syrians for whom the only certainty right now is uncertainty.

This should not, however, prevent us from thinking concretely about the question that should be on everyone's mind: what is to be done? How can the Syrian conflict be resolved? For these basic questions there are no immediate or simple answers. Fragmentation, both of Syria's territorial integrity and of the coherence of the various regime and rebel forces fighting one another, has ensured that the resolution to the Syrian conflict will not be an easy one. In the context of increasing violence and a humanitarian crisis that is occurring in parallel to the disintegration of the state and the carving up of Syrian territory into competing administrative units, where can a solution be found?

Under these circumstances a solution to the Syrian crisis cannot be thought of as a single problem, that is, as part of a large bargain that addresses all of the country's social, political, and economic problems. Such was the case in neighboring Lebanon when the Ta'if peace accords to end the civil war resulted in a postconflict order that looked much like the conflict order it sought to replace, minus civil violence. A solution to the Syrian crisis must be thought of then in much more holistic terms and in ways that address the multilayered complexities and problems wrought by the conflict. One of the main problems with the Geneva process, for example, was that it isolated certain elements of the conflict, particularly the issue of political transition, at the expense of others. Moreover, the Geneva process had by design excluded many of the local actors who were a part of the conflict and who had the power to shape its trajectory. Any solution must begin from the premise of being the outcome of an inclusive process that engages all of the major parties to the conflict, both domestic and international.

Given the multilayered complexity of the conflict, it is extremely difficult to think of singular solutions. Most serious observers of the Syrian conflict have long ago rejected the idea that it has a quick fix (Haddad, 2015; Heydemann, 2013a,b). Furthermore, it is a challenge to think of solutions when one must necessarily involve the very domestic and international actors who have caused the conflict in the first place. In most conflicts around the world, the main approach to resolution is to bring together the different parties, typically under international auspices, to negotiate some sort of collective agreement that satisfies nobody and everybody at the same time. This has been the basic premise of the Geneva framework, for example, and other similar proposals for a solution to the crisis.

In the remainder of this chapter, I would like to propose thinking about a solution to the Syrian crisis in very different terms. While I strongly believe that it is important to include all the major parties to the conflict in any agreement I believe that framing any resolution in terms of winners and losers poses serious problems for long-term stability, as this does not seriously address the grievances that gave rise to the conflict in the first place. Neither does it address those that arose during the course of the conflict. Instead of framing a solution in terms of who wins or loses, or who is included in the postconflict order, I would like to propose instead some foundational ideas for what a postconflict Syria would look like.

Throughout the course of this book I have emphasized the complexity and multilayered nature of the conflict. I believe that this complexity has to be embraced and engaged directly in any conversations about solutions. With this in mind, I believe that any solution(s) should address the four main problems that were addressed throughout this book: the fragmentation of the country, the social and humanitarian crisis, and the lack of political inclusion, and the need for a political transition process. In my view, any solution has to address these four problems. By definition, any singular bargain cannot address them all. In the pages that follow, then, I do not attempt to sketch out how a peace process can integrate all of these elements into a solution. Instead, I map out different ways in which solutions to these problems can be thought out.

In the subsequent section, I will delve deeper into the liberal peace approach to conflict resolution and discuss some of the plans (beyond the Geneva and Moscow processes) that have been proposed to resolve the Syrian crisis. While many of these proposals are genuine in their desire to end the violence and bring about a political transition, they have many blind spots and do not sufficiently address the many problems associated with the conflict. I will then transition to a discussion of the four main problems raised above and offer some possible ways in which they can be addressed. It is my strong belief that in the absence of any resolution to these problems the Syrian conflict will remain intractable.

Approaches to Solving the Syrian Conflict

The approach preferred by the international community to solve violent conflicts is that of liberal peace. This takes as its starting point the need to integrate multiple actors into the post-conflict state. It is highly problematic in conflict spaces and would accomplish very little toward alleviating the Syrian crisis. Unfortunately, it has been a preferred model of the international community and formed the basis of many ideas about transitional government as a solution to the crisis. In the liberal peace approach, planners argue that the establishment of strong state institutions is the best means of resolving conflict. This is what Beswick (2009) calls the "single sovereign" problem. Planners attempt to reinscribe sovereignty into the postconflict state by strengthening state institutions and integrating former adversaries into the new state. In this model, conflict is disincentivized by offering the material and political benefits of institutional access to the former conflict participants through their cooptation and integration into the postconflict order. These rewards come in the form of official positions, bureaucratic appointments, and so on. One only needs to look to Syria's neighbor Lebanon for an excellent example of a liberal peace approach to conflict resolution. The logic of this approach is simple: economic and political power accrued from integration into the state outweigh the benefits of conflict. Strengthening state institutions makes the sovereign state the locus of deliberation and debate (rather than the battlefield), the central provider and distributor of services and aid, and reestablishes the state's monopoly on violence.

These approaches are based on the faulty assumption that conflict occurs solely because different actors seek access to the state. This premise is extremely problematic in most conflict spaces but especially so in Syria, where the conflict has evolved from demands for political rights and regime change to a complicated violent conflict in which different groups pursue radically different and competing agendas, very few of which have anything to do with integrating into a postconflict state order. Today, the conflict requires resolution on multiple levels, beyond a single bargain between the major regional powers or a political agreement that integrates warlords and oppositionists into a rejuvenated state.

To this end, a number of new and old formulas have been proposed by commentators to solve the Syrian conflict. The diverse range of policies includes a commitment to arming the rebels, relegitimizing the regime and making it a counterterrorism partner, economically and administratively supporting nonregime areas, military intervention, reinvigorating the Geneva process, or linking resolution of the Syrian conflict to a larger regional settlement.

Yet, these policies aimed at resolving the Syrian conflict do not meaningfully address the underlying causes and the consequences of its violent evolution. Any steps toward sustainable long-term resolution need to take as a central point the role of the Syrian regime and its repressive apparatus, both before and after the uprising began. Similarly, the deteriorating socioeconomic conditions wrought by the years of marketization and agricultural neglect and their impacts on Syria's social stratification must be addressed. Any plan for resolution must also centralize the humanitarian issue and the safe and secure repatriation of Syrian refugees. Finally, any solution to the conflict must address how federal-governorate relations will look like in light of the emergence of different and competing administrative projects throughout Syria. Unfortunately, in the liberal peace mode of conflict resolution there is very little space for the articulation of such goals and wider societal needs in the context of conflict and postconflict politics. The goal of most peace agreements is simply to stop violence and not to rectify the social and political catastrophes wrought by it.

For the remainder of this book I intend to highlight what some approaches to the four main problems wrought by the conflict—fragmentation, social and humanitarian crisis, political transition, and violent armed groups—may look like. In doing so, I want to encourage a holistic understanding of such a solution and how it can be brought about. I am fully aware that such a holistic approach has not been taken in other contexts and that the severity of the Syrian crisis demands an immediate cessation of violence before all else. However, we should be weary, or at least wary, of any solutions that propose deflecting action on key issues for the future. We have seen in Lebanon, Iraq, Afghanistan, and countless other conflict zones how the desire to stop violence simply breeds more grievances, resentment, and, in the end, violence. Any solution to the Syrian crisis must begin from the idea that the solution must be permanent and not just a temporary measure.

Fragmentation

Syria is rapidly being divided into competing centers of authority and control. The country's northwestern, southern, and northeastern areas are being divided from one another and from the central heartland of the country north up through the coastal areas. The liberal peace approach to conflict resolution would view such decentralization as a problem to be corrected. In particular, in the aftermath of conflict, local political and administrative projects would be sidelined and the sovereign reach of the state extended throughout the country. This entails a dismantling of the formal and informal institutions of authority and governance that were established throughout a conflict.

In the case of Syria, the decentralization of authority should be institutionalized and integrated into any post-conflict order. Decentralization does not have to entail the emasculation of the sovereign state or the consecration of federal-governorate conflict into the postconflict order, such as has been the case between the federal Iraqi government and the Kurdistan Regional Government (KRG). Rather, decentralization can entail a clear and coherent division of powers between the federal, governorate, and local levels. Such a division of powers should reflect some of the main strengths of the local and village councils' activity during the course of the conflict, which ranges from providing municipal services to administering justice. The integration of the experiences and expertise of those who provided governance during the course of the conflict would be a first step toward alleviating some of the conflict conditions, providing social buy-in and acceptance of the post-conflict order, and recognizing the efforts of the activists and volunteers who held Syrian society together in the face of violent conflict.

More important, however, institutionalizing decentralization can help reestablish an effective public sector in a postconflict situation. Typically in postconflict spaces the collapse of the central state renders public service delivery ineffective, thus perpetuating some of the hardships experienced during the conflict. In this context, a number of studies have argued that decentralized local government can play an extremely important role in mitigating these negative effects and can actually improve governance, enhance public service delivery, and increase the credibility and legitimacy of the postconflict political order (Fox, 2007; Siegle and O'Mahony, 2006). Institutionalizing decentralization into any postconflict order would also satisfy local demands for greater control of their political affairs. Syria's social mosaic demands a nuanced political architecture that allows for the exercise of decision-making on the local level, of which, for decades under the Ba'ath Party, Syrians were deprived, as they were governed by a series of appointees and governors whose loyalty to the party, and not necessarily their administrative acumen, determined their suitability for the job.

Such an approach to postconflict resolution has been underway with modest success in many other parts of the world. In Uganda, for example, five different projects have been developed that link either the federal government or international organizations to local governments and which empower the latter to provide services to their communities (Boex et al., 2010). This model has recognized the importance and utility of local government providing postconflict services and is premised on the idea that recovery is essential to postconflict stability. Other examples of institutionalizing decentralization include embedding decentralization into the political resolution of the conflict (Macedonia) or relying on decentralized authorities to deliver infrastructure or public services in the postconflict period, effectively replacing the central state (Cambodia) (Boex et al., 2010). In the Arab and Islamic context, especially Afghanistan and Iraq, the tendency has been to promote centralization rather than decentralization. Such a strategy in Syria would have disastrous consequences for the ability of authorities to provide social services and for the legitimacy and credibility of the postconflict order.

Thus, any approach to the resolution of the Syrian conflict should consider the key question that emerged during the course of the conflict: how to institutionalize decentralized authority. Everything from local councils to localized curriculums to new judicial systems has emerged in the nonregime areas. Capturing these modalities, rather then peripheralizing them, can help bring about a solution and should be an essential component of any attempts to solve the conflict.

Social and humanitarian crisis

The demands of ending violence in many conflict zones usually outweighs agreement over other key areas of postconflict life. In many postconflict countries, social policy is severely neglected at the expense of establishing the state's monopoly on violence and disarming armed groups. To put it simply, postconflict planners focus almost exclusively on the political and institutional arrangements of the state at the expense of thinking about key questions of social provision and social policy more broadly. Here, social policy refers to policies that directly affect the lives of those in postconflict zones, whether related to housing, food distribution, employment, services, or, in the case of displaced people, repatriation. Many of these areas are severely neglected in postconflict spaces; in perpetrating such neglect, planners unintentionally reproduce grievances and problems associated with the conflict.

In Iraq, for example, the Coalition Provisional Authority (CPA) had no defined social policy when it took over control of Iraq. The set of ideologically driven policies pursued by the CPA (Abboud, 2008) emasculated the state and dramatically reduced the capacity of the public sector to engage in the reconstruction process. Despite years of displacement under the Saddam Hussein regime, the CPA did not even develop a policy for the repatriation of refugees. Unfortunately, such experiences for the displaced have been replicated in many other conflict zones.

While any solution to the Syrian conflict must engage the political grievances and dynamics of the conflict, I contend that addressing the social and humanitarian crisis should be given importance equal to that of the political solution. This would require a concerted and long-term commitment from the international community, including states and INGOs, to the provision of resources and support services to local government bodies and civil society to provide postconflict reconstruction services. Social policy must address multiple crises at once: the brain drain, the collapse of the health care system, unemployment, refugee and IDP repatriation, and the physical reconstruction of homes, among other crises. Doing so requires more than just the coordination of federal, governorate, and local bodies within Syria, but a sustained effort on the part of the international community to channel needed resources to these bodies in order to assess, develop, and implement reconstruction plans that address the humanitarian crisis.

Although such programs may not be contained in the provisions of a peace agreement, they are nevertheless prerequisites for addressing the conflict and preventing it from being intractable. Reinvigorating Syria's social service provision system and establishing a strong social safety net would not only encourage repatriation but would foster social stability and help Syrians return to some degree of normalcy in the years and decades after the conflict ends. A commitment from international donors and actors to the longterm social stability of Syria will be as important to the stability of the country than any political agreement hatched in Geneva or elsewhere. Social stability in Syria will not follow from a political agreement to end the conflict. Such stability requires a material basis. As Cocozelli (2006) has argued, social policy is largely absent in postconflict reconstruction plans, where planners typically focus on normative macroeconomic indicators to assess the economic well-being of the country.

Moreover, when social policy is incorporated into postconflict plans it is often done on a project basis and is not pursued holistically in relation to other social issues.

Any solution to the Syrian conflict must thus take social policy seriously and incorporate a robust, holistic plan to address the short- and longterm social and humanitarian crisis wrought by the conflict. This will necessarily include engagement with local, national, and international actors. While such engagement will certainly raise coordination and financing issues, progress on social issues will be a vital component of stability in Syria after the conflict ends. Rather than building from scratch, any solution should engage the ongoing efforts of Syrian civil society (discussed in the previous chapter) and of informal social networks to provide social services and relief to Syrians. Working through these existing networks will not only strengthen them but will incorporate diaspora and local activists into the postconflict order.

Political transition

Almost all of the parties to the Syrian conflict agree that there is no military solution and that the preferred path is through a political process that ends the conflict. These pronouncements have come from both regime supporters and rebel groups, even while they continue to support violence and armament. The question of political transition, or, to put it more broadly, how the postconflict political system will be structured in the aftermath of the conflict, is a difficult and problematic one. Given the regime's history of cosmetic political reforms it is unlikely that the main decision-makers would, given the current stalemate, submit to a political transition that undermines their current power. This is likely to change as the conflict evolves and the regime inner circles absorb pressure from the armed opposition and, perhaps, their international patrons, for a negotiated solution.

With the notable exception of ISIS, which rejects the idea of the sovereign Syrian state (Nielsen, 2015) all of the major armed and nonviolent actors have some stake in the survival of the Syrian state. Many of these groups, from the PYD to

JAN to the regime, have a substantial social base that cannot be peripheralized as part of any political solution to the conflict. Currently, many of these groups reject the very idea of a political process inclusive of the other. Such is the case for the regime and for many of the rebel groups. This impasse and the rejection of the other as a part of any postconflict arrangement in Syria has to be overcome in order for there to be a viable solution. While it may be the case that supporters of the regime and of the FSA deplore the idea of incorporating the other into any political settlement, there is no alternative given the military stalemate.

Unfortunately, the current stalemate has rendered politics dead. All parties to the conflict have committed to a military solution while paying lip service to a political solution. Yet the latter has to be based on some sorts of political compromise that regime and rebel forces are unwilling to make. Where does this leave space for politics and how can a political transition be taken seriously and accepted by all sides? The answer to this question may lie in the issue of decentralization discussed earlier. The incorporation of various administrative structures, such as local councils or Sharia councils, may placate supporters of the armed groups and place enough pressure on them to accept a political compromise. Ultimately, both the regime and rebel groups generate their legitimacy from their social bases. Targeting these bases with political arrangements and institutional structures, particularly decentralization and enhanced local decision-making, could enhance the legitimacy of any solution and enable postconflict political order.

Too often political settlements focus on the incorporation of warlords or other conflict elites into a postconflict order. Such incorporation misses the larger picture and fails to address the needs of the social bases of support that different parties to a conflict enjoy. The larger issue with a political transition in Syria will not be the creation of a parliament or political system that distributes power according to sect or other fixed identities that do not hold the same meaning in the Syrian context as they may hold elsewhere in the region. We have seen how the attempts to create a political system based on sectarian and ethnic representation in Iraq have gone wildly wrong and led to a worsening of the violence and a near-total breakdown of the state in that country. The imposition of a political model of representation that fulfills Western imaginaries about how Syrian society is stratified and organized must be rejected in any sort of political solution in favor of political models that address the social, political, and geographic realities of Syrian support for different parties to the conflict. Any attempt to impose a sectarian model on Syria as a resolution to the conflict will likely breed the same hostilities, violence, and grievances that have occurred in Iraq.

All of this means that a political transition must be inclusive of all parties to the conflict. A political solution must include a very clear delineation of powers between different levels of government and specific and identifiable mechanisms for the incorporation of different social groups into the Syrian state and political system. Doing so need not rely on sectarian formulas of representation; it can rather address the political needs and grievances of a wide range of Syrians, whether they are supporters of the regime or of the PYD.

Conclusion

At the risk of ending the story I have been telling with a chimerical proposition, I believe that any solution to the Syrian conflict, let alone any discussion of one, must begin with Syrians themselves. While the space for such discussion is currently circumscribed in many ways, the only way in which a longterm solution to the Syrian conflict that addresses the major needs around fragmentation, the social and humanitarian crisis, and the need for an inclusive political transition, can be achieved is if it emerges from the Syrians who have suffered so tragically during the course of the conflict. How such a space can be cultivated on a national level is difficult to fathom under the current circumstances, but one only has to look to the work of Syrians inside and outside of the country, who have attempted to rescue their nation from ruin while simultaneously putting forth ideas for a new Syria, to find promise for the emergence of such space.

Whereas prior to the conflict Syrian discussions of citizenship and political life had been severely repressed by the regime, they occur today with frequency and vigor. Media organizations such as Radio Souriali contain programming targeting all Syrians, regardless of sect or locale, and have placed great emphasis on telling the story of the Syrian uprising from the perspective of average Syrians. Similar media projects have been put forth by Syrians in the diaspora (Anden-Papadopolous and Pantti, 2013). Relief organizations, from the White Helmets to SAMS, provide services that have buttressed against total social collapse and they have often done so with minimal support from the outside and under the dual pressures of sustained regime bombardment and the mistrust of rebel groups. Throughout the course of the conflict there are countless examples of Syrians coming together in ways that provide an alternative vision and path to the violence and humanitarian tragedy being inflicted on the country today.

How this alternative can become the mainstream or at least a viable substitute to the current madness is a difficult question. On the one hand, support for the conflict is very low among Syrians, many of whom want the violence to end and for there to be any solution, regardless of how potentially flawed, that can provide some reprieve from besiegement, violence, and displacement. Discontent with the conflict from both regime and rebel supporters is an important factor that may propel the parties toward a negotiated solution, although this is unlikely in the short term. All Syrians, regardless of affiliation, have in common the objective fear of living in a conflict zone fraught with violence and the constant threat of violence. On the other hand, the Syrian conflict is deeply embedded in regional rivalries and has emerged as a proxy for playing out regional conflicts. The pressures of such rivalries mean that the decisions and possibilities to end the conflict are increasingly out of the hands of Syrians themselves. Such a prospect is indeed a frightening one and does not bode well for the immediate future of the country.

Today, the conflict is at a painful stalemate in which a political solution seems far outside of the realm of possibility. David Lesch's claim that a protracted stalemate was one scenario for the future of the Syrian conflict has unfortunately been realized (2013). Until the space for such a solution becomes larger the prospects for an end to the conflict will remain small. Unfortunately, until then, Syrians will continue to suffer as the dreams, hopes, and goals that gave rise to the uprising in the first place become more and more unattainable.

References

Abbas, H. (2011) The dynamics of the uprising in Syria. *Jadaliyya*, 19 October.

Abboud, S. (2008). The transitions paradigm and the case of Syria. In S. Abboud & F. Arslanian, *Syria's Economy and the Transition Paradigm*. St. Andrews, Scotland: Lynne Rienner Publishers.

———. (2009). Syrian trade policy. S. Abboud and S. Said, *Syrian Foreign Trade and Economic Reform*. St. Andrews, Scotland: Lynne Rienner Publishers.

———. (2012). Economic transformation and diffusion of authoritarian power in Syria. In Sadiki, L. and Heiko Wimmonen (eds.). *Unmaking Power: Negotiating the Democratic Void in the Arab Middle East*. London: Routledge, 159–77.

———. (2013). Capital flight and the consequences of the war economy. *Jadaliyya*, 18 March.

———. (2013b). Syria's business elite: Between political alignment and hedging their bets. *SWP Comments*. August 2013.

———. (2015). Locating the "social" in the social market economy. In Hinnebusch, R., and Tina Zintl (eds.), *Syria: From Reform to Revolt*. Syracuse, NY: Syracuse University Press, 45–65.

Abboud, S. & Muller, B. (2012). *Rethinking Hizballah: Legitimacy, Authority, Violence*. Farnham, U.K.: Ashgate.

Abushakra, R. (2013). Main Syrian opposition group in exile chooses government. *The Wall Street Journal*. 12 November.

Abu Hamed, A. (2014). Syria's local coordination committees: The dynamo of a hijacked revolution. In *Knowledge Programme Civil Society in West Asia Special Bulletin, 5*, May 2014.

Al-Ayed, Abdulnasser (2015). *Jihadists and the Syrian Tribes: Transient Hegemony and Chronic Dilemmas*. Arab Reform Initiative.

Al-Wasl, Z. (2015). Interim govt. faces severity of financial crisis as funds deplete. *The Syrian Observer*, 24 March.

Alagha, J. (2006). *The Shifts in Hizbullah's Ideology*. Amsterdam: Amsterdam University Press.

Ali, Abdallah Suleiman (2015). Translated by Rani Geha. Jabhat al-Nusra slammed for not severing ties with al-Qaeda. *Al-Monitor*, March 11. Accessed March 15.

Ali, Nour (2011). "Syrian regime steps up propaganda war amid bloody crackdown on protests." *The Guardian*. 20 July.

Allison, R. (2013). Russia and Syria: Explaining alignment with a regime in crisis. *International Affairs* 89(4): 795–823.

Anden-Papadopolous, K., & Pantti, M. (2013). The media work of Syrian diaspora activists. *International Journal of Communication*, 7, 2185–206.

Anna, C. (2015). Report says 640,200 Syrians live under siege. *The Columbian*. 20 March.

Aranki, D., & Kalis, O. (2014) Limited legal status for refugees from Syria in Lebanon. *Forced Migration Review*, 47 (Sept) pp. 17–19.

Aras, B., & Falk, R. (2015). Authoritarian "geopolitics" of survival in the Arab Spring. *Third World Quarterly*, 36(2): 322–36.

Asseburg, M. & Wimmen, H. (2014). Geneva II—A Chance to Contain the Syrian Civil War. *SWP Comments*, 10 (January): 1–7.

Bank, André Roy Karadag (2013). The "Ankara Moment": The politics of Turkey's regional power in the Middle East. *Third World Quarterly*, 34(2): 287–304.

Barmin, Y. (2015). Moscow's 11 principles for peace in Syria. *Russia Direct*. 29 January.

Batatu, H. (1999). *Syria's Peasantry, the Descendants of Its Lesser Rural Notables, and Their Politics*. Princeton, NJ: Princeton University Press.

Benraad, M. (2011) Iraq's tribal "Sahwa": Its rise and fall. *Middle East Policy Council*, Spring 18(1).

Boex, J., Kimble, D. & Pigey, J. (2010). Decentralized local government as a modality for post-conflict recovery and development: An emerging natural experiment in Northern Uganda. Urban Institute Center on International Development and Governance. *IDG Working Paper No. 2010–01*.

Byman, D. (2014). Sectarianism afflicts the New Middle East. *Survival: Global Politics and Strategy*, 56(1): 79–100.

Carpenter, Ami, Anu Lawrence & Milburn Line (2013). Contested authorities alternatives to State law and order in post-conflict Guatamela. *Journal of Law and Conflict Resolution*, 5(3): 48–61.

Carter Center The. (2013). *Syria Countrywide Conflict Report #1*. Atlanta: The Carter Center.

Charap, S. (2013). Russia, Syria and the doctrine of intervention. *Survival: Global Politics and Strategy* 55(1): 35–41.

Coles, I. (2015). Iraqi Kurds say Islamic State used chlorine gas against them. *Reuters*. 14 March.

Dahi, Omar. S. & Munif, Y. (2011). Revolts in Syria: Tracking the convergence between authoritarianism and neoliberalism. *Journal of Asian and African Studies*, 47(4): 323–32.

Dannreuther, R. (2015). Russia and the Arab Spring: Supporting the counter-revolution. *Journal of European Integration*, 37(1): 77–94.

Daoud, D. (2014). Hezbollah: The party of Iran, not Lebanon. *The Washington Institute*. 3 December.

Dark, E. (2014). Syrian regime ignores supporters' rising anger. *al-Monitor*. 7 October.

De Châtel, F. (2014). The role of drought and climate change in the Syrian uprising: Untangling the triggers of the revolution. *Middle Eastern Studies*, 50(4): 521–35.

Dreyfuss, B. (2014). US Should Back Syria's Assad Against ISIS. *The Nation*. 3 July.

Droz-Vincent, Philippe (2014). "State of Barbary" (Take Two): From the Arab Spring to the return of violence in Syria. *Middle East Journal*, 68(1): 33–58.

Durac, V. (2015). Social movements, protest movements and cross-ideological coalitions: The Arab uprisings re-appraised. *Democratization*, 22(2): 239–58.

El-Hokayem, E. (2007). Hizballah and Syria: Outgrowing the proxy relationship. *Washington Quarterly*, 30(2): 35–52.

El-Husseini, R. (2012). *Pax Syriana: Elite Politics in Postwar Lebanon*. Syracuse, NY: Syracuse University Press.

Evans, D. & Karouny, M. (2013). Iranian Guards commander killed in Syria. *Reuters*. 14 Feb.

Farouk-Alli, A. (2014). Sectarianism in Alawi Syria: Exploring the paradoxes of politics and religion. *Journal of Muslim Minority Affairs*, 34(3): 207–26.

Fisher, N. (2014). Foreword: The inheritance of loss. *Forced Migration Review*, 47(Sept.): 4–5.

Fox, W. (2007). Fiscal decentralization in post-conflict countries. *Fiscal Reform and Economic Governance Project: Best Practice.* (http://www.fiscalreform.net/)

Gelvin, J. (1999). *Divided Loyalties: Nationalism and Mass Politics in Syria at the Close of Empire.* Berkeley: University of California Press.

Gladstone, R. (2012). Resigning as envoy to Syria, Annan casts wide blame. *New York Times.* 2 Aug.

Goodarzi, J. (2009). *Syria and Iran: Diplomatic Alliance and Power Politics in the Middle East.* London: I.B. Tauris.

———. (2013). Iran and Syria at the crossroads: The fall of the Tehran-Damascus axis? Viewpoints, 35: Wilson Center.

Gorenburg, D. (2012). Why Russia Supports Repressive Regimes in Syria and the Middle East. PONARS Eurasia Policy Memo 198. June 2012.

Gorman, S., Malas, N., and Bradly, M. (2014). Brutal efficiency: The secret to Islamic State's success. *The Wall Street Journal.* 3 September.

Guardian (2012). Syrian forces shell central Homs, breaking cease-fire, activists claim. *The Guardian.* 14 April.

Haddad, B. (2004). The formation and development of economic networks in Syria: Implications for economic and fiscal reforms, 1986–2000. In Heydemann, Steven (ed.), *Networks of Privilege: Rethinking the Politics of Economic Reform in the Middle East,* New York: Palgrave, 39–78.

———. (2011). *Business Networks in Syria: The Political Economy of Authoritarian Resilience.* Stanford, CA: Stanford University Press.

———. (2012). Syria, the Arab uprisings, and the political economy of authoritarian resilience. *Interface,* 4(1): May, 113–30.

———. (2012b). Syria's state bourgeoisie: An organic backbone for the regime. *Middle East Critique,* 21(3): Fall.

———. (2015). Four years on: No easy answers in Syria (Part II). *Jadaliyya.* 30 March.

Hashem, A. (2015). Iran's new strategy in Syria. *al-Monitor.* 15 May.

Hassan, H. (2013). The Gulf states: United against Iran, divided over Islamists. Barnes-Dacey, Julien, and Daniel Levy (eds.). *The Regional Struggle for Syria.* European Council on Foreign Relations, 17–24.

Henderson, E. & Singer, D. (2002). New wars and rumors of new wars. *International Interactions,* 28(2): 165–90.

Heydemann, S. (1999). *Authoritarianism in Syria: Institutions and Social Conflict 1946–1970*. Ithaca, NY: Cornell University Press.

———. (2007). Upgrading authoritarianism in the Arab world. In *The Saban Center for Middle East Policy at the Brookings Institution, 13* (Oct.).

———. (2013a). The big picture: Envisioning a best possible peace for Syria—and what it will take to reach it. *Foreign Policy*. 6 December.

———. (2013b). Syria and the future of authoritarianism. *Journal of Democracy*, 24(4): 59–73.

Hinnebusch, R. (1989). *Peasant and Bureaucracy in Ba'athist Syria: The Political Economy of Rural Development* (Westview Special Studies on the Middle East). Boulder, CO: Westview Press.

———. (1990). *Authoritarian Power and State Formation in Ba'thist Syria: Army, Party, and Peasant* (Westview Special Studies on the Middle East). Boulder, CO: Westview Press.

———. (2001). *Syria: Revolution from Above*. London: Routledge.

———. (2009). The Political Economy of Populist Authoritarianism. In *The State and the Political Economy of Reform in Syria*, edited by Raymond Hinnebusch and Søren Schmidt. St. Andrews, Scotland: St. Andrews Papers on Contemporary Syria, Boulder: Lynne Rienner Publishers.

———, ed. (2010). *Agriculture and Reform in Syria*. Boulder, CO: Lynne Rienner.

———. (2012). Syria from "authoritarian upgrading" to revolution? *International Affairs*, 88(1): 95–113.

Hokayem, E. (2013). *Syria's Uprising and the Fracturing of the Levant*. London: Routledge.

Hsu, Carolyn L. (2007). *Creating Market Socialism: How Ordinary People Are Shaping Class and Status in China*. Durham, NC: Duke University Press.

Hubbard, B., Krauss, C., and Schmitt, E. (2014). Rebels in Syria claim control of resources. *New York Times*. 28 January.

Hughes, G. A. (2014). Syria and the perils of proxy warfare. *Small Wars & Insurgencies*, 25(3): 522–38.

International Crisis Group (2013). Syria's Kurds: A struggle within a struggle. *Middle East Report 136*. 22 January.

———. (2014). Flight of Icarus? The PYD's precarious rise in Syria. *Middle East Report #151*. 8 May.

Ismail, Salwa (2011). The Syrian uprising: Imagining and performing the nation. *Studies in Ethnicity and Nationalism*, 11(3): 538–49.

———. (2013). Urban subalterns in the Arab revolutions: Cairo and Damascus in comparative perspective. *Comparative Studies in Society and History*, 55(4): 865–94.

Kahf, M. (2014). The Syrian revolution, then and now. *Peace Review: A Journal of Social Justice*, 26(4): 556–63.

Kaldor, M. (1999). *New and Old Wars: Organized Violence in a Global Era*. Stanford, CA: Stanford University Press.

———. (2012). *New and Old Wars: Organized Violence in a Global Era*, 3rd ed. Cambridge: Polity.

Khaddour, K. (2014). Securing the Syrian regime. *Sada*, Carnegie Endowment for International Peace. 3 June. (http://carnegie endowment.org/sada/index.cfm?fa=show&article=55783&solr _hilite=)

Khoury, Philip S. (1983). *Urban notables and Arab nationalism: The politics of Damascus 1860–1920*. Cambridge: Cambridge University Press.

Kirisci, K. & Salooja, R. (2014). Northern exodus: How Turkey can integrate Syrian refugees. *Foreign Affairs*. 15 April.

Kleinfeld, R. (2013). The case for arming Syrian rebels. *The Wall Street Journal*. 24 February.

Kurdistan National Congress (2014). Canton based democratic autonomy of Rojava: A transformation process from dictatorship to democracy. May. (https://peaceinkurdistancampaign.files .wordpress.com/2011/11/rojava-info-may-2014.pdf)

Landis, J. & Pace, J. (2007). The Syrian opposition. *Washington Quarterly*, 30(1): 45–68.

Lawson, F. (1997). Private capital and the state in contemporary Syria. *Middle East Report 203: Lebanon and Syria, The Geopolitics of Change*. 8–13, 30.

Leenders, R. (2012). Collective action and mobilization in Dar'a: An anatomy of the onset of Syria's popular uprising. *Mobilization*, 17(4): 419–34.

Leenders, Reinoud & Heydemann, Steven (2012). Popular mobilization in Syria: Opportunity and threat, and the social networks of the early risers. *Mediterranean Politics*, 17(2), 139–59.

Lekas Miller, A. (2014). Syria's White Helmets—The most dangerous job in the world. *Waging Nonviolence*. 25 Sept.

Lesch, D. (2013a) *Syria: The Fall of the House of Assad*. New Haven, CT: Yale University Press.

———. (2013b). The unknown future of Syria. *Mediterranean Politics*, 18(1): 97–103.

Lund, A. (2012). *Syrian Jihadism. UI brief #13*, Swedish Institute of International Affairs.

———. (2015). Who are the pro-Assad militias? *Carnegie Endowment for International Peace*. 2 March.

Lynch, M., Freelon, D., and Aday, S. (2013). Syria in the Arab Spring: The integration of Syria's conflict with the Arab uprisings, 2011–2013. *Research & Politics* 1(3).

Macias, A. and Bender, J. (2014). Here's how the world's richest terrorist group makes millions every day. *Business Insider*. 27 August.

Mackreath, H. (2014). The role of host communities in north Lebanon. *Forced Migration Review*, 47 (Sept.): 19–21.

Malantowicz, A. (2013). Civil war in Syria and the "new wars" debate. *Amsterdam Law Forum*, 5(3): 52–60.

Miles, T. (2014). WFP suspends food aid for 1.7 million Syrian refugees. *Reuters*. 1 December.

Moret, E. (2015). Humanitarian impacts of economic sanctions on Iran and Syria. *European Security*, 24(1): 120–40.

Mufti, Malik (1996). *Sovereign Creations: Pan-Arabism and Political Order in Syria and Iraq*. Ithaca: Cornell University Press.

Nielsen, R. (2015). Does the Islamic State believe in sovereignty? *Islamism in the IS Age*. 17 March, 28–31.

Norwegian Refugee Council. (2015). Failing Syria: Assessing the impact of UN Security Council Resolutions in protecting and assisting civilians in Syria. Oslo: Norway.

Oesch, L. (2014). Mobility as a solution. *Forced Migration Review* 47 (Sept.): 48.

O'Toole, J. (2012). Billions at stake as Russia backs Syria. *CNN Money*, 10 Feb.

Oweis, Khaled Yacoub (2015). *The Last Bastion of the Syrian Revolt: Southern Syria Offers Non-military Venues to Strengthen the Moderates*. SWP Comments #5. Berlin: German Institute for International and Security Affairs.

Owen, R. (2012). *The Rise and Fall of Arab Presidents for Life*. Cambridge, MA: Harvard University Press.

Perthes, V. (2001) The political economy of the Syrian succession. *Survival: Global Politics and Strategy*, 43(1): 143–54.

Phillips, C. (2015). Sectarianism and conflict in Syria. *Third World Quarterly*, 36(2): 357–76.

Pierret, T. (2013). External support and the Syrian insurgency. *Foreign Policy*. 9 August.

Pierret, T. and Selvik, K. (2009). Limits of "authoritarian upgrading" in Syria: Private welfare, Islamic charities, and the rise of the Zayd Movement. *International Journal of Middle East Studies*, 41(4): 595–614.

Pizzi, M. (2015). Syrian opposition to snub Moscow peace talks invite. *Al Jazeera.* 17 January.

Podder, Sukanya (2014). Mainstreaming the non-state in bottom-up state- building: Linkages between rebel governance and post-conflict legitimacy. *Conflict, Security & Development,* 1–31.

Rawan, B., and Imran, S. (2013). Framing the Syrian uprising: Comparative analysis of *Khaleej Times* and *The New York Times. Journal of Social Sciences and Humanities,* 21(1).

Rubenstein, L. (2011). Post-conflict health reconstruction: Search for a policy. *Disasters* 35(4): 680–700.

Ruiz de Elvira, L. (2013). The Syrian civil society in the face of revolt. In *TEPSIS Papers,* Oct. 2013, 1–5.

Saadullah, V. (2014). Syrian Kurdish refugees struggle to find affordable housing. Trans. S. Utku Bila. *Al Monitor.* 6 Oct.

Sadiki, L. (2011). The Bouazizi "big bang." *Al Jazeera.* 29 Dec.

Sadjadpour, K. (2013). Iran's unwavering support to Assad's Syria. *Carnegie Endowment for International Peace.* 27 August.

Sahner, C. (2014). *Among the Ruins: Syria's Past and Present.* Oxford: Oxford University Press.

Salloukh, B. F. (2013). The Arab uprisings and the geopolitics of the Middle East. *The International Spectator: Italian Journal of International Affairs,* 48(2): 32–46.

Sayigh, Y. (2012) Above the state: The officers' republic in Egypt. Paper, Carnegie Middle East Center.

Seale, Patrick (1990). *Asad: The Struggle for the Middle East.* London: University of California Press.

Seeberg, P. (2014). The EU and the Syrian crisis: The use of sanctions and the regime's strategy for survival. *Mediterranean Politics,* 1–18.

Seifan, Samir (2010). *Syria on the Path to Economic Reform.* Boulder: Lynne Rienner.

Shaery-Eisenlohr, R. (2008). *Shi'ite Lebanon: Transnational Religion and the Making of National Identities.* New York: Columbia University Press.

Siegle, J. & O'Mahony, P. (2006). Assessing the merits of decentralization as a conflict mitigation strategy, Office of Democracy and Governance, USAID, Washington DC.

Slavin, B. (2015). Shiite militias mixed blessing in Iraq, Syria. *Al Monitor.* 2 Feb.

Sood, A. & Seferis, L. (2014). Syrians contributing to Kurdish economic growth. *Forced Migration Review,* 47 (Sept.): 14–17.

Sottimano, A. (2008). Ideology and discourse in the era of Baathist reforms: Towards an analysis of authoritarian governmentality."

Hinnebusch, Raymond (ed.), *Changing Regime Discourse and Reform in Syria*, Boulder, CO: Lynne Rienner.

Staniland, Paul (2012). States, insurgents, and wartime political orders. *Perspectives on Politics, 10*(2): 243–64.

Steenkamp, Christina (2014). *Violent Societies: Networks of Violence in Civil War and Peace*. London: Palgrave.

Stein, A. (2015). Turkey's evolving Syria strategy: Why Ankara backs Al-Nusra but shuns ISIS. *Foreign Affairs*. 9 February.

Strategic Comments. (2012). Russia's Syrian stance: Principled self interest. *Strategic Comments, 18*(7): 1–3.

Suleiman Ali, A. (2015). Noose tightens around Jabhat al-Nusra. Trans. S. Abboud. *Al Monitor*. 18 March.

Syrian Center for Policy Research (2015). *Syria Alienation and Violence: Impact of Syria Crisis Report 2014*. Damascus: Syrian Center for Policy Research.

Taylor, P. (2015). "It's God's gift." Islamic State fills coffers with Iraqi government cash. *The Guardian*. 21 April.

Trombetta, L. (2014). The EU and the Syrian crisis as viewed from the Middle East. *The International Spectator: Italian Journal of International Affairs, 49*(3): 27–39.

United Nations High Commission for Refugees (2014). *Syria Response Plan*. New York: United Nations.

United Nations Children's Fund (2013). *Syria's Children: A Lost Generation?*

USAID. (2015). Crisis in Syria. (http://www.usaid.gov/crisis/syria)

Utas, M. (ed.) (2012). Introduction: Bigmanity and network governance in Africa. In *African Conflict and Informal Power: Big Men and Networks*. London: Zed Books, 1–34.

Valeriano, B., & Marin, V. (2010). Pathways to interstate war: A qualitative comparative analysis of the steps to war theory. *Josef Korbel Journal of Advanced International Studies, 2,* 1–27.

Von Maltzahn, N. (2013). *The Syria-Iran Axis: Cultural Diplomacy and International Relations in the Middle East*. London: I.B. Tauris.

Wall Street Journal (2011). Interview with Syrian President Bashar al-Assad. 31 January.

Wezeman, P. (2013) Arms transfers to Syria. In *SIPRI Yearbook 2013 Armaments, Disarmament and International Security*. Oxford: Oxford University Press, 269–73.

Wieland, C. (2012). *Syria—A Decade of Lost Chances: Repression and Revolution from Damascus Spring to Arab Spring*. Seattle, WA: Cune Press.

Windrem, R. (2014). Who's funding ISIS? Wealthy Gulf "angel investors," officials say. *NBC News*. 21 September.

White, B. (2012). *The Emergence of Minorities in the Middle East: The Politics of Community in French Mandate Syria*. Edinburgh: Edinburgh University Press.

Yilmaz, N. (2013). Syria: The view from Turkey. *Commentary*. European Council on Foreign Relations. 19 June.

Index

Abbas, Hassan, 63, 75
Abboud, S., 35–6, 37, 40, 43, 75, 79, 114, 123, 131, 206, 222
Abdel-Nasser, Gamal. *see* Nasser, Gamal
Abu Hamed, A., 212
Abushakra, R., 181
activists, 68–69. *see also* protesters
  Ba'ath Party and, 24–7
  networks of, 9, 45, 71
  political, 65
  repression of, 51
Afghanistan, U.S.-led war in, 39
Aflaq, Michel, 23, 24–5
agrarian reform policies, 22–3
agricultural subsidies, decline of, 37–8
agriculture
  landownership and, 15–16
  shifting away from, 5, 37–9
  social stratification based on, 17–19

Ahrar al-Sham, 97
  Jabhat an-Nusra and, 97, 99–100
Ahrar as-Sham, 140, 142
  in Geneva II process, 153
al-Assad, Bashar
  assumption of power of, 51
  foreign relations under, 39–40
  political crackdown and economic liberalization under, 14
  rise of, 34–5
  rule of, 35–40
  Wall Street Journal interview of, 56
al-Assad, Colonel Riad, 88
al-Assad, Hafiz, 25
  corrective revolution of, 29–30
  death of, 34
  liberalization under, 32–4
  revolution and rule of, 13–14
al-Atrash, Sultan, 20
al-Baghdadi, abu Bakr, 106–7, 172–3

al-Bateesh, Mithaq, 90
al-Din al-Bitar, Salah, 23
al-Fajr movement, 142
al-Hariri, Rafik, assassination
        of, 52–3
al-Hawrani, Akram, 22–3
al-Julani, Abu
        Mohmmaed, 106
al-Jundi, Abd al-Karim, 25
al-Maliki, Nouri, 106
al-Qaeda groups
    ideology of, 97–8
    transnational goals of, 140
al-Qaeda in Iraq, 104–6
    forming Majlis Shura
        al-Mujahideen, 106
al-Qusayr assault, 113–14
al-Sisi, Abdel Fattah, 124
al-Thani, Hamad bin
        Khalifa, 123–4
al-Thani, Tamin bin
        Hamad, 123–4
al-Watan coalition, 76
Alagha, J., 131
Alawi community, 26, 29, 183
Aleppo
    ceasefires in, 156, 157
    Councils in, 180
    militarized opposition in, 95
    refugees from, 195
Aleppo Shari'a Committee
        (ASC), 177
Ali, Nour, 57
Allison, R., 127
alternative governance, 163–4
Amal party, 40
Anden-Papadopolous, K. 227
Annan, Kofi, 150–52
Arab Ba'ath Socialist Party, 23
Arab Gulf countries,
        rapprochement
        with, 30–1

Arab League, in Libya
        intervention, 121
Arab nationalism, 20–1, 22,
        25
Arab Socialist Party (ASP), 23
Arab Spring, 55
Arab states, in Syrian
        conflict, 10, 118,
        121–6, 144. see also
        specific countries
Arab unity, 25–6
Arab uprisings, 54–5
    militarization of, 56
Aranki, D., 202
Aras, B., 79, 127
armed opposition, 83–108
    fragmentation of, 92–7
    proliferation of, 118–19
    rivalries among, 95–7
arms industry, concern with
        regional
        instability, 129–30
army
    loyalty of, 31–2
    purges in, 22
Army of Islam, 84
Arsal, abducted soldiers
        in, 203–4
Assad, Asma, 44
Asseburg, M., 151
authority, decentralization
        of, 220–2
Ayyam al-Hourriya (Freedom
        Days), 71

Ba'ath Party, 9
    Arab nationalism and, 22
    assumption of power by, 12
    coming to power, 26–8, 29
    emergence of, 3
    fragmentation of, 26–7
    instability preceding, 13

interests of, 21
pillars of power of, 31–2
pro- and anti-unionists
   in, 25–6
radicalization of, 25–6
reestablishing structures
   of, 24–5
rise of, 24–8
rural-minoritarian leadership
   in, 26–7, 29
social base of, 27–8
Ba'athist coup, 3, 8, 28–9
Bahrain protests, 55–6
Bank, André, 40
Barmin, Y., 159
barrel bombs, 147
Barzani, Massoud, 102
Batatu, H., 23, 27
Bender, J., 107
Benraad, M., 105
Beswick, D. 218
"blowback" fear, 139
Boex, J., 221–2
Bogdanov, Mikhail, 158
Bouazizi, Mohammed, self-
   immolation of, 54–5
Brahimi, Lakhdar, 150, 152–6
brigades, 9–10. see also under
   Free Syrian Army (FSA);
   specific brigades
Britain, arming rebels policy
   of, 138–9
Building the Syrian State
   party, 76
business community, 43–4,
   45–6
   losses in, 191
   rapprochement with, 32–3
Byman, D., 142, 183

Caliphate, 163, 171, 172–3,
   175, 186

Canton Based Democratic
   Autonomy of Rojava
   (CBDAR). see Rojava
   administration
capitalism, global system
   of, 15–16, 18
Carpenter, A. 163
ceasefires, negotiating, 156–8
Cedar Revolution, 52–3
Cezire Canton, 168–9
Charap, S., 127
charitable associations
   state-licensed, 40–4
   before uprising, 70–1
chemical weapons, 144–8
China, opposition of to Geneva
   I process, 152
citizen journalists, 68
Civic Defense Council, 179
civic society associations
   issue-based, 41
   state licensed, 40–4
civil society
   informal groupings in, 42–3
   intellectual and elite let, 42
   resiliency of, 71–2
   restricted, 40–6
   since uprising, 70–3
civil society forums, 51
civil society organizations
   charitable, 41
   providing aid and wartime
      services, 72
   providing authority and
      security, 71–2
   in uprising, 49, 70–3
civil war, 2, 75
   parallel with revolution, 2–3
civilians, in armed
      conflict, 85–6
class conflict, in Ottoman
      period, 16

Coalition Provisional Authority
    (CPA), 222–3
Cocozelli, F. 223–4
Coles, I., 148
Communist Party, 21
Convention on the
    Disarmament and
    Destruction of Chemical
    Weapons, 146–47
corporatism, 31, 46
corrective revolution
    (1970), 13, 29–32
cultural organizations, 44–5

Dabis, Abdel Majid, 90
Dahi, Omar S., 6, 37
Damascus, protests in, 56–7
Damascus Declaration, 52–3,
    65
Damascus Spring of 2001, 51
Dannreuther, R., 128, 129
Daoud, D., 131
Dar'a
    Free Syrian Army in, 179
    protests in, 56, 80
Dark, E., 81
"Day of Anger," 56
De Châtel. F., 6
de Mistura, Staffan, 150,
    156–8
decentralization, 220–1
    institutionalizing, 221–2
Declaration of one
    Thousand, 41
Democratic Autonomy, 168
Democratic Union Party
    (PYD), 101–4
    in Aleppo, 95
    areas controlled by, 162,
        164–71
    in Geneva II process, 153
    Rojava project of, 168–71

disease, spread of, 196–7
displaced persons, 188–9,
    191–6
    inaccessibility to education
        of, 200
doctors, shortage of, 197
Dreyfuss, B., 138
Droz-Vincent, 84
Druze, 29
Dur al-Din Zanki
    Battalions, 142
Durac, V., 6

economic liberalization, 14
economic reforms, 29, 32–3
    market-based, 34–5
economic transformation, 4
economy
    diversification of, 5
    impact of conflict on, 189–
        91
education crisis, 198–200
Egypt
    political union with, 23–5
    Qatar and Saudi Arabia
        in, 124
    uprising in, 55
el-Hokayem. E., 131
el-Husseini, R., 39
el-Seif, Riad, 41–2
Emergency Law, repeal of, 59
European Union
    ineffective Syrian policy
        of, 135–7
    refugee crisis in, 209–10
    sanctions of, 136
Evans, D., 132

Fahd, Ziad, 90
Faisal, King, deposition of, 17
Falk, R., 79, 127
Farouk-Alli, A., 183

fighting units, 9–10
financial crisis (1986), 14
fiscal crisis, liberalizations
    and, 32–4
Fisher, Nigel, 188–9
foreign actors. see also Arab
    states; European Union;
    West; specific nations
  geopolitical interests
    of, 161–2
  sectarianism and, 184
Forum for National
    Dialogue, 41–2
Foursan al-Haq brigade, 178
Fox, W., 221
fragmentation, 2, 4
  approach to, 220–2
  of opposition, 74–5, 81, 87,
    91, 93–5, 155, 160
  sectarian, 75, 183–6
  territorial, 10, 84, 93, 100,
    164–82
France, arming rebel policy
    of, 138–9
Franco-Syrian Treaty of
    Independence, 20
Free Syrian Army (FSA), 74,
    76
  in Aleppo, 95
  areas controlled by, 178–80
  brigades of, 96
    arming of, 139–40
    fragmented, 93–4
    Jabhat an-Nusra
      and, 176–7
  creation of, 83
  decentralization of, 91–2
  declaration of, 88
  failure of, 96–7
  fluid affiliations of, 141
  fragmentation of, 87–8,
    93–4

General Command of, 90–2,
    93
  geographical diffusion
    of, 88–9
  infighting in, 89, 92
  Joint Command of, 90
  in Moscow process, 160
  resource deficiencies
    of, 88.89
  rise of, 87–92
  weaknesses and limitations
    of, 89–90
French rule, 17–21. see also
    Mandate (French)
  resistance to, 19–20
Friends of Syria, 133–4, 138,
    139
Front for Authenticity and
    Development
    (FAD), 142
Fronts, 93–95. see Islamic
    Front
  fluid affiliations of, 140–1
  in Geneva II process, 153

Gelvin, J. 17
Geneva process, 216
  Geneva I, 150–2
  Geneva II, 152–6
  reinvigorating, 219
Ghazaleh, Rustom, murder
    of, 61
Ghouta chemical weapon
    attacks, 144–5
Golan Heights, occupied, 4–5
Goodarzi, J., 130, 132
Gorenburg, D., 129
Government Non-
    Governmental
    Organizations
    (GONGOs), 44–6
Great Revolt (1925), 19–20

Gross Domestic Product (GDP), loss of, 190–1

Haddad, B., 32, 33, 37, 78, 216
Hama, attack on, 50
Hashem, A., 132
Hassan, H., 89
Hazm Movement, 100
health care crisis, 196–8
health workers, shortage of, 197
Henderson, E., 85
Heydemann, Stephen, 6, 23, 24, 31, 57–8, 63, 78–9, 84, 216
Higher State Security Court, abolishment of, 59
Hinnebusch, Raymond, 17–18, 26, 27, 29, 31, 34, 37, 38, 50, 78
Hitto, Ghassan, 181
Hizbollah, 40, 108
  Iran and, 131–2
  in Syrian conflict, 10, 112–15, 145
Hokayem, E., 6, 7, 130–1
hospitals, destroyed or damaged, 197
Hsu, C. 35
Hughes, G. A., 2
human rights activists, 65
human rights organizations, 44–5, 51
humanitarian aid, 149, 210–13, 227
humanitarian crisis, 1, 10–11
  approach to, 222–4
  disrupted education in, 197–200
  economic, 189–91
  in health care, 196–8

refugee and displaced persons in, 191–6, 200–10
  scale of, 188–9
  Syrians' response to, 210–13

Idriss, General Salim, 90, 125
Imran, S., 3
independence period, 3, 20–1
  instability of, 13, 21–2
interim government, 180–82
internally displaced persons, 191–6
  Iraqi, 209
  repatriation of, 223
international alliances, shifting, 79
international community, in Syrian conflict, 10, 118–19
internet service, shutdown of, 59–60
investment law, 33
Iran
  Russian relations with, 128–9
  sanctions on, 131
  Saudi rivalry with, 130–1, 185–6
  support of Moscow process by, 160
  in Syrian conflict, 4, 10, 118, 130–2
Iranian Nuclear Programme, Comprehensive Agreement on, 131
Iraq
  Arab Sunni community in, 106
  postconflict social policy in, 222–3
  refugees in, 194–5, 207–9

roots of ISIS in, 104–5
Sahwa movement in, 104–6
Syrian relations with, 39–40
U.S.-led war in, 39
weapons flow from, 138
Iraq Accord Front, 106
ISIS. *see* Islamic State in Iraq and al-Sham (ISIS)
Islamic Front, 84
in Geneva II process, 153
Islamic Liberation Front (ILF), 94
Islamic State in Iraq (ISI), 106–7
Islamic State in Iraq and al-Sham (ISIS), 64, 84, 94
administrative goals and structure of, 172–3
advances of in Syria and Iraq, 107
areas controlled by, 162, 171–5
creating new Caliphate, 163
formation of, 106–7
in Iraq, 209
Kurdish fighters against, 103, 104
oil fields controlled by, 107
pro-regime fighters against, 112–16
split of with Jabhat an-Nusra, 175–6
transnational goals of, 140
U.S. aerial bombing of, 144
war economies and expansion of, 173–5
warlords in, 175
Western policies toward Syrian regime and, 137–8

Islamic State in Iraq and as-Sham (ISIS), 2, 104–8
Islamist brigade coalition, 95–6
Islamist fighters, 50, 97–100. *see also* jihadists; Salafist-jihadists
arming of, 140
cooperative relations between, 97–9
infighting among, 97–8
Islamist Fronts, fluid affiliations of, 140–1
Islamists, political, 64–5
Ismail, S., 65, 75, 183
Israel, in Syrian conflict, 144

Jabhat an-Nusra (JAN), 64, 84, 94, 97–100
in Aleppo, 95
alliances of, 99–100, 176–7
areas controlled by, 175–6
arming, 140
expansion of into Syria, 106–7
governance strategy of, 177–8
military strategy of, 176
split of with ISIS, 175–6
Jaish al-Islam, 94
Jaish al-Mujahideen (Mujahideen Army), 96
Jama'at Zayd (Zayd Group), 43–4
Jamal Atassi Forum, 42
Jamiyyat Ghiras al-Nahda (Association of the Seeds of Resistance), 212
Jedid, Salah, 25
jihadists, 64. *see also* Islamist fighters; Salafist-jihadists
arming of, 140
fear of, 78

Joint Command for the
Revolution's Military
Council, 90–1
Jordan
hostility to refugees in,
195–6
refugees in, 207

Kafr Nabel Shari'a Court, 178
Kahf, M., 6, 53–4
Kaldor, Mary, 84–5
Kalis, O., 202
Karadag, Roy, 40
Karouny, M., 132
Kataib Hizbollah (Hizbollah
Forces), 115
Kerry, John, 160
Khaddam, Abdel Hallim, 53
Khaddour, K., 110, 111
Khashanah, 7
Khoury, Doreen, 67–8
Khoury, P. S., 15, 16
kinship based social
networks, 63–4
Kirisci, K., 205
Kleinfeld, R., 143
Kurdish community, 5, 100
under Assad regime, 166
autonomy of, 168
citizenship extended to, 59
fleeing to Iraq, 208
under French Mandate,
164–5
in Geneva II process, 153
in Ottoman period, 164–5
political organizations of, 4,
100–4
regime cooptation of,
166–7
in Rojava, 164–71
self-rule of, 159
in uprising, 166–7

Kurdish Democratic Party
(KDP), 102
Kurdish National Council
(KNC), 101–2, 170,
171
Kurdish opposition, 52, 53,
65
Kurdish parties, Syrian, 4
Kurdish-regime alliances,
103–4
Kurdish Regional Government
(KRG), 102
Kurdish Workers Party
(PKK), 101, 166, 185
Kurdistan Regional
Government
(KRG), 220

Land Code of 1858, 15–16
land laws, 38
land reforms, under UAR, 24
Landis, J., 52
landlord-merchant class, rule
of, 12–13
landownership
class structure based on, 17–
19
concentration of, 15–16
Lavrov, Foreign Minister, 160
Law of the provinces, 16
Lawson, F., 33
leadership
lack of, 62–3
multiple, 73–77, 81
League of Arab States (LAS)
diplomatic efforts of, 121–2
sanctions against Syria,
122–3
suspension of Syria's
membership in, 122
League of Nations, Mandates
granted by, 16–17

Lebanon
  Cedar Revolution in, 52–3
  hostility to refugees in, 195–6
  open-door policy of, 201–2
  refugees in, 200–4
  residency restrictions in, 201
  spillover of violence
    into, 113, 134–5, 196,
    201, 203–4
  in Syrian conflict, 112–15
  Syrian presence in, 4, 39–40
  weapons flow from, 138
Leenders, R., 57–8, 63, 84
leftist groups, 65
Lekas Miller, A., 211
Lesch, David, 6, 228
liberal peace approach, 218
liberalization, political and
  economic, 32–4
Libya
  civil war in, 56
  NATO-led intervention
    in, 121, 127, 143–4
  protests in, 55
lijan shaabiyya (popular
  committees), 109–10
Liwa al-Tawhid (Tawhid
  Brigade), 93–4, 142
Local Coordination
  Committees (LCCs), 6,
    49, 80
  central role of, 9
  decentralized structures
    of, 74–5
  functions of, 68–9
  governance function of,
    69
  in mobilization, 66–70
  nonviolent position of, 76
  providing humanitarian
    aid, 211–13

Local People's Protection
  Committees (PPC), 102
Lolu, Zaki, 90
"lost generations," 196–7,
  198–9
Lund, Aron, 109, 139
Lynch, M., 6

Macias, A., 107
Mackreath, H., 203
Maghawir Forces, 141
Majilis Qiyadat al-Thawra
  al-Surriya (Syrian
  Revolutionary
  Command Council), 94
Majlis inqadh al-Anbar
  (al-Anbar Salvation
  Council), 104–6
Majlis Shura al-Mujahideen
  (MSM), 106
Majlis Thawar (Revolutionary
  Councils), 69
Makhlouf, Hafez, exile of, 61
Mandate (French), 3, 17–21,
  46
  Kurdish population
    under, 164–5
  powers of, 12
  state expansion under, 3–4
Mandates, 16–17
marginalized groups, 65–6
Marin, V., 60
marketization, 8–9, 14, 34–5,
  36
  civil society groups
    and, 43–4
  deteriorating socioeconomic
    conditions from, 219
  unemployment and, 65
Marxism, 25–6
media programming, 227
medicines, shortages of, 198

merchant class, emergence of, 18
middle classes, 63
Middle East Peace Process, Syria in, 4
migration, of unemployed, 65–6
Miles, T., 192
militarization, 9, 72–3, 81, 83–4
  causes of, 87
  Free Syrian Army in, 87–92
  ISIS in, 104–8
  Islamist fighters in, 97–100
  networked rebel groups in, 92–7
  opposition to, 76
  PYD in, 100–4
  regime violence and, 108–17
  sectarianism in, 184
militias, pro-regime, 108–12, 115–17, 118
non-Syrian, 112–16
minority communities, 4. see Kurdish community
  in Ba'ath Party, 26
  supporting opposition, 185
mobile health clinics, 197
mobilization
  of 2011, 48–9
  civil society forums in, 51
  Local Coordination Committees in, 66–70
  nonviolent versus militarized, 81
Moret, E., 136
Morsi, Mohammed, 124
Moscow process, 158–60
Movement for Social Peace, 42
Mubarak, Hosni, resignation of, 55, 124
Mufti, 20–1

Mujahideen Shura Council, 177
Muller, B., 114, 131
Munif, Y., 6, 37
Muslim Brotherhood, 21, 31–2, 64, 124
  repression of, 50
Mussalaha (Reconciliation), 71

Najda Now (Assistance Now), 71, 212
Nasrallah, Sayyed Hassan, 114
Nasser, Gamal, 23
Nasserism, 25
National Bloc, 20, 21
National Coalition
  defection of allies from, 153
  in Geneva II process, 155, 156
  interim Prime Minister of, 181
National Coordination Body for Democratic Change (NCB), 179
  nonviolent position of, 76
National Defense Forces (NDF), 84, 110–11
  Hizbollah fighters and, 115
  institutionalization of, 118
National party, 21
National Progressive Front (NPF), 30, 50
National Provisional Government, 20
National Salvation Front (NSF), 53
nationalism, 17
  commitment to, 25
  territorial, 20–1
nationalization, 29, 37
NATO, Libyan intervention of, 56, 121, 143–4

neoliberal policies, 38–9
networks of solidarity, 67–8
"new wars" theory, 84–5
Nielsen, R., 224
no-fly zone, in northern
    Syria, 133
nobility-based order, 18
  uprooting of, 13
nongovernment organizations
    (NGOs), 211–12
nonviolence, advocacy of, 76
nonviolent mobilization, 81

Obama, Barack, on Syrian
    chemical weapons,
    144–6
Obama Administration
  ineffective Syrian policy
    of, 137
  policy of on arming
    rebels, 138
Öcalan, Abdullah, 166, 168
Oesch, L., 200
oil monarchies, rapprochement
    with, 30–1
O'Mahony, C. 221
Omran, Mohammed, 25
opposition, 49–53. see also
    rebel groups
  coalition of, 52–3
  exiled, 53, 74, 75–6
  fragmentation of, 74–6, 81,
    92–7
  in Geneva II process, 152–5
  lack of political strategy
    of, 76
  legitimacy deficit of, 75–6,
    181
  militarization of, 83–4, 184
  mistrust among, 74–5
  in Moscow process, 160
  plurality of, 52–3

providing humanitarian
    aid, 211–12
  shifting alliances of, 2
  suppression of, 50–1
  weakness of, 79–80
organizers, 68
O'Toole, J., 129
Ottoman Empire, 3
  collapse of, 3, 15–17
  reforms in, 12–13
  reforms of, 14–15
Oweis, K. 179
Owen, R., 55

Pace, J., 52
Palestine, loss of, 21
Palestinian factions, Syrian
    support of, 4
Pantti, M., 227
paramilitary groups, 66
parliament, 17, 19, 30
patrimonial state, 13–14
Pax Syriana, collapse of, 52
peasant politics, rise of, 22–3
peasant proprietorship, decline
    of, 15–16
peasants, landless, 18
Peninsula Shield Force, 55–6
People's Defense Corps
    (YPG), 102, 103–4
People's Party, 21
Perthes, V., 34
pharmaceutical industry,
    destruction of, 197–8
Phillips, C., 112, 183
Pierret, T., 43, 46, 141, 142
pillars of power, 9, 13–14, 31,
    46
Pizzi, M., 158
PKK. see Kurdish Workers
    Party (PKK)
Podder, S. 163

political community making, 75
political dissent, repression of, 48–51
political instability, post-independence, 21–2
political parties, suppression of, 49–51
political radicalization, 22
political transition, 224–6
population displacements, 193
private sector
  investment in, 36
  regime rapprochement with, 32–3
protest movement, 6
  decentered and leaderless, 62–3
  Local Coordination Committees in mobilizing, 66–70
  militarization of, 60, 72–3
  organization of, 57
  repression of, 58–9
  social groups participating in, 63–6
  spread of, 59–60
  in Tunisia, 54–5
  unorganized, 53–4
protest-repression cycle, 54
protesters
  escalating violence against, 59–60
  social and political backgrounds of, 62–6
  social networks of, 49, 63
public planning, 29
PYD. see Democratic Union Party (PYD)

Qatar
  arming rebel groups, 138, 142–3
  financing and organizing opposition, 123–4
  Saudi Arabia and, 124–5
  supporting Free Syrian Army, 91–2
  in Syrian conflict, 118, 121–2
  Turkey and, 134
Quanaitra, Free Syrian Army in, 178–9

Radio Souriali, 227
Rawan, B., 3
rebel groups. see also Islamist fighters; Salafist-jihadists
  areas controlled by, 162
  arming of, 138–43, 219
  fluid affiliations of, 140–2
  moderate-extremist split in, 140
  networked, 92–7
  private donations to, 141–3
  Qatari arming of, 125
  rivalries among, 95–7
  Turkish support of, 133–4
reconstruction services, postconflict, 223
reforms, 54, 58
refugee camps, 194–6
  lack of in Lebanon, 201, 202
refugees, 191–6
  demographic breakdown of, 192–3
  in Europe, 209–10
  familial and social networks of, 194, 202–3
  fleeing to Turkey, 133
  hostility from host countries toward, 195–6
  humanitarian aid to, 149
  inadequate food and services for, 196

in Iraq, 207–9
Iraqi, 209
in Jordan, 207
in Lebanon, 200–4
legal protections for, 205–6
repatriation of, 223
tensions between host
    countries and, 203–4
in Turkey, 60, 204–7
regime (Assad)
accommodationists in, 61
adaptability and resilience
    of, 49, 77–80, 80–1
areas controlled by, 108–9
behaviors during conflict, 6
chemical weapons agreement
    of, 146–8
conflicts and reshufflings
    in, 60–1
crackdown on protests
    by, 57–9
dual strategy of, 54, 58–9
framing of protest movement
    by, 58–9
hardliners in, 60–1
international isolation of,
    79
pillars of power of, 9
relegitimizing, 219
response of to protests, 54
Russian support of, 126–30
sanctions against, 136
violence of, 108–17
regime-rebel relations, 7–8
regional conflicts, 118–19
regional geopolitics, 7, 85,
    171
regional settlement, 219
relief work, 67–72, 179–80,
    198, 203–5, 210–13
Republican Party, 21
revolution, parallel with civil
    war, 2–3

Rojava administration, 162,
    164–71, 186
cantons of, 168–70
Rojava Democratic Society
    Movement (TEV
    DEM), 169
Rojava Project, 102–3, 104
Ruiz de Elvira, L., 212
rural economy, shift away
    from, 37–9
Russia
concern of over Western
    intervention, 126–7
military and economic ties
    with Syria, 129–30
negotiating chemical
    weapons
    agreement, 145–7
obstruction of UNSC
    intervention, 128, 135
opposition to Geneva I
    process of, 152
regional rivalries of with
    U.S., 128
relations of with Iran, 128–9
in Syrian conflict, 10,
    126–30, 158–60

Saadullah, V., 208
Sadiki, L., 55
Sadjadpour, K., 132
Sahner, C., 6
Sahwa (Awakening)
    movement, 104–6
Salafi al-Islam Brigade, 141
Salafist-jihadists, 10, 97–100,
    135, 186
fear of, 78–9
network of, 175–6
spreading through
    region, 126, 127–9, 130
Salafist rule, 78
Salloukh, B. F., 7

Salooja, R., 205
Saudi Arabia
  arming rebel groups, 138,
    142–3
  Iran rivalry with, 130–1
  Qatar and, 124–5
  rivalry of with Iran, 185–6
  supporting Free Syrian
    Army, 91–2
  in Syrian conflict, 118,
    121–2
  Turkey and, 134
Sayigh, Y. 74
schools, destruction of, 199
Seale, Patrick, 30, 31
sectarianism, 183–6
  fear of, 75, 78, 79
  Saudi-Iranian rivalry
    in, 185–6
security apparatus, 9, 31–2
Seeberg, P., 6, 136
Seferis, L., 207–8
Seifan, S. 38
Selvik, K., 43
September 11 attack, aftermath
    of, 39–40
shabiha (thugs), 58, 66, 109–
    10
  fostering of, 184
  in NDF, 132
Shaery-Eisenlohr, R., 131
Shafik, Ahmad, 124
share-croppers, 18
Sharia councils, 225
Shi'a fighters, against
    ISIS, 115–16
Shishakli, Adib, purges of, 22
Shuhada al-Islam Brigade, 141
Siegle, S. 221
Singer, D., 85
single sovereign problem, 218
Slavin, B., 115

Social Contract, charter
    of, 168
social crisis, approach to, 222–
    4
social groupings, 63–6
social market economy, 35–6,
    38, 43
social mobility, reduction
    of, 37
Social Movement Theory, 6,
    84
social networks, in
    uprising, 49, 62–6
social services,
    reinvigorating, 223–4
social stratification, 3–4, 219
socialism, 25–6, 29
society
  segmentation of, 62
  stratification of, 183–4, 187
Sood, A., 207–8
Souqour al-sham brigade, 178
Souriya Bil Alwan (Syria in
    Colors), 212
Staniland, P. 7
state
  bureaucracy of, 18–19, 31
  consolidation of, 29–32
  seismic shifts in, 3
  social realities in, 3–4
state institutions
  factionalization of, 23
  growth of, 22
  strengthening, 218
Statement of 1,000, 51–2
statist economic
    development, 34–5
Steenkamp, C. 85, 86
Stein, A., 133
strategic crop incentives, 38
Sufi al-Habib al-Mustafa
    Brigade, 141

Sunni tribal militias, 112
Supervision and Follow-up
    Council, 179
Supreme Kurdish Council
    (SKC), 102, 103
Supreme Military Command
    (SMC), 142
  factionalization of, 125–6
  hopes for U.S.
    intervention, 146
Suqoor al-Sham, 94
Syria
  borders of, 5, 162, 164–5,
    168
  decentralized authority
    in, 163–4
  economic sanctions
    against, 122–3
  geographic fragmentation
    of, 117, 162, 187, 215–
    16
  regional role of, 4
  southern, 178–80
Syrian American Medical
    Society (SAMS), 211–12
Syrian Arab Army (SAA)
  emasculation and contraction
    of, 84, 112, 116
  Hizbollah fighters and, 114,
    115
  marginalization of, 108
  regime's reliance on,
    109–10
Syrian Association for Women's
    Role in
    Development, 44
Syrian Civil Defense, 211
Syrian conflict
  approaches to, 218–28
  Arab states in, 118, 121–6
  arming of rebels in, 138–43
  causes of, 219

chemical weapons
    controversy in, 144–8
  complexity and fluidity
    of, 5–8
  complexity of, 2–3, 217
  holistic approach to, 216
  internationalization of, 118–
    19, 120–1, 160–1
  Iran in, 130–2
  Moscow process in, 158–60
  regional players in, 7, 118
  Russia in, 126–30
  Turkey in, 132–5
  UN and, 148–58
  Western intervention
    in, 135–9
Syrian diaspora
    organizations, 211–12
Syrian Economic Society
    (SEC), 42
Syrian Human Rights
    Committee (SHRC), 45
Syrian Interim Government
    (SIG), 181–2
  financial problems of, 182
Syrian Islamic Front (SIF), 94,
    141
  arming, 140
Syrian Islamic Liberation Front
    (SILF), 93–4, 95
Syrian National Coalition
    (SNC), 121–2
  Qatari and Saudi influence
    over, 124–5
Syrian National Council
    (SNC), 72, 73, 74
  divisions and conflicts in, 73
  in Geneva II process, 153
  lack of material support
    of, 75–6
  support of Western
    intervention by, 76

Syrian Network for Human Rights (SNHR), 147
Syrian Observatory for Human Rights, 45
Syrian Revolutionaries Front (SRF), 94, 98, 100
  in Aleppo, 95
  in Geneva II process, 153
Syrian Social Nationalist Party (SSNP), 21, 111
Syrian Trust, 44
Syrian Women Observatory, 44

Ta'if Accord, 52
Tansiqiyyat. see Local Coordination Committees (LCCs)
Tanzimat reforms, 14–15, 16–17
Taylor, P., 173
teachers, shortage of, 199
territorial control, 7–8, 86, 117
trade, severe restriction of, 189–90
tribal leaders, 64
tribes, 63–4
Trombetta, L., 135, 136–7
Tunisian uprising, 54–5
Turkey
  advocacy of regime change, 133–4
  arming rebel groups, 138
  changing policy of toward Syrian regime, 133–4
  entry into Europe through, 210
  evolving refugee policy of, 205–6
  intervention of in Syria, 144
  Kurds and, 4, 101, 166

  military involvement of in Syrian conflict, 134–5
  open-door policy of, 205
  rebel support through, 90, 133–4
  refugees in, 194–5, 204–7
  regional relations of, 134–5
  Russian relations with, 129
  in Syrian conflict, 10, 118, 132–5
  Syrian money in, 206–7
  Syrian relations with, 39–40
  weapons flowing from, 125, 132–3

ulama, 45–6
unemployment, 6, 65–6
Union of Syrian Medical Relief Organizations (UOSSM), 71, 198, 211–12
United Arab Republic (UAR)
  declaration of, 23–4
  failure of, 24–5
United Nations
  Geneva I initiative of, 150–2
  Geneva II initiative of, 152–6
  humanitarian assistance of, 149
  negotiating local freezes, 156–8
  resolution 1973 of, 127
  resolution 2165 of, 149
  resolution 2191 of, 149
  Syrian conflict deliberations of, 149–50
  UNSCR 2139 and 2013 of, 147–8, 149
  Western-Russian/Chinese split on Syrian conflict in, 58

World Food Programme
(WFP) of, 192
United States
aerial bombing of ISIS
by, 144
chemical weapons policy
of, 144–7
ineffective Syrian policy
of, 137–8
Middle East interventions
of, 126–7
regional policies of, 128
uprising
context of, 6, 46–7
early period of, 9, 48–9,
53–61
growth of civil society
since, 70–3
militarization of, 83–4
multiple leadership in,
73–7
repression of, 9
Utas, M., 85

Valeriano, B., 60
violence
of armed opposition, 83–
108
civilianization of, 85–6
in modern war, 84–5
multiplicity of, 86
networks of, 10
of regime, 108–17
in Syrian context,
84–6
von Malzhan, N., 130

war
civilianization of, 85–6
economies of, 86, 173–5,
190–1
political orders of, 7–8
warlords, in postconflict order,
225–6
West
arming rebel groups, 138–9,
140–1
disunity of over Syrian
conflict, 135–8
in Geneva I process, 151–2
military interventions of
case for, 76
Russian skepticism
toward, 126–7
in Syria, 10, 135–9
reluctance of to
intervene, 143–4
sanctions against Syria, 135
Wezeman, P., 125
White, B., 165, 183
White Helmets, 211, 212
Wimmen, H., 151
Windrem, R., 141, 143
women's rights organizations,
44

Yilmaz, N. 134
Youth of March 15, 57
Youth Party, 21

Zawahiri, Ayman, 107
Zayd Group, 43–4
zu'ama (political leaders), 1